Intercultural Transmission in the
Medieval Mediterranean

Intercultural Transmission in the Medieval Mediterranean

Edited by Stephanie L. Hathaway
and David W. Kim

Continuum International Publishing Group
A Bloomsbury Company

The Tower Building	80 Maiden Lane
11 York Road	Suite 704
London	New York
SE1 7NX	NY 10038

www.continuumbooks.com

British Library Cataloguing-in-Publication Data
A catalogue record for this book is available from the British Library.

ISBN: HB: 978–1–4411–3908–5

Library of Congress Cataloging-in-Publication Data
A catalog record for this book is available from the Library of Congress.

Typeset by Fakenham Prepress Solutions, Fakenham, Norfolk NR21 8NN
Printed and bound in Great Britain

Contents

Musicians and scribes at the court of Alfonso X, from the prologue of the *Cantigas de Santa Maria*, 5r.

Preface

It was late Spring 2008, a few months before submitting our PhD theses, that Stephanie and I had a chance to share the progress of each other's research, which comprised many common points in historical and literary perspectives. Several of us, humanities postgraduates at the University of Sydney, met specifically to discuss the common threads in the material we were working on and would like to work on, though we come from different disciplines: history, medieval literature, religious studies and archaeology. We realized that although our individual research was from slightly different eras as were the primary documents, the geographical region of influence was around the Mediterranean Rim, and the main subject was the transmission of medieval culture among diverse societies or communities. After a coffee and a long conversation, we agreed that not enough studies were undertaken on the theme of cultural transformation, especially in an interdisciplinary, Mediterranean concept, and that our new project, a study of intercultural transformation of the area and timeframe, would be entirely useful in terms of offering a fresh method of re-evaluating the study of the life of medieval people. After raising this issue with colleagues, and at conferences, we found that many scholars were in agreement. As our research developed, so did our group, and we were encouraged by the demand for scholarly pursuit in this area, and we took up this study together.

The result is a collaborative volume that includes writings of scholars from different fields to focus on this issue from different angles. Some works are the products of long-term research projects while others are still in their beginning phases, and some make salient cases for further study by way of collaborative scholarship, and all offer value to research in medieval studies. That each scholar in his or her own field addresses this idea of transmission attests to the active interest in how ideas moved across time and space during this era. Approaching intercultural transmission in this way, from various perspectives, will advance a better understanding of the cultures that together formed foundations for the ethics and traditions of the first modern Europe that society still holds valuable today.

While there exist criticisms in the fields of study in early to late medieval literature, history, archaeology, architecture and religious studies, little has been done to bring them together and present them alongside each other beyond the conference panel or workshop. However, as each author individually explores the socio-political issue of medieval society, this collective book not only seeks to fill some gaps between different academic fields of research, but will also cover the evidence of topics or issues on the change or development of the medieval community in the history of the Mediterranean region. This interdisciplinary material is a product of text-based research for those professional readers who are interested to observe the phenomena of the cultural transmission from a literary approach and students who try to draw a picture of the era in people's lifestyle and beliefs.

The range of topics includes the study of knights, women, chivalry, love poetry, clothes, buildings, language, romance, royalty, faith and destiny, and will reflect the socio-political direction of medieval literature. Thus, this is not a book to be read for a comprehensive history of medieval culture, but as a reference work it will answer questions regarding the genre and rhetoric of the texts. The main concern of this book is to comprehend the contemporary interpretation of medieval texts.

This research-based work includes ancient and medieval languages, such as Greek, Middle High German, Coptic, Latin and medieval French. Based on the study of primary texts, this collection will make comparative and critical use of documents from Persia, al-Andalus, the Roman Empire, Byzantium, Greece, and the Angevin and Rhineland courts of Europe. This volume as a whole will complement the research being undertaken in early Christian and medieval history, contribute to new views on Byzantine studies, Europe's history with the Islamic World, and the landscape of power, etiquette and power-play as depicted in these texts, and in relation to the medieval Church.

David W. Kim
Edinburgh

Acknowledgements

Among many people involved in this project, we are thankful to each author who has contributed to this volume. Although they live and teach in different parts of the world, in different time zones, and speak different languages, they have all supported this project with one heart.

We would like to give our special thanks to Professor Annette Volfing, Rhodri Mogford and Michael Greenwood, and in particular to Megan Kerr whose confidence and objectivity lent much-needed support to our project at a time when it was greatly needed.

Abbreviations

Ac.	Book of Acts
Acts Thom.	*Book of Acts of Thomas*
CD	Damascus Document
Gal.	*Epistle of Galatians*
Gos. Thom.	*Gospel of Thomas*
Jn.	*Gospel of John*
ms., mss.	manuscript(s)
Mt.	*Gospel of Matthew*
NHC	*Nag Hammadi* Codices
NT	New Testament
P. Oxy.	Oxyrhynchus Papyrus
Q	*Quelle*, Source
Rom.	Paul's Book of *Romans*
Thom. Cont.	*Book of Thomas the Contender*

Introduction

The great surge in literary composition and copying, in commerce, the exchange of ideas, and in the use of vernacular languages that marked the twelfth and thirteenth centuries, were to redefine the cultural landscape of the Mediterranean Rim. Great social and economic changes, and increased intercultural contact signalled a blossoming of the expression of a modern Europe. But the medieval Mediterranean and its surrounding area was only the fulcrum, since it is upon this pivotal space in time and place that the transmission of ideas stretched both forward and backward in time, from pre-Christianized, and Classical Persian and Greco-Roman civilizations through Christian Rome, the rise of Islam and extensive caliphates, the rise and fall of the Byzantine Empire, Carolingians and Capetians, to the early Renaissance and the development of the first modern tourism and pilgrimage. It stretched East and West, North and South, from the farther reaches of Asia Minor, the Frankish Levant and Persia to the Iberian peninsula, from the desert regions of Tunisia and Egypt to the temperate British Isles, from the bustling port of Bordeaux to the dense forests of Germany. Elements evident in literature, art, religion and architecture reveal that the active transmission of ideas across the political and cultural borders throughout the Mediterranean Rim and beyond played an important and central role in the developing cultures of Christian Europe and the Byzantine and Arab civilizations, and since even before the first century AD, setting in motion a quiet undercurrent of multiculturalism.

In the later centuries of the Roman Empire multicultural communities were forming which were represented by diverse languages and ethnicities, a phenomenon that was to increase in the centuries following as the political and religious landscape changed and trade increased. Following the advent of Islam in the seventh century AD the Arab world served as a key agent for the transmission and reshaping of ideas westward from Asia Minor and the many ancient cultures that had left their marks there. Even if Europe had little immediate knowledge of the Arabo-Islamic culture before the conquest of Jerusalem in the twelfth century, it had, through trade and relations in Spain and the Mediterranean Rim, and especially the French participation in the *Reconquista*, been influenced by it.[1]

Influences on and interaction of these cultures that criss-crossed the Mediterranean reached far into Europe. Even Albertus Magnus (1193–1280), perhaps the greatest German scholar of the Middle Ages, had an insatiable curiosity that led him to study Jewish, Greek and Arabic texts, and his interest in the cooperation of different cultures, classes and nationalities is legendary. Further influences of the eastern regions on Europe during this time are apparent in things as various as the use and stock of horses, clothing and hairstyles, music, musical instruments and performance, and spices. Leisure pursuits from the Orient also became popular with nobility, such as poetry, cards, chess, hunting and polo. The impact on women in Aquitaine was apparent in legal matters; in many cases they had inheritance rights as well as a right to autonomous rule over lands owned. As had their Visigothic predecessors as well as their Mediterranean neighbours, Aquitanian ladies participated in social affairs alongside their men, and were 'renowned for their elegance in dress, yet censured by the Church for their painted cheeks, their charcoal-rimmed eyes and their oriental perfumes',[2] as well as a lax attitude towards morality and adultery. Chivalric customs, clothing and styles of oral performance, both sacred and profane, also made their way between Europe's courts and cultural centres in the Near East.

Text translation was also taking place widely, spreading the knowledge and philosophies of ancient texts, as well as glosses and commentaries, far into Europe and Asia Minor. Literature and poetry were influenced in form, metre and subject matter. Ideas, materials, texts, art and languages passed along trade, slave and pilgrimage routes as well as with embassies, *troubadours* and crusading armies, spanning the fifth to sixteenth centuries. Religion, another key conduit for the transmission of ideas that occurred throughout Europe in the early Middle Ages, from the beginnings of the Roman Church, is evidenced in the spread of Christianity both eastward and westward from Jerusalem. Spiritual ideas and practices were interconnecting through the wide-ranging communities of Jewish peoples in Europe and the Mediterranean, the waxing and waning political strength of the Eastern Christian Church in Byzantium and the Coptic Church in Egypt, the Norman and Frankish territories and Angevin France, and the growing Arabic empire and the spread of Islam.

Constantinople, the seat of the Eastern (Roman) Empire, had, like the Arab world, largely preserved much of the classical knowledge from its ancestral territories, while also using it to assert power over its realm. As the larger empires of Eastern and Western Europe and of Asia Minor grew, swallowing older cultures, new communities were being formed. Among a growing populace with increasing multicultural communities, these ancient and classical ideals were subject to reinterpretation as they served to unite communities in both cultural past and political present. Many texts exploited the cultural heritage of the classical world, such as those of alchemy and Aristotlean theory, that are now known to have only purported to be translations of Greek or Coptic to lend credibility and prestige to their contents.

Texts show this multilingual, multicultural merging, reshaping and transmission of ideas from one era to another, from one place to another, and from one community to a new one; they are both mirrors of the journey of these ideas as well as the tools by which these ideas were disseminated, transformed and reshaped for use in a particular community. In this way, the study of different and special aspects from a panoply of texts from around the medieval Mediterranean supports the perspective of scholarship favouring an established East–West connection rather than merely interaction of divided groups. The range of disciplines in which these texts have been investigated demonstrates the landscape of mutual influence, reciprocity, and an historical process of cross-fertilization in the Mediterranean and its areas of influence from the Roman Empire to the advent of the Renaissance.

Twentieth-century criticisms have shown us that medieval literature has as much to offer the cultural historian as it does the pure philologist, and scholarship has benefited from the proliferation of criticism on a great number of original texts, many only rediscovered during the previous century. However, the greater part of research being undertaken on the interconnection between the medieval European cultures and the myriad cultures of the Mediterranean Rim has been done by scholars whose main field did not originate in literature, linguistics or history; for example, John Tolan or Rudolph Fahrner whose works attempt to span the East–West intellectual divide, the travel author Habeeb Salloum, or the quasi-historical work on Arabian knights by Sharif Abdunnur. In addition, the work of Phillip Bennett and Finn E. Sinclair on Saracen women in Old French texts has opened up broader avenues for investigation of the 'other', and Albrecht Classen's publications that further the concept of what may be identified as foreign in medieval literature show a desire to view from new perspectives medieval cultural interaction around the Mediterranean, that great cultural crossroads and beyond.

These new perspectives have been open to exploration, especially since María Rosa Menocal published *The Arabic Role in Medieval Literary History: A Forgotten Heritage* in 1987, and the impetus set out in the conference: *Die*

Begegnung des Westens mit dem Osten: 4. Symposions des Mediävistenverbandes in Köln 1991 aus Anlass des 1000. Todesjahres der Kaiserin Theophanu. In the field of religion, the research into the effect of pagans, mixed Christian/non-Christian communities and converts on canon law advances our understanding of the historical landscape, such as that of Lawrence G. Duggan, James Muldoon, Benjamin Z. Kedar or Allan Cutler, and much recent research has been undertaken on Sufism and spiritual chivalry by authors such as Qamar-ul Huda, Arley Loewen and Seyyed Hossein Nasr. Why, then, does the boundary still exist between scholars of the Iberian and Islamic world and those scholars of medieval European texts? Why does the transmission of ideals such as chivalry and spirituality across not only the Mediterranean but also across religious and cultural borders remain within these limitations for the medievalist as well as for the scholar of late classicism?

There have been some detailed publications on medieval Iberian chivalry, such as those incorporating medieval law and society studies by Jesús Rodríguez-Velasco, though these do confine their scope to Spain. One set of conference proceedings published in 2007 focuses on the archaeological significance of texts and literacy in medieval Europe: *Text and Transmission in medieval Europe*, ed. Chris Bishop (Newcastle: Cambridge Scholars, 2007). Two sets of conference proceedings are to be published. One focuses on the transformation of texts between cultures: *Vehicles of Transmission, Translation, and Transformation in Medieval Textual Culture* (Cursor Mundi) by Carlos Fraenkel, Jamie Fumo, Faith Wallis and Robert Wisnovsky (Brepols, 30 August 2011); and the other will comprise a collection of articles from some of the presentations given in specific fields of study at the symposium: *Cultures, Communities and Conflicts in the Medieval Mediterranean; Second Biennial Conference of the Society for the Medieval Mediterranean* (University of Southampton, 4–6 July 2011).

These publications reflect a relatively new area of medieval studies in that they attempt to bring together scholars from various fields; that is not without obstacles. Some groups work in collaboration, while some pose their research alongside that of their colleagues from other disciplines, which can mean that fewer language-based studies are possible. In addition, in the broad field of Medieval Studies, there are always the recurring issues of bringing together research from different time periods and geographical areas in such endeavours, and the 'greater' Middle Ages is now accepted as that time between Late Antiquity and the Renaissance. This time span alone comprises many cultural, political and linguistic changes that must be brought together under a specific focus so that it serves better to advance the studies in each field.

This volume focuses on the transmission of ideas in the Mediterranean Rim during the period of the 'greater' Middle Ages with nine highly specific studies, each interrelated. Although we approach this concept from different angles, our research merges in the development of medieval cultures and their impact on groups and communities. In the following chapters, the perception of intercultural transmission across this area is investigated by examining a specific set of primary texts with a focus on language, form and content. A wide range of genres are represented. Part I focuses on religious and canon documents, Part II on chivalry, Part III on poetry, verse and theatrical works, and Part IV on the art forms represented by architectural treatises and commercial and material goods.

The result of these studies is the demonstration of how texts of various genres reflect and are themselves the products of transforming, and multicultural, multilinguistic communities revolving around the medieval Mediterranean Rim. The interaction of these transforming communities through their expression in text, social structure, architecture, performance, language, religious practice and clothing is illuminated, as are the ways in which these groups established their cultures, making use of historical manifestations, such as texts, legends and architecture, as well as combining cultural, social and religious practices from those Mediterranean cultures with which they came into contact, to project their identity geographically and chronologically.

The interpretation and formation of texts in merging cultural communities, and texts that reflect a multicultural populace, is the focus of Part I, 'Faith and Spirituality'. With an analysis of the *Nag Hammadi Codex*, or Thomas Gospel, David Kim (Chapter 1) traces the textual evidence of Thomasine Christians in Jerusalem, questioning the theories about Pella, Antioch and Edessa as geographical locations for the community. As he investigates the need for and use of this text for a canonical community that comprised early practising Christians, including Jews, Romans and Greeks, Kim also lays bare the cases for Syriac, Aramaic and Greek as the original languages for the text of the *Gospel of Thomas*. Kim deduces that, in translating from a source for a specific Judaeo-Christian/Greek community in need of a text for religious practice, the translator made the decision to put the gospel into the Coptic language, a language that would be commonly understood by a new, diverse and growing community. Because of a need for unity in a multicultural community, the texts that were used reflect cultures influenced by Christian texts as well as texts incorporating the cultural history of a community. The unity and continuity of a community of early Christians in the Byzantine Empire with Greek or other pagan religions required a text incorporating their own cultural history as well as transmitting that of their religion. The transmission of the story of St Michael of Chonai, the legendary figure of Christianity in the Eastern (Roman) Empire, is the subject of Chapter 2 by Alan Cadwallader, as demonstrating the importance of cultural memory in communities. By tracing the characterization of Michael via Greek and Jewish gods, Cadwallader shows how paganism and pagan elements in this text are used both to endorse the Christian faith by adopting and adapting sacred matter, and to advance the power of the Byzantine Church over the following centuries.

The merging of values from different cultures into an ideal and an institution transcending political and religious boundaries is the subject investigated in Part II, 'Chivalry', from two differing perspectives in scholarship. In Chapter 3, Milad Milani presents a study of Persian Sufism and chivalry against the backdrop of the rise of the Arabian caliphates in Asia Minor, showing how the chivalric ideal brought a practical approach to Sufi spirituality and Persian cultural continuity. Milani discusses the origins of chivalry as it came to Persia and Persian culture under the Abbasid rulers, proposing that chivalric orders originated in the Middle East. Furthering his investigation of the spiritual aspects of Sufi chivalry, *fûtûwwat*, Milani explores the differences in interpretation between Arabic and Persian chivalry, and how the new Islamic Iranian spiritual chivalry incorporated Persia's ancient spiritual tradition, using Persian-Arabic religious texts as an example of the use of languages that reflect the history of the community and the newer multicultural population. From the medieval European perspective, Stephanie Hathaway (Chapter 4) investigates the introspective aspects of chivalry as they are seen to develop in twelfth-century Europe, considering influences from the East, and paralleling chivalry's depiction in literature. Focusing on the transformation of the material of the *chanson de geste Aliscans* to its Middle High German version *Willehalm*, she presents an integrated reading of the character of Rennewart/Rainouart in terms of his development from buffoon to knight to chevalier.

Part III, 'Love and Literature', begins in Umayyad Spain and makes the journey back to Byzantium and Greece. In Chapter 5, following on the concept of troubadours as vehicles for the transmission of poetry and its forms, Jerónimo Méndez shows the transformation of the courtly love ideal through the journey of the Arabic poetry of Abu Nuwās to Spain and beyond the French frontier, offering a contrast between jocular obscenity and virginal love. Investigating the representation of love in these works, Mendez shows how ideals of chaste love were set opposite eroticism, excess and hedonism to depict the movement of the fourteenth and fifteenth century towards anti-courtly sentiments. Making a case for transmission of textual material in the direction West–East, Andrew Stephenson (Chapter 6) introduces a comparison of Byzantine and French *lais* in his survey, and a collation of the findings of some investigations of this material. By categorising the arguments of critics, he supports that more analysis along the lines of comparison of Byzantine to French literature needs to be undertaken.

Remaining in the Eastern Mediterranean, Amelia Brown (Chapter 7) shows how the performance of Aeschylus' *Oresteia* in Carthage changed over time into the Middle Ages to incorporate the interests, values, legislations and even languages of cultures other than that of its origins. Brown makes a study of the manuscript tradition of *Oresteia* as a dramatic art, revealing how its medieval performance was gradually modified to take on other forms and genres, reflecting a multicultural community in its format, patronage, costumes and the design of the stage itself.

Part IV, 'Material Culture', brings together aspects of architecture, art and clothing. Constantine's rebuilding of Constantinople as the new capital is the subject of Gordana Fontana-Giusti's chapter on how this city, as an artistic, architectural and cultural fusion of the past and present was constructed to envisage the future. Fontana-Giusti begins with a comparison of Byzantine texts on the construction of Constantinople ranging from classical Greece to those of the eighteenth century on recovering lost antiquities, before investigating the aspects of Constantine's creation of the 'new Rome' and the use of statuary and effigies, philosophy, public spaces and architecture, as well as memory and rhetoric to create a civic identity that held both ancient knowledge and modern significance.

There is no question of the importance of the robe as a garment to cultures across the medieval world, from monarchs to patriarchs, from troubadours to merchants, from priests to philosophers, in commerce, investiture, politics and theatre, and also in that facet of community which permeates all levels of culture: religion. This garment had more than a symbolic significance, as the *soufis* and the striving for spiritual chivalry in Sufism, but also a canon function and symbol of eminence, as in Hebrew, Byzantine, Christian and pagan religious rites. It is therefore fitting that the material culture of the robe in language comprises the subject of investigation for the final chapter (Part IV). It marks a unity in itself not only of Part IV, but in the compilation and demonstration of a tangible phenomenon of intercultural exchange across the Mediterranean Rim in space and time, a chapter within which all points of this volume converge. The relations between the Eastern and Western Roman Empires and all of the cultures with which they came into contact is the setting for Timothy Dawson's linguistic investigation of clothing terminology and cultural fashion as he demonstrates how these changed over time and distance, following the transmission of loan words and the integration of orthography and meaning from Persian to Greek to Arabic to English, and back again eastwards to Byzantium.

Together, these studies illustrate the cross-fertilization and reciprocal relationships apparent in historical events, cultural memory, written and material culture, prominent figures, art, oral transmission, performance, and architecture through text. Setting these articles side by side brings new light to the understanding of the issue of the scholarly reception of intercultural transmission and its historical influence and contribution. This is supported further in the common threads that are traced throughout this volume: religious and spiritual practice, chivalry, material culture, art, architecture and performance, which all have proven fertile ground for connections between diverse fields of study. This volume, then, will demonstrate and develop the idea that the textual transmission of ideas and culture across borders began much earlier than the Crusades and continued far beyond the twelfth century.

The influence of the texts of this era continues to stretch both forward and backward in time, as it has done since they were first written down, reflecting a landscape of multicultural and multilingual transmission of ideas, shared cultural inheritance, and communities that persists despite the cultural schism that seems to have taken hold between East and West after the thirteenth century. Each community is reshaping their cultural inheritance and adapting it to sustain their new environment. Just as Arabic texts translated from the Persian and Greek made their way to Spain, France and further to the British Isles, so too did their ideas, cultures and ethos travel the Mediterranean Rim and beyond, leaving their permanent mark on the Europe that would later extend its influence to the farther reaches of the globe.

S. L. Hathaway
Oxford

Notes

1   Elisséeff, Nikita. 'Les échanges culturels entre le monde musulman et les Croisés à l'époque de Nur ad-Din b. Zanki (m. 1174)'. In *The Meeting of Two Worlds: Cultural Exchange between East and West during the Period of the Crusades*, ed. Vladimir P. Goss, 39–52. Michigan: Medieval Institute Publications, 1986.

2   Weir, Alison. *Eleanor of Aquitaine: By the Wrath of God, Queen of England*. London: Jonathan Cape, 1999.

Part 1

Faith and Spirituality

1

Thomasine Metamorphosis:

Community, Text and Transmission from Greek to Coptic

David W. Kim

The Thomas people were initially a branch of the Jesus movement, composed under the individual leadership of Thomas, based on his own revelation and belief. If this is so, some questions should be considered, such as: What was the social policy of the Graeco-Roman Empire in which the leader(s) of the community had to make decisions about the texualization of the community canon? Where was the geographical and religio-cultural genesis of the Thomasine community? What was the initial language of the ancient text? And why did they choose that language among many other languages of the era? The three fragments of the *Oxyrhynchus Papyrus* 654, 1, 655, together with the *Nag Hammadi Codex* II, 2.32.10–51.28, not only present a new perspective on the genetic DNA of the Thomas people, but also reconfirm the linguistic insight that the Greek *Thomas* was cross-culturally translated into Coptic for those outsiders of ancient Christianity.

The Jesus people were persecuted from the time of the Founder to the reign of Constantine (AD 313). Many of the Roman Emperors, as well as the local rulers of the Eastern region, impacted directly or indirectly upon the process of the Christian persecution during their official period.[1] Domitian (AD 81–96)[2], after his father Vespasian (AD 69–79) and his brother Titus (AD 80–81), continuously afflicted Christians in connection with other Jews in various ways, although Richardson and Moreau doubt the separate identities of Christians and Jews in the time of Domitian.[3] When the Caesar, for example, compelled the two groups to pay the temple tax to the Jerusalem temple of Jupiter (Zeus),[4] Christians were executed for refusing to offer sacrifices before Domitian's image (AD 92).[5] The cruel behaviour of Domitian is likewise applied in the event of the capital punishment of his own family: the charge of atheism that was made against his own cousin, the consul Flavius Clemens, and his wife Domitilla, was presumably about their being Christians or Christian sympathizers (*Roman History*, LXVII[6]).

The persecution by the imperial authority did not stop, but extended to the reign of Trajan (AD 98–117). The persecution of Ignatius, Bishop of Antioch, who was martyred for his Christian faith (AD 108), was representative as the spread of the new Christian religion separate from Judaism motivated the Roman citizens to complain about unemployment among pagan temple-servers.[7] Trajan also instructed Pliny the Younger (Caius Caecilius Secundus) not to pay attention to anonymous denunciations of Christians when the Governor of Bithynia had asked for advice about Christians being the source of the social trouble in the north of Asia Minor (*Letters* 10.96–97: AD 112).[8] The mistreatment that occurred during the religious conflict in the local society eventually caused a socio-political revolt against the Romans at the end of Trajan's reign. At this time, there was also considerable internecine strife between Christians and Jews, particularly in Cyrene and Cyprus (AD 117).[9]

The Roman law forbidding circumcision in the land of Judaea became a major factor in the AD 132 to 35 revolt in which 580,000 men from anti-Roman groups (presumably including the converted Jewish-Christians) were slain during the reign of the next emperor, Hadrian (AD 117–138).[10] The Christian persecutions from the second half of the first century (AD 69) to the first half of the second century (AD 138) were not the first time in history that the Roman Empire exerted such pressure, but were simply the ongoing condition of the Christian communities, demonstrating that the post-Jewish War period AD 69–138 was not the right time for the textual project of Thomas.[11]

If the reigns of Tiberius (AD 14–37), Gaius (Caligula: AD 37–41) and Claudius (AD 41–54) were not also the actual time of the textualization of the Thomas Gospel, but were only oppressed times for the members of the community, the Jesus Logia project must have been transformed into written form during the first half of the reign of the next emperor, Nero (originally called Lucius Domitius: AD 54–68), who hated Christians intensely and executed the leaders and members of the Christian community as proof of his socio-political strategy.[12] The initial five years (called the quinquennium) of the 16-year-old emperor's reign, with the assistance of Seneca[13] and Burrus,[14] were peaceful.[15] But this peace did not last; rather, it changed into a dictatorship under the despotic advice of Tigellinus, when Nero officially became an adult (at age 21) in AD 59. The number of victims under the persecution of Nero is uncertain. The fire on 19 July AD 64, which burned 'more than half of Rome' and its property,[16] was one of the major historical incidents blamed on the new Christian movement.[17] The actual cause has not been identified, but the disaster was used by the corrupt Caesar as a method of self-protection against his political opponents. Cruel persecution reached its climax in the history of the pre-Constantine era under Nero. The situation is clearly expressed in the writings of P. Cornelius Tacitus:[18]

> [T]herefore, to overcome this rumour [about the cause of the fire], Nero put in his own place as culprits, and punished with most ingenious cruelty, men whom the common people hated for their shameful crimes and called *Christians* … they were not only put to death, but subjected to insults, in that they were either dressed up in the skins of wild beasts and perished by the cruel mangling of dogs, or else put on crosses to be set on fire, and as day declined, to be burned, being used as lights by night. Nero had thrown open his gardens for that spectacle, and gave a circus play, mingling with the people dressed in a charioteer's costume or driving in a chariot.
>
> (*Annals* XV, 44.2–8)[19]

During the neronian persecution, Peter was crucified and died in Nero's circus. He was buried in a large cemetery nearby in the summer of AD 64. These facts have not only been archaeologically verified in recent days,[20] but also the fourth canonical gospel credibly explains how Peter died.[21] Nero's persecution extended to Paul (AD 65) who was beheaded with a sword on the Ostian way and was then buried in a pine wood nearby (Sulpicius' *Chronicle* ii.29.15).[22] If the elite of the Thomasine community were not yet concerned about the significance of the Jesus tradition for preservation and transmission, it should be postulated that the community had not even existed in the AD 45 to 60 period[23] because the crisis for the Christian groups unpredictably increased from the beginning of the sixties AD and ultimately reached its peak at the fall of Jerusalem (AD 70).[24]

The genesis of Thomas

So where was the home town of the Thomas people? Contemporary readers customarily determine the Logia text within the Gnostic ambiance, disregarding the primary principle embodied in the Jesus tradition of Thomas (Table 1.1).

Reader	Period	Provenance	Community DNA	Language
Koester	AD 50s–60s	Edessa		Greek
Cameron	AD 50–100	Syria		Greek
Patterson	AD 70–80	Eastern Syria		

Reader	Period	Provenance	Community DNA	Language
Morrice	End of the 1st AD (approx. AD 80–90)	Syria (in or around Edessa)	Syriac-speaking Christian	Aramaic, Syriac
Vööbus (Valantasis)	AD 105–115 (AD 100–110)[25]	Edessa	Jewish-Christian	
Crossan	1st AD	Edessa	Eastern Syriac-speaking Christian	(Syriac)
Blatz	(AD 1st–150)	Syrian provenance		
Quispel	AD 140	Edessa	Jewish-Christian	Greek
Perrin	AD 173–200	Syrian provenance	Syriac Christian	Syriac
Layton	Before AD 200	Edessa		Greek (and Syriac)

Table 1.1 Contemporary research data on Thomas[26]

These scholars, who are generally interested in the time of writing, provenance and original language of the Logia text, have proposed their own conclusions about the Thomasine community. These are often contradictory because the external content of the text is not formed in a chronological or narrative way, but in a doctrinal style as an early Christian community instruction. Koester and Cameron's assumption of the date of the text is a revolutionary and pioneering challenge to other readers, yet the evidence is still insufficient for demonstrating the community DNA of Thomas.[27] Patterson, who asserts the similarity between Thomas and John in that they both have gnostic traces,[28] disregards the simplicity of the text with Q (known as written sources of the canonical writings). In addition, although two views of 'Syriac-speaking Christian' and 'Jewish-Christian' are suggested, most do not take the community identity as a focal point; instead, they focus more on the linguistic profile of the *Gos. Thom.*, divided into the two different cultures of Greek and Syriac.[29] If so, where is the most likely location for the establishment of the Thomasine community?

There are three major theories supported by contemporary readers. First, the view of Pella community that a Jewish-Christian group started to settle down in the town of Pella in the Gentile region of Decapolis (also called Transjordania) is considered to be the foremost hypothesis for the origin of the Thomas people.[30] The city of Pella was quite a reasonable place for the Jewish-Christian refugees of Jerusalem because it was not under the control of the Roman soldiers and was located on the other side of the Jordan River.[31] The ancient testimony of the *Ecclesiastical History* supports the Pella-flight tradition:

'the whole body, however, of the church at Jerusalem, having been commanded by a divine revelation ... before the [Jewish] war, removed from the city [of Jerusalem] and lived at a certain town beyond the Jordan [river] called Pella' (3.5.3).[32] Epiphanius of Salamis also describes the exodus of Christ's disciples from Jerusalem and the emigrant life in Pella: 'After all those who believed in Christ had generally come to live in Perea, in a city called Pella of the Decapolis of which it is written in the Gospels'.[33] The Pella-flight story, however, is very controversial, being viewed by some as historical and by others as unhistorical. Brandon, for example, denies the history of the flight to Pella, based on the assumption that the Jerusalem Christians in the pre-AD 70 period were affected by the plot of the Zealots and were destroyed during the war, while Munck presumes that the Jewish-Christians of Pella were not originally from the Jerusalem community, but were just part of a local post-AD 70 Jewish-Christian group.[34] Further, whether the Thomas community was part of the Pella refugees or not, the view that the Thomas text was written during the flight process of the religio-political war is not logically comprehensible in the context.[35]

Second, the viewpoint of a Hellenistic Christianity in Jerusalem and (later) in Antioch has related the Thomas followers.[36] The narrative of the seven ordained deacons (Stephen, Philip, Prochorus, Nicanor, Timon, Parmenas and Nicolas) in the *Book of Acts* informs readers about the weak position of the Hellenistic widows in the Jerusalem-Christian community.[37] Because of that there arose a complaint against the Hebrews by the Jerusalem Hellenists. The social concern that equal welfare was not being given to the Hellenistic widows was granted by the Twelve when the multitude of the disciples was summoned to a place in Jerusalem.[38] The author of the *Book of Acts* also recounts the rapid growth of the new Antiochene church: 'And the disciples were first called Christians in Antioch.'[39] The major members of the Christian community in the capital city of Syria were not Jews, but those who were called Gentiles by the traditional Jewish people.[40]

These Hellenistic sources claim that the initial Thomasine community was fundamentally a Gentile group that adopted the Jesus religion during the time in which the Jerusalem church was growing in the Hellenistic society. However, Nock has correctly pointed to the lack of evidence on the Hellenistic influence of early Christianity,[41] and the Hellenistic community cannot be determined with accuracy as being of Thomas' group because the inference of the Gentile community is based on unconvincing evidence. In the same way, the fact that there is no Gentilistic tradition in the *Gos. Thom.* is consistent with the less Gentilistic root of the community, if one accepts the notion that the context of a text is always incorporated into the DNA of the community membership and its customs when an author writes the community doctrine. The social culture of the early Christians agrees with Esler's concept of early Christian society in that 'the creation of the early Christian communities with their distinct modes of organisation, behaviour and symbolism provides an example of externalisation'.[42]

Third, with reference to the community, the city called Edessa in northern Mesopotamia east of the Euphrates, the capital of the independent kingdom of Osrhoëne between the Roman and the Parthian Empires, is frequently suggested (with Arbela[43]) as the epicentre of Thomas. The Edessa origin of the Thomasine community, for those who assume the textual dependence on the canonical Gospels, is based on various literary and archaeological sources. Along with the Indian legend of Thomas (fundamentally constructed by the *Acts Thom.*),[44] the Christian faith of Edessa emerged. This theory is maintained within the supposition that the new anti-Jewish religion of Jesus was preached to Agbarus, the prince of Edessa in the apostolic age, by the devoted effort of Thaddaeus, who was one of the 70 disciples,[45] and that Mar Peqidha, the first Bishop of Adiabene, who converted to Christianity, ruled between AD 105 and 115.[46] The legendary story of the successor of Thomas, for which Eusebius does not provide any datable source, is, in a slightly different era (half a century later), reintroduced in the book called *The Doctrine of Addai the Apostle*,[47] another form of the same tradition.[48] This Addai tradition proposes that one of the original copies of Thomas was brought to Edessa in the second half of the second century (AD 150–190). It is socio-politically reasonable since the region was outside the Roman Empire until AD 216.[49] Therefore, the Christian movement was formed during the independent period of Edessa, which seems to be the core point for the Edessa hypothesis.

In further detail, Addai, who had a Galilee and Jordan background, on reaching Edessa, stayed with a Palestinian Jew called Tobias until received by the local ruler of Edessa (Abgar VIII Bar Ma 'nu: AD 179–214).[50] The target of Addai in the kingdom was not only the king, the members of the royal family and the nobles, but included the people of many country villages.[51] His successor, Palut (c. AD 200), had to visit Antioch for episcopal ordination from the diocesan Serapion (AD 190–211).[52] Such historical data, nevertheless, leads one to conclude that there is no certain picture of a Christian structure or organization having been born within which a writing project could have been launched for the new belief. Rather, the Christian community of Edessa seems to have been formed during the last decades of the second century AD, based on evidence that the pioneer(s) of the community brought a copy of the community canon from their holy city Jerusalem to 'the satellite mission field'.[53]

Thus, the ancient writings of Christians and non-Christians, such as Hippolytus (AD 222–235), Origen (AD 233), Mani (AD 250), Eusebius (the first decades of the fourth century AD), the Jerusalem Cyril (AD 348), Jerome (late fourth century AD), Ambrose (late fourth century AD) and Philip of Side (AD 430), prove the existence of the *Gos. Thom.*,[54] but no record offers proof either for the Thomasine community in Edessa or for the publication of the *Logia* text in the non-Jewish town of strangers. The Thomas tradition, then, should be perceived as having been transported from one of the original Jesus movements, since the earliest Christians were almost 'Judaic-Christians'[55] in that the first disciples of Jesus were Jews and the original church was in Jerusalem. The question 'Where was the original dwelling place of the Thomasine community?' should be answered by tracing its origins from the city of Jerusalem, where the first Christian council was also held in AD 49. The Judaic-Christian community that was born pre-AD 45 grew to a certain size before the Jewish war (AD 66–70) among other Christian communities.[56] The following four factors support the hypothesis of the Jerusalem Judaic-Christian community: James' reputation with Thomas, the Jerusalem population, *Logion* 13, and the relevant figure with Q (the pre-canonical written sources).

34:25 **ⲡⲉϫⲉⲙ̅ⲙⲁⲑⲏⲧⲏⲥⲛ̅ⲓ̅ⲥ̅ ϫⲉ ⲧⲛ̅|**
34:26 **ⲥⲟⲟⲩⲛ ϫⲉ ⲕⲛⲁⲃⲱⲕ`ⲛ̅ⲧⲟⲟⲧ̅ⲛ̅ ⲛⲓⲙ` ⲡⲉ|**
34:27 **ⲉⲧⲛⲁⲣ̅ ⲛⲟϭ ⲉϩⲣⲁⲓ̈ ⲉϫⲱⲛ ⲡⲉϫⲉⲓ̅ⲥ̅ ⲛⲁⲩ|**
34:28 **ϫⲉ ⲡⲙⲁ ⲛ̅ⲧⲁⲧⲉⲧⲛ̅ⲉⲓⲙ̅ⲙⲁⲩ ⲉⲧⲉⲧⲛⲁ|**
34:29 **ⲃⲱⲕ` ϣⲁⲓ̈ⲁⲕⲱⲃⲟⲥ ⲡⲇⲓⲕⲁⲓⲟⲥ ⲡⲁⲉⲓⲛ̅ⲧⲁ|**
34:30 **ⲧⲡⲉ ⲙⲛ̅ ⲡⲕⲁϩ ϣⲱⲡⲉ ⲉⲧⲃⲏⲧϥ̅**

The disciples said to Jesus, 'We know that you will depart from us. Who is to be our leader?' Jesus said to them, 'Wherever you are, you are to go to James the righteous, for whose sake heaven and earth came into being.'

Gos. Thom. 12: NHC II, 2.34.25–30[57]

The *Oxyrhynchus* fragments do not contain this part of the Logion, but the *Nag Hammadi* Text (NHC II, 2) in the context of the 'Judaic-Christian element' defines **ⲓ̈ⲁⲕⲱⲃⲟⲥ ⲡⲇⲓⲕⲁⲓⲟⲥ** (James the Righteous)[58] to be the answer to **ⲛⲓⲙ` ⲡⲉⲉⲧⲛⲁⲣ̅ ⲛⲟϭ ⲉϩⲣⲁⲓ̈ ⲉϫⲱⲛ** (Who is to be our leader?), who thus becomes the leader after Jesus in the new religious movement (AD 44–62). Although the Judaic-Christians called 'the sect of the Nazoreans (*Ac.* 24.5) or Ebionites'[59] evidently continued until the end of the second century AD, the perspective that the figure of Ⲓⲁⲕⲱⲃⲟⲥ ⲡⲇⲓⲕⲁⲓⲟⲥ was well recognized in the Thomasine community clearly echoes the interactive relationship of James with Thomas in the Christian Assembly of Jerusalem.[60] Paul also testifies to the key leadership of Ⲓⲁⲕⲱⲃⲟⲥ ⲡⲇⲓⲕⲁⲓⲟⲥ as 'one of three pillars' by whom Paul (with Barnabas) was sanctioned to preach to the Gentiles in the land of Syria: 'James, Peter and John, those reputed to be pillars, gave me [Paul] and Barnabas the right hand of fellowship … They agreed that we should go to the Gentiles.'[61] In this respect it is certain that ⲑⲱⲙⲁⲥ is not excluded from the numbers of ⲙ̅ⲙⲁⲑⲏⲧⲏⲥⲛ̅ⲓ̅ⲥ̅. The concept that the authority of the Jesus leadership for the new anti-Jewish movement was passed on to Ⲓⲁⲕⲱⲃⲟⲥ ⲡⲇⲓⲕⲁⲓⲟⲥ[62] also predicts that the sub-authority of the leadership would possibly be re-imparted to Thomas by ⲡⲇⲓⲕⲁⲓⲟⲥ, when the Jerusalem Christian community was unaccountably growing and unexpectedly extended. Eisenman, in the direct appointment scenario, views the historical James as 'the Bishop of Bishops' or 'Archbishop', advocating the role of Thomas as a regional bishop of Jerusalem.[63] The report of Luke on the new religious revival reflects the effect of the disciples' leadership in Jerusalem: 'So the word of God spread. The number of disciples in Jerusalem increased rapidly, and a large number of priests became obedient to the faith.'[64] Lapham suggests that in the narrative 'the Twelve were generally to be found about their missionary tasks,'[65] supporting the independent work of Thomas as one of the 12 disciples of the new *Christ* movement.

The story that the earliest Judaic-Christians travelled and established local churches throughout Palestine (*Gal.* 1:22; *Ac.* 9:31) and the Diaspora (*Ac.* 9.1) in the context of 'Jewish Christians outside Palestine' is addressed in the *Letter of James*, especially in his mention of 'the twelve tribes that are in the Diaspora' (1.1). But if one considers the population of Jerusalem in the first century AD (approximately 80,000),[66] the location of the Thomasine community should be placed somewhere in Jerusalem.[67] The remarkable growth of the Jerusalem church in the scene of *Ac.* 6:7[68] indicates that about half of the population of Jerusalem, or one-third, was converted to the new doctrine of Jesus. Luke's account of the Christian population of Jerusalem – 'The number of the men came to be about five thousand (5,000)'[69] – at least helps to estimate the number of 20,000 followers from the supposition that women and children were not included in the population count in the Jewish society of the first century AD, and one family may be said, in general, to be composed of four members: father, mother and two children (*Mt.* 14.21).[70] Further, another demonstration of the growing numbers of the Christian population in Jerusalem – 'multitudes of men and women, were constantly added to their number', possibly up to the 5,000[71] – divulges that the Christian population in Jerusalem was apparently between 20,000 and 40,000 in the period of pre-AD 62, before the death of ⲒⲀⲔⲰⲂⲞⲤ ⲠⲀⲒⲔⲀⲒⲞⲤ. If the combined size of the Christian groups is connected with the meaning of 'the whole church',[72] the apostles and elders at the first Jerusalem council must have been representatives of many regional churches or communities in which the average membership of a single group would have been between 1,600 and 3,200. Although it is risky to speculate on the exact number in an early Christian group, especially in the first century AD, the Thomasine community, which is presumed to have at least 400 to 800 families, was a mega-church that needed its own version of the Jesus tradition based on the memories and experiences of the community's founder, Thomas.

Thomas, in the scene of Logion 13, is exalted by Jesus because of Thomas' humble attitude, though it is still not clear whether the word 'Master' or the statement ϩⲟⲗⲱⲥ ⲧⲁⲧⲁⲡⲣⲟ ⲛⲁϣⲁⲡϥ` ⲁⲛ ⲉⲧⲣⲁ ϫⲟⲟⲥ ϫⲉ ⲉⲕⲉⲓⲛⲉⲛ̄ⲛⲓⲙ` ('my mouth is wholly incapable of saying whom you are like') was important to the founder of the new sect, Jesus. The external figure to the scene recalls a similar picture in the Matthean text (16.13–20), which was written for a Jewish-led Christian community. The narrator of the text, based on rumours of Jesus as 'John the Baptist, Elijah, Jeremiah or one of the prophets', starts the account with Jesus asking about His own identity, continues by hearing the response of His followers, and concludes as Jesus encouraged and exhorted the only man who gave the best speech about him. Simon's confession of ὁ Χριστὸς ὁ υἱὸς του θεου του ζωντος (Christ, the Son of living God) satisfied Jesus' mind; this phrase is comparable with Jesus' self-acknowledgement as ⲡϣⲏⲣⲉ ⲙ̄ⲡⲉⲧⲟⲛϩ (the son of the living one) in Logion 37 of *Thomas*.[73] The other part of Logion 13 ('ⲁⲩⲱ ⲁϥϫⲓⲧϥ̄ ⲁϥⲁⲛⲁⲭⲱⲣⲉⲓ| ⲁϥϫⲱ ⲛⲁϥ ⲛ̄ϣⲟⲙⲧ`ⲛ̄ϣⲁϫⲉ; and he took him, he withdrew, he spoke to him three words') states that Thomas, among the disciples, was particularly given ⲛ̄ϣⲟⲙⲧ`ⲛ̄ϣⲁϫⲉ (three words) that had to be kept secret, even from his fellow disciples, while Simon Peter and Matthew were depicted as being unable to comprehend the nature of Jesus.[74] Puech suggests that the ⲛ̄ϣⲟⲙⲧ`ⲛ̄ϣⲁϫⲉ (three words) were the Names of Father, Son and Holy Spirit, disagreeing with Wilson who argues that they were definitely 'blasphemous to Jewish ears'.[75] This particular section seems to exalt the community founder Thomas (like Judas of Tchacos Codex 47.1–53.7)[76] more mystically than any other eyewitness disciple of Jesus and also implies that the Thomasine community was unique in being unusually privileged and having been given the secret instructions[77] from the historical figure of Jesus. In this context, the last saying ('When Thomas returned to his companions, they asked him, what did Jesus say to you?') can be interpreted as that the

Ⲛ̄ϢⲞⲘⲦ` Ⲛ̄ϢⲀϪⲈ (three words) were the special revelation for Thomas' ministry, independent from the rest of the Christian communities of Jerusalem. Patterson attests the independence campaign as a growing phenomenon in the early Church, in that '[Logion 13] suggests a time … when local communities had begun to appeal to the authority of particular well-known leaders … to guarantee the reliability of their claims'.[78]

Furthermore, tracking the similarity of Thomas with external and internal figures of the Q (the pre-canonical *Jesus* tradition) community is another method by which one can evaluate the credibility of the Thomas group.[79] The Q community that is centrally concerned about the Torah, the Hebrew ethics of life and the term 'living Jesus', pursues the same or familiar community purpose with the Thomasine people.[80] The community of Q practised the Law of Moses, but 'the community preferred a less burdensome application of the Law'.[81] This is revealed in the case where the passage of Q (*Mt.* 23.4//*Lk.* 11.46) arraigns the Pharisees and scribes for binding 'heavy burdens' on the shoulders of the ordinary Jews. In this regard, Jesus in Logion 39 of *Thomas* warns: 'you, however, be as wise as serpents and as innocent as doves', after saying that 'the Pharisees and the scribes have taken the keys of knowledge and hidden them. They themselves have not entered, nor have they allowed to enter those who wish to.'[82] The story of Jesus dividing the Law into two primary commandments of 'love God and love your neighbour' (Q/*Lk.* 10.25–28) expresses a similar attitude towards the Law being lightened or loosened. The ethical behaviour of the Q community, which was based on moral exhortations, corresponds to the ultimate concepts of the Thomas people, such as loving one's enemies, resisting evildoers, not judging others, seeking God rather than wealth, and following the teachings of Jesus.[83] The literary Gattung of Q, which is congruous with *Thomas*, supports the point that the two communities of early Christianity would probably have known each other or at least existed in the same period before AD 60. Therefore, the existence of many diverse Christian groups, 'with different shades of Christology', indicates that the major Jewish Thomasine community was an urban group centred in Jerusalem and co-existed with other Jewish or Gentile-Christian communities (*Ac.* 6.1).[84]

The linguistic policy of Thomas

What, then, would be the linguistic policy of the ancient group for their canonical project in such a socio-political environment? In this regard, when

Jesus was crucified, the signpost placed on the cross was written in three languages of Aramaic, Latin and Greek (*Jn.* 19.19–20).[85] Why is that? It is generally known that Aramaic was the local language of Jews, that Latin was the official language of the Roman Empire (military), and that Greek was the most common language of the Empire; thus all the residential people of Jerusalem and surrounding areas would have understood the case of Jesus. Among those languages, Aramaic, which was divided into several dialects, including Jewish-Aramaic (Galilean), Christian-Palestinian Aramaic and Samaritan, according to Brock,[86] was used as the daily conversational language of the lower classes. The large number of bilingual people in the local towns using Aramaic as their mother tongue indicates that the language was limited only to Jews, and not to the outsiders.[87] Quispel claims that the origin of *Thomas* is Aramaic, in that the author of the text lived around AD 140 and integrated the Gospel tradition of Judaic Christian origin. Quispel, in analysing a unique character of Thomas in Logion 9,[88] found an Aramaic tradition (*'al urha*) in the Coptic word ⲈⲬⲚ̄ (on), but he did not connect the Logion with Greek; instead, he disregarded the influence of the worldwide communicational medium because of the Gentile communities that spoke Aramaic.[89] While Quispel failed to prove the close relationship between Aramaic and Greek in the multilingual world of *Thomas*, Frend assumes the existence of the Aramaic text of *Thomas* used among the Greek-speaking Christians and further suggests that the Aramaic text was spread among Syriac dialect-speaking groups.[90] Yet this view fails to address the purpose of the *Thomas* compiler in terms of the impact of the Greek language in the Hellenized regions of Jewish-Christian communities.

Likewise, Yamauchi, one of those who believe that *Thomas* depicts a pre-Christian gnosticism, claims that the *Gos. Thom.*, like the *Acts Thom.*, was originally written in Syriac. His perspective is supported by Davies who states that the *Acts Thom.* is 'a Syrian pious novel' and that the *Thom. Cont.* is 'a fictional Syrian dialogue between Thomas and Jesus'.[91] Further, the Syriac origin of *Thomas* based on the hypothesis of Thomas' dependence on the synoptic tradition is demonstrated in relation to the *Diatessaron of Tatian* (written in about 170 AD). Perrin argues that the character of Thomas' catchwords not only fits within a Syriac milieu but is also shared in the *Odes Sol.*[92] The variants shared by Thomas and the *Diatessaron*, compared against the Greek Mss. of the Gospels, constituted more evidence for Perrin that the *Diatessaron* was one of Thomas' sources. The view that *Logia* 14, 45 and 45 are dependent on the *Diatessaron* became further material for Perrin.[93] However, Perrin's linguistic analysis, which depends on the *Nag Hammadi Thomas*, is much diminished in the light of the three *Oxyrhynchus* fragments. Greenlee carefully overturns this view, stating that the *Diatessaron* was composed in Greek or translated from a Greek original.[94]

If there is limited evidence that the Aramaic and Syriac languages were the original languages of *Thomas*, the stream of thought holding to the anti-gnostic influence and the independence of *Thomas* from the canonical texts has more potential within a hypothesis of a Greek origin, since the complete *Nag Hammadi* text was translated from a Greek text.[95] The *Thomas* text preserved in Greek and Coptic should, therefore, be more credible,[96] rather than following assumptions of non-existing texts (no Aramaic or Syriac *Gos. Thom.* exists at present) – just as the questions suggest a negative response, despite unclear traces of both languages contained in those texts: whether any NT text, including Paul's *Letters*, was originally written in Aramaic or Syriac; or whether the original Q was written in one of these languages. No objections among Q scholars, including Kloppenborg, have been made against the view that Q was originally written in Greek. Since Q and *Thomas* are valued on an equal level in studies of the Jesus *Logia* tradition,[97] this view should also be adopted with regard to the original language of *Thomas*. The existence of the *Oxyrhynchus* Greek fragments themselves justifies the possibility that the *Logia* text in the first edition was concerned not only with the Jewish-Christians who were the bilingual members of the community but also with the newly converted Gentiles. The composition of the Thomasine community, which was mainly Jewish-Christian with an increasing percentage of Gentile-Christians, is significant in that the post-disciple leader of the community had to decide whether to use the prevailing Greek language within the Eastern Roman Empire.

The meaning of gnosis in the Coptic phrase ⲯⲚ̄ⲰⲀⲰⲦ`Ⲛ̄ⲦⲄⲚⲰⲤⲒⲤ (the keys of knowledge: Logion 39)' is also not derived from any dialect of Aramaic or particularly Syriac, but from the Greek term γνῶσις ; this is consistent with the fact that 60 per cent of the words of the Coptic text were derivatives of Greek words.[98] Where the sacred names became the major Greek loan words in Coptic, the word ⲒⲤⲬ the abbreviation of ⲒⲎⲤⲞⲨⲤ (Jesus), which was derived from the abbreviation ⲒⲤ̄ from Ἰησους, is one of the most representative Greek loan words in Coptic, just as ⲒⲎ̄Ⲗ̄ for ⲒⲤⲢⲀⲎⲖ (Israel: Logion 52), ⲠⲚ̄Ⲁ̄ for ⲠⲚⲈⲨⲘⲀ (spirit: Logia 14, 29, 44, 53 and 114), and ⲢⲘ̄ for ⲢⲰⲘⲈ (man: Logia 4, 7, 8, etc.), while ⲤⲒⲘⲰⲚⲠⲈⲦⲢⲞⲤ (Simon Peter), ⲘⲀⲐⲐⲀⲒⲞⲤ (Matthew), ⲀⲆⲀⲘ (Adam), ⲤⲀⲖⲰⲘⲎ (Salome) and ⲘⲀⲢⲒⳀⲀⲘ (Mary) came directly from the Greek.[99] Regarding the shortening of a word in the process of translating, Greenlee demonstrates four common forms: *contraction*, omitting the middle part of a word; *suspension*, omitting the last part of a word; *ligature*, combining two or more letters into one syllable; and *symbols* like '&' for 'and' as a practical skill of handwriting. These linguistic phenomena are frequently applied in the *Nag Hammadi* text, which has already been depicted in the *Oxyrhynchus Papyri*.[100]

For example, the *Logiographer* of the *Gos. Thom.* demonstrates the manner of emphasising a character's identification by using a nickname. The ⲡⲆⲓⲕⲆⲓⲟⲥ (the *Just*) of Logion 12 is not that person's real name, but a nickname supporting the real name Ïⲁⲕⲱⲃⲟⲥ (James), so everyone easily recognized Ïⲁⲕⲱⲃⲟⲥ as the ⲆⲓⲕⲆⲓⲟⲥ. This is repeated in Ïⲱϩⲁⲛⲛⲏⲥ ⲡⲃⲁⲡⲧⲓⲥⲧⲏⲥ (John the Baptist); ⲡⲃⲁⲡⲧⲓⲥⲧⲏⲥ of Logion 46 was the major activity of Ïⲱϩⲁⲛⲛⲏⲥ. In the same way, the official name of Thomas, ⲆⲓⲆⲩⲙⲟⲥ ÏⲟⲩⲆⲁⲥ ⲑⲱⲙⲁⲥ (Didymus Judas Thomas),[101] may be understood through the principle of the power of his first name, if the Coptic translator thought about non-Jewish Greek-speaking Christians in the Hellenistic society. As the reputation of the author of a text in ancient times easily expanded the range of readership, the initial name of the author symbolized his background: where he came from or what kind of social position or status he possessed. The three synoptic narrators, without mentioning Thomas' real name, use the Aramaic-originated nickname Thomas only once throughout their entire texts as well as in the *Book of Acts* (*Mt.* 10.3; *Mk.* 3.18; *Lk.* 6.15; and *Acts* 1.13), which indicates that the major target of the synoptic narrators was presumably the converted Jewish-Christians and their communities.

From this perspective, the *Nag Hammadi* text should announce ⲑⲱⲙⲁⲥ or ÏⲟⲩⲆⲁⲥ ⲑⲱⲙⲁⲥ as the author of the text, which is the proper order (the real name + Aramaic nickname), but the Coptic translator more logically used the Greek nickname ⲆⲓⲆⲩⲙⲟⲥ before the official name. Why did he use such a stylistic order for Jude's name? Was it just coincidental, or did he place it that way intentionally? These questions have led to various ideas in the minds of both ancient and modern readers. The manner of writing ⲆⲓⲆⲩⲙⲟⲥ ÏⲟⲩⲆⲁⲥ ⲑⲱⲙⲁⲥ, according to Cullmann, is close to a Syrian tradition as found in the Syriac translation of the *Gospel of John* (*Jn.* 14.22),[102] but he does not provide any clearer ideas on the purpose of the order of Jude's name, instead pointing to the linguistic power of Greek as the major communicational tool in the Graeco-Roman world. Since the Aramaic nickname ⲑⲱⲙⲁⲥ is located after the full name for ÏⲟⲩⲆⲁⲥ,[103] the propriety of the Coptic translator being mainly concerned with Greek-speaking Christians, on the other hand, is a more acceptable view because the Aramaic-speaking Christians were already confident and dominant in the community, so that the new textualising project should not be forced only on the original members, but also on the new Greek-speaking 'outsiders', including 'God-worshippers',[104] coming into the community. The structure of the full name ⲆⲒⲆⲨⲘⲞⲤ ⲒⲞⲨⲆⲀⲤ ⲐⲰⲘⲀⲤ, which is translated as 'the Twin Judas the Twin' (the Greek nickname + the real name + the Aramaic nickname) in two different languages,[105] is most likely owing to the notion that the major Greek-speaking group including the Jews of Egypt could not read Aramaic, while the initial members of the community who were from an Aramaic background were bilingual users of the Greek language.

The name of Ἰούδας Θωμας in the *Oxyrhynchus Papyri* 654, written not by a native Greek speaker but by a semi-native Greek speaker of Aramaic origins (of the so-called 1.5 generation of Jesus), simply reflects the fact that the *Logiographer* disregarded the range of the readership in the period of textualising the verbal Logia, as he only followed the traditional way of naming the person. It is unlikely that the Coptic translator would want to emphasize the mainly biological as well as spiritual and psychological twinship with the historical person, Jesus, since not only is the character of Jude drawn in the double terms ⲆⲒⲆⲨⲘⲞⲤ and ⲐⲰⲘⲀⲤ, reminding readers that ⲒⲞⲨⲆⲀⲤ is the real name of the person, but s/he has also advertised the credibility and originality of her/his community in connecting it with the Founder of the Christ movement.[106] Although Mani (AD 215–276), according to the writings of the Manicheans (*CMC* 69.9–70.9), received his *syzygos*, the spiritual twinship with Jesus from the heavenly father figure,[107] the twinship of Thomas in a spiritual sense is not clear in the case of the three synoptics and *Book of Acts*, which do not present the real name Ἰούδας, but the Aramaic nickname Θωμας only.[108] If the word Θωμας was really pointing to the spiritual twinship with Jesus, those canonical writers would likely have added the term Θωμας, whether before or after the real name, to the names of the other disciples such as Andrew (the Twin), Philip (the Twin), Bartholomew (the Twin), Matthew (the Twin), etc. The other term, 'the doubting Jude', instead of 'Jude the Twin', is, though in a negative way, another choice that the redactor of the text could have used to describe the uncertain belief about the character's status, if the twinship of Thomas was psychological. Instead of causing one to despise the twin brother of Jesus by way of the three concepts above, the picture of touching the wounds of the resurrected Jesus in the *Gospel of John* exalts Ἰούδας (Judas), who had had an extraordinary experience that left a deep impression he felt throughout his life. This is consistently connected with the moment in which Thomas himself acknowledges Jesus' divinity by saying, 'My Lord and my God'.[109] This view of the secret of the official name of the Thomasine author, as intended by the *Logiographer*, is validated in Koester's assertion that 'attribution of authorship to Didymus Judas Thomas situates the text at a time … to secure the identity and guarantee the reliability of the tradition'.[110]

Further, if one considers Table 1.2, the omitted words or phrases of the Greek text, the added words or phrases of the Coptic text, and the textual alteration in the process of transmission prove not only the effects of the translation, but also the extension and development of the Thomasine Christianity in the cross-cultural context of the Graeco-Roman world.[111]

Logion number	P. Oxy. Omitted	NHC II, 2 Altered	Added	Note
Prologue	(1)		(1)	
Logion 1				
Logion 2	(1)	(3)	(1)	
Logion 3	(4)	(4)	(2)	
Logion 4	(1)			
Logion 5	(1)			
Logion 6		(2)	(2)	
Logion 7				Two parts of *P. Oxy.* 654 (the beginning and the end parts) are critically damaged, so these parts cannot be compared with the Coptic Logion.[112]
Logion 24				The beginning part of *P. Oxy.* 655 was lost, so it cannot be compared with the Coptic text.[113]
Logion 26		(1)		The beginning part of *P. Oxy.* 1 was lost.
Logion 27	(1)			
Logion 28				The last part of *P. Oxy.* 1 was lost.[114]
Logion 29		(1)		A large part of the beginning of *P. Oxy.* 1 is missing.
Logion 30	(2)	(2)		The last part of *P. Oxy.* 1 is relocated to the end of the Coptic Logion 77.
Logion 31		(1)		
Logion 32		(1)		
Logion 33		(1)		The last part of *P. Oxy.* 1 is missing.
Logion 36	(3)	(1)		
Logion 37	(1)	(2)		The last part of *P. Oxy.* 655 is missing.
Logion 38		(1)		
Logion 39		(1)		

Table 1.2 A comparison between the Greek text and the Coptic text

The comparison of the Greek text[115] with the Coptic version[116] would not be entirely effective or fruitful, since the three fragments of *P. Oxy.* 1 (Logia 26–33), *P. Oxy.* 654 (Prologue-Logia 7) and *P. Oxy.* 655 (Logion 24 and Logia 37–39) are not derived from the same text[117] and each fragment was seriously damaged.[118] In fact, if one regards the external arrangement of *P. Oxy.* 1 and *P. Oxy.* 655, one might assume that *P. Oxy.* 1 (Logia 26–33) is supposed to be located in between Logion 24 and Logia 37–39 of *P. Oxy.* 655. However, as the constitutional survey of Logion 24 of *P. Oxy.* 655 is recorded on the verso[119] of Logia 37–39, and *P. Oxy.* 1 (Logia 26–33) is not placed in between them but written on a completely different papyrus, this implies the different historical background of *P. Oxy.* 1 and *P. Oxy.* 655.[120]

Furthermore, when one investigates each one of the *Oxyrhynchus* Logia, it is more than probable that the Coptic text must be a translated version intended for the ancient community of Egypt.[121] Table 1.2[122] shows that most (17) of the Greek Logia, except for four Logia (1, 7, 24 and 28),[123] have been changed in some aspects of the literal composition. Among them, the nine Greek Logia (Prologue, 2, 3, 4, 5, 27, 30, 36 and 37) were omitted and the four Coptic Logia (Prologue, 2, 3 and 6) were extended. The 13 Logia of the Greek text were intentionally re-edited by the Coptic translator.[124]

The modernity of the Coptic text is well seen in the phenomenon of omission or addition. For instance, the Greek phrase 'who is also' in the Prologue is omitted in the Coptic *Gospel of Thomas* (*C.G. Th*). Instead, the translator of the *C.G. Th*, as previously mentioned, added the Greek nickname Didymus before his real name Judas, in consideration of the dominant Greek influence even in the Coptic society. When the Greek conjunction 'and' in Logion 2 was skipped, the Coptic phrase 'he will be astonished, and' was added. The four Greek parts ('that', 'of the sea', 'of God', and 'whoever knows himself will discover this. And') of Logion 3 are deleted, but the new phrases of 'to you' and 'then you will become known, and' functioned to make the context of the Coptic text clearer.[125] Where the Greek phrases 'and the last will be first' (Logion 4) and 'nor buried that will not be raised' (Logion 5) are left out,[126] the *C.G. Th* added the two parts 'to him' and 'and nothing covered will remain without being uncovered' in Logion 6.[127]

Likewise, if one explores the alterations in each Logion, the three Greek parts: 'be amazed', 'amazed' and 'and once he has ruled, he will attain rest' (Logion 2) were changed into the forms: 'become troubled', 'troubled' and 'over the all'.[128] The words 'under the earth', 'enter it preceding you', 'and', and 'you are sons of the living father' (Logion 3) are changed into the words 'in the sea', 'precede you', 'Rather',[129] and 'it is you who are the sons of the living father'. The question 'how shall we fast?' (Logion 6) is compared to 'do you want us to fast?'[130] The connecting words 'and then' (Logion 26) are reduced to 'then'.[131] The Greek present tense verb 'makes' (Logion 29) is compared to the form of the present perfect tense verb 'has made'.[132] Similarly, the words 'country' (Logion 31), 'built' (Logion 32) and 'of mine' (Logion 38) are transformed into 'village', 'being built' and 'which I am saying to you', while the phrases 'that which you (sg.) hear in one of your (sg.) ears, preach' (Logion 33),[133] 'He' (Logion 37), 'disrobe and are not ashamed' (Logion 37)[134] and 'who were about to come in' (Logion 39) are corrected to 'preach from your housetops that which you (sg.) will hear in your (sg.) ear', 'Jesus', 'disrobe without being ashamed' and 'who wish to'. The exegetical analysis of the Thomas texts produces the result that 15 parts of the Greek text were omitted in the Coptic version, that the translator added six parts of the four Logia (Prologue, 2, 3 and 6), and that 21 parts of the Greek text have been reduced or extended in the religio-cultural transformation. A linguistic comparison between the *G.G.Th* and *C.G.Th* cannot be accurate, since it is uncertain that the present *G.G.Th* texts are historically the actual reference for the present *C.G.Th*. Nevertheless, such a literal observation still ensures that the key point of each Logion has not been altered radically, even in the process of transmission, and that the textual shift of the Logia tradition is from Greek to the Coptic version.[135]

Conclusion

In the end, the hypothesis that the canonization of Thomas is primarily related to the circumstances of the era's history is justified by the interrelationships of the religio-political environment of the Graeco-Roman world. Imperial persecution and the regional criticism of the anti-Christian Jews support the period of AD 45 to 60 as being the most appropriate time for the textual project of Thomas.[136] There is no certain indication either that the Thomas school was deliberately established for the project of the textualization or that the canonical project of Thomas brought about the formation of the community institution, but it is worthwhile to speculate about their previous achievements when the Jewish Christians were in the Holy City before the unwanted war. The historical and textual evidence commonly draw the picture of the Judaic-Christian community of Thomas in Jerusalem. The linguistic transformation is also revealed in the fact that the Greek language was not their mother tongue, and yet they did not hesitate to use that common medium of communication of the Graeco-Roman world for Thomas' textualization. Many major components of the Coptic language support the argument that the ultimate decision the *Logiographer* made for the language of Thomas was not an unusual case but was part of the socio-cultural precedent of the era for the generalization, popularization and officialization of the community canon. If the Thomasine community was such a systematic group in terms of its goal of global mission, one should not underestimate the religio-political identity of the early Christian movement.

Notes

1 Rome's anti-Christian Emperors were: Tiberius (AD 14–37), Hadrian (AD 117–138), Antoninus Pius (AD 138–161), Marcus Aurelius (AD 161–180), Septimius Severus (AD 193–211), Maximin the Thracian (AD 235–238), Decius (AD 249–251), Valerian (AD 253–260), Gallienus (AD 260–268) and Diocletian (AD 284–305).

2 Domitian was one of the 'evil emperors' represented in the writings of Suetonius (*Domitian 13*). Barrett, *The New Testament Background: Selected Documents*, 19–20.

3 Richardson, *Israel in the Apostolic Church*, 40–41. The Christian sect was first distinguished from Judaism in the time of Nero (AD 64).

4 The most dominant Greek gods – Zeus, Hera, Poseidon, Artemis, Athena, Hermes, Ares, Aphrodite, Demeter, Dionysus and Hephaestus, but not Apollo – were identified with the Roman gods respectively: Jupiter, Juno, Neptune, Diana, Minerva, Mercury, Mars, Venus, Ceres, Bacchus and Vulcan. Spivey and Smith, *Anatomy of the New Testament: A Guide to Its Structure and Meaning*, 34–45.

5 Williams, *Chronology of the Ancient World: 10,000 B.C. to A.D. 799*, 314–15.

6 'Domitian slew, along with many others, Flavius Clemens the consul, although he was a cousin and had wife Flavia Domitilla, who was also a relative of the emperor's. The charge brought against them both was that of atheism, a charge on which many others who drifted into Jewish ways were condemned.' Cary, *Dio's Roman History VIII*, 349–350. Ayer, *A Source Book for Ancient Church History: From the Apostolic Age to the Close of the Conciliar Period*, 11–12.

7 The tradition of Ignatius' death is that he was thrown to the lions in the arena. His saying of 'suffer me to be eaten by the beasts, through whom I can attain God' shows that Ignatius was ready to die for his Christian belief. See *The Epistle of Saint Ignatius to the Romans IV.1*, in Everitt, *Part III: The Christian Testament Since the Bible*, 23–5.

8 The Younger Pliny, *The Letters of Pliny*, 97–99. Sher Win-White, *Fifty-Letters of Pliny*, 68–71. Bull, *The Rise of the Church*, 154–6. Ayer, 19–23.

9 Williams, 321. De Ste Croix, 'Early Christian Attitudes to Property and Slavery', in *Church Society and Politics: Papers Read At the Thirteenth Summer Meeting and the Fourteenth Winter Meeting of the Ecclesiastical History Society*, 1–38.

10   Although this looks like a matter concerning the traditional Jews only, if one
      considers the Christian communities as being Jewish-led in the history of early
      Christianity, the 580,000 men could be not only Jews, but Jewish-Christians as
      well. Dio Cassius, *Roman History LXIX.* 12: 4–45. Eusebius, *Historia Ecclesiastica*
      IV, vi: 1–4. See Cary, 446–9. Freeman, *Egypt, Greece and Rome: Civilizations of the
      Ancient Mediterranean*, 418–21.

11   The archaeological evidence of the *Oxyrhynchus Papyrus*, which has already
      generalized the production of the original Logia as having occurred at least in the
      period pre-AD 140, indicates that this was improbable during the reigns of the
      post-Hadrian emperors as well. See Yamauchi, *Pre-Christian Gnosticism*, 89–90.

12   Merrill, *Essays in Early Christian History*, 82–130. Spence, *Early Christianity and
      Paganism: A.D. 64 to the Peace of the Church in the Fourth Century*, 40–63. Klauck,
      The Religious Context of Early Christianity: A Guide to Graeco-Roman Religions,
      306–8.

13   He was known as one of the most articulate proponents of Roman Stoicism ('a
      single brotherhood of the world'). Gallio, who was Seneca's brother, was also
      Governor of Greece during this period (*Acts* 18:12). Freeman, 408–11.

14   He was 'the prefect of the praetorian guards'. Ferguson, *Backgrounds of Early
      Christianity (Third Edition)*, 34.

15   See Paul's *Rom.*, 13.

16   The fire, which began among the shops filled with wares, raged for six days and
      seven nights. Numberless palaces and important buildings were consumed. A full
      account is presented in *Annals of Tacitus* (XV.2). See Johnson, *The Writings of the
      New Testament*, 97. Spence, 42–4. Barnes, *St. Peter in Rome and His Tomb on the
      Vatican Hill*, 84–6.

17   Williams, 300–1.

18   It covers Roman history between AD 14 and 68.

19   Although Tacitus (AD 52–117) was not an eyewitness of the persecution and was a
      pagan historian, that his information was entirely accurate and trustworthy is the
      common view of modern readers. Miller, *Tacitus Annals 15: Annalivm Liber XV*,
      24. Ayer, 6–7. Clark, *The Rise of Christianity*, 14. Barrett, 15–16.

20   Frend, 'The Archaeologist and Church History', 259–65.

21   'When you were younger you dressed yourself and went where you wanted; but
      when you are old you will stretch out your hands, and someone else will dress you
      and lead you where you do not want to go. Jesus said this to indicate the kind of
      death by which Peter would glorify God' (21.18–19).

22   Quoted in Barrett, 17. See Andel, *The Christian Concept of History in the
      Chronicle of Sulpicius Severus*, 40, 52, 68, 111, 121–2. Stancliff, *St. Martin and His
      Hagiographer: History and Miracle in Sulpicius Serverus*, 80–95.

23   Based on Josephus' interpretation of 'when the city [Jerusalem] was in very great
      peace and prosperity' (*The Jewish War* 6.5.5 [300]), the period for Thomas may

be up to 61 or early 62, if the Thomasine community had already launched the textualization work before then.

24   The four-year duration of the Jewish war (AD 66–70) would also likely not have been the most appropriate time during which a group or an individual might engage in religious writing. See Pliny, *Natural History*, 17. 5. Ellis, 'New Directions in the History of Early Christianity', 71–92. Robinson, *Reading the New Testament*, 13–30. William, 300–305. Brandon, *The Fall of Jerusalem and the Christian Church: A Study of the Effects of the Jewish Overthrow of A.D. 70 on Christianity*, 154–66.

25   Valantasis insists that Thomas has common points with John and Ignatius, so that the text was written around AD 100–110, but he still advocates the independence of Thomas from those texts. Valantasis, *The Gospel of Thomas*, 1–27.

26   These scholars, including Uro, represent the contemporary Thomas readers as offering 'the creative reader-response ideology'.

27   Koester, 'The Text of the Synoptic Gospels in the Second Century', in *Gospel Traditions in the Second Century: Origins, Recensions, Texts and Transmission*, 19–37. Cameron, *The Other Gospels: Non-Canonical Gospel Texts*, 23–5.

28   Patterson, *The Gospel of Thomas and Jesus*, 1993. Dunderberg also assumes that Thomas was written in the period of AD 70–100. Dunderberg, 'Thomas' I-Sayings and the Gospel of John', in *Thomas at the Crossroads: Essays on the Gospel of Thomas*, 33–64.

29   An exception to this is Morrice's view of Aramaic. Morrice, *Hidden Sayings of Jesus: Words Attributed to Jesus Outside the Four Gospels*, 23–5, 63–9.

30   See Pritz, *Nazarene Jewish Christianity*, 122–7.

31   Gwatkin, *Early Church History to A.D. 313 (Volume 2)*, 1–18. Robinson, 16–25.

32   Eusebius, *Ecclesiastical History*, translated by C. F. Cruse, 70.

33   The phrase of *Panarion*, 30.2.7. quoted by Saint (Bp. Of Constantia in Cyprus) Epiphanius, *The Panarion of Epiphanius of Salamis Book I (sects 1–46)*, edited by Frank Williams, 121.

34   Lüdemann, 'The Successors of Pre–70 Jerusalem Christianity: A Critical Evaluation of the Pella-Tradition', 161–173. McLaren, 'Christians and the Jewish Revolt, 66–70 A.D', in *Ancient History in a Modern University (Volume 2: Early Christianity, Late Antiquity and Beyond)*, 53–60.

35   The views that James was 'the Teacher of Righteousness' in the *Dead Sea Scrolls* and that James was called ⲡⲇⲓⲕⲁⲓⲟⲥ (the Righteous) in Logion 12 of the *Gos. Thom.* sustain the argument of Eisenman that the Pella refugees of Jerusalem were the 'Jamesian community'. Eisenman, *James the Brother of Jesus*, xx–xxii.

36   The third-largest city of the Roman Empire, Antioch was primarily composed of many mingled races, but the leading classes of the society were of Greek-speaking Hellenistic background, which indicates that the Antioch Church was

the first Gentile Christian community (*Ac.* 11.20–26). Metzger, *The Text of the New Testament: Its Transmission, Corruption, and Restoration*, 4–10. Burkett, *An Introduction to the New Testament and the Origins of Christianity*, 94–6.

37 'There arose a complaint against the Hebrews by the Hellenists …' 'and he [Saul] spoke boldly in the Name of the Lord Jesus and disputed against the [Judaic] Hellenists'. The *Acts* reports that the converted Saul returned to Jerusalem and introduced the Gospel of Jesus to his former fellows in Judaism, but was rejected by them (*Ac.* 9:29). Stephen's party of Christianity was mainly 'the Hellenists' (*Ac.* 6.1). Brown and Meier, *Antioch and Rome: New Testament Cradles of Catholic Christianity*, 32–36.

38 The human rights issue of the Hellenists in the Jerusalem church (*Ac.* 6.1–7) implies that the Gospel was also open to non-Jews. But the open mind of the Jerusalem Church opposes the policy of the Thomas community, since the Thomas text does not appear to show any concern for outsiders.

39 *Ac.* 11.26.

40 The 'Greek culture and thought' were generally understood as Hellenistic. Nock, *Early Gentile Christianity and Its Hellenistic Background*, 2–22. Elliott-Binns, *The Beginnings of Western Christendom*, 29–41.

41 Nock, 87–9 and 100–4.

42 Esler, *The First Christians in Their Social Worlds: Social-Scientific Approaches to New Testament Interpretation*, 7.

43 Details in Metzger, 7–10. The *GTh-1: Contemporary Research Data on Thomas* shows that readers such as Koester, Vööbus (Valantasis), Crossan, Quispel and Layton support this view for Thomas.

44 The ministry of Thomas was extended to Edessa, Parthia, Persia, and India where he died in AD 72. This is still considered a legend today. See Koester, 'GNOMAI DIAPHOROI: The Origin and Nature of Diversification in the History of Early Christianity', in *Trajectories Through Early Christianity*, 126–32. Klijn, *The Acts of Thomas*, 1962.

45 'And I was chosen, together with my fellows, to be a preacher'. Labubna, *The Teaching of Addai*, 17. However, the two interpretations of Eusebius' Thaddaeus and Addai are doubtful, since the two texts were written at least 200 years later (around AD 325–360). Eusebius, *Ecclesiastical History*, 29–32, 36. Wilson, *Are These the Words of Jesus?: Dramatic Evidence from Beyond the New Testament*, 56–67.

46 Despite Metzger's argument that the young Syrian community was not limited to 'urban people' but included the evangelization of 'country-folk' as well, the question of how they avoided the Christian persecutions of Domitian (AD 81–96), Trajan (AD 98–117) and Hadrian (AD 117–138), after Nero (AD 54–68), is still a mystery. Vööbus, *Early Versions of the New Testament: Manuscript Studies*, 68–70.

47   Phillips, *The Doctrine of Addai the Apostle*, 1876.

48   Metzger, 35–8.

49   The kingdom of Osrhoëne, including Edessa, was occupied by the Roman
      Emperor Trajan between AD 115 and 118. Burkitt, *Early Christianity Outside the
      Roman Empire*, 8–16. Lincoln, 'Thomas-Gospel and Thomas-Community: A New
      Approach to a Familiar Text', 65–76.

50   Addai's Palestine-Syrian origin is also indicated by his Aramaic and Greek-
      speaking background. Vööbus, 67–73. The testimony of Addai (Addaeus)
      regarding the church rules of Edessa emphasizes the authentic authority of the
      Jewish-Christian leadership in Jerusalem. See Phillips (1876). It is also called 'The
      Teaching of Addaeus the Apostle'. Labubna, *The Teaching of Addai*.

51   However, rural Christianity, according to Liebeschuetz, was not established in
      the Syrian area before Constantine. Liebeschuetz, 'Problems Arising from the
      Conversion of Syria', in *The Church in Town and Countryside*, 17–24.

52   Aggaeus, the second Bishop of Edessa, was not able to lay his hand upon Palut,
      because he suddenly died by the cruel hand of one of Abgar's contumacious sons.

53   In addition, being a strong Jewish diaspora city, Alexandria was once assumed
      to be a place in which the Greek Thomas text was read and used, before being
      relocated to the region of Nag Hammadi. Akagi presumes the Alexandria
      Christianity which pioneered a satellite community in Nag Hammadi. Akagi, *The
      Literary Development of the Coptic Gospel of Thomas*, 43–77.

54   Layton, *The Coptic Gnostic Library; Nag Hammadi Codex II, 2–7 (with XII,2, BRIT.
      LIB. OR. 4926(1), and P.OXY. 1, 654, 655)*, 103–9.

55   Those Judaic-Christians, including the Thomas people, were Jews not merely
      by race but also in religion. *Ac.* 1.15, 2.9, 4.1. Freeman, 483–493. Edwards,
      Christianity: The First Two Thousand Years, 8–51.

56   The Hebrew ceremony of circumcision was kept, but applied creatively in the
      new religious faith, affirming that the Saviour Jesus came to the world and was
      resurrected from the dead as the promised Messiah of the Hebrew Canon. See
      Logion 53's notion of 'circumcision' that is similar to *Ac.* 15:6–21. Symes, *The
      Evolution of the New Testament*, 1–10.

57   See Robinson, and the Department of Antiquities of the Arab Republic of Egypt,
      The Facsimile Edition of the Nag Hammadi Codices: Codex II, 1974.

58   According to Hegesippus (AD 120–180), in *Hypomnemata*, James' devotional life
      was expressed in the saying 'his knees grew hard like a camel'. James, the brother
      of Jesus in a Jewish-Christian setting, was regarded as the leader following Jesus.
      Lapham, *An Introduction to the New Testament Apocrypha*, 23. Frend, 'The
      Gospel of Thomas: Is Rehabilitation Possible?', 13–26. Bruce, *Jesus and Christian
      Origins Outside the New Testament*, 117–18. Conzelmann, *History of Primitive
      Christianity*, 48–63.

59 Irenaeus' *Against Heresies*, 1.26.2., 'Those who are called Ebionites agree that the world was made by God.' See also the *Dialogue*, 46–7 of Justin, written in the middle of the second century A.D.

60 Wilson's five Jewish-Christian examples for the independence of Thomas from the synoptic Gospels contain Logion 12 with other Logia 27 (*P. Oxy.* 1), 30, 80, 95. Wilson, *Studies in the Gospel of Thomas*, 117–32.

61 *Gal.* 2:9. Paul never opposes James' legitimate right or 'the fact of his authority'. Eisenman, 51–60.

62 Logion 12 tells of the direct appointment of James by Jesus, though Clement of Alexandria (AD 150–215), as reported by Eusebius, indicates an election by the Apostles. Ibid., 9–12. The quotation of Hegesippus in *Ecclesiastical History*, 2.23.4–7 refers to James the Righteous: 'I sent each one of them to a different place. But I myself went up to Jerusalem … that I might acquire a share with the beloved ones who will appear.' Meyer, *Secret Gospels: Essays on Thomas and the Secret Gospel of Mark*, 74.

63 Eisenman's interpretation of James' leadership in Jerusalem in the context of the Qumran community and the Damascus Document (CD) is a new approach, still problematic to the readers of Thomas. Eisenman, 200–4.

64 *Ac.* 6.7.

65 Lapham, 22.

66 The population of Jerusalem, 80,000 in the first century A.D., is quite understandable in terms of the fact that the population of Rome was approximately 1,000,000 and over 750,000 people were living in Antioch, the third largest city of the Roman Empire, where the first Gentile Christian church was born. Bull, 58–72. Diema and Armstrong, 'Jerusalem at the Time of Jesus', 46–56.

67 During the Passover, Succoth and Shavuoth, the people of Jerusalem, including visitors, numbered between 100,000 and 250,000. Ivor, *The Birth of the Church: From Jesus to Constantine AD 30–312*, 19–21, 36–8.

68 'The number of disciples in Jerusalem increased rapidly, and a large number of priests became obedient to the (Christian) faith.'

69 *Ac.* 4.4.

70 'The number of those who ate was about five thousand men, besides women and children'.

71 *Ac.* 5.14.

72 *Ac.* 15.22.

73 *Mt.* 16.16. The *P. Oxy.* 655.i.17–23 matches NHC 39.27–40.02, but this part is omitted in the *Oxyrhynchus* text.

74 Peter and Matthew, according to Hurtado, were the representatives of the 'Judean Christianity or Palestinian Christianity' around the towns of Judea and Galilee (the land of Palestine). Catchpole, 'Tradition History', 165–79. Hurtado, *Lord Jesus Christ: Devotion to Jesus in Earliest Christianity*, 452–85. Metzger, 155–75. Brandon, 31–53.

75   Hippolytus, in *Refutation of All Heresies*, 5. 8. 5. R. See Grant and Freedman, *The Secret Sayings of Jesus: According to the Gospel of Thomas*, 31–57. Wilson, 111–12.

76   Kasser, Rodolphe and Wurst, Gregory, *The Gospel of Judas, Critical Edition: Together with the Letter of Peter to Philip, James, and a Book of Allogenes from Codex Tchacos*. Washington, DC: National Geographic, 2007, 213–25.

77   The 'three secret instructions' ('knowledge', *gnosis* in Greek) of Jesus given to Thomas is one of the main phrases for those who hold up the gnostic theory of Thomas.

78   Patterson also believes that this kind of rivalry occurred in the first century AD rather than later. Patterson, Robinson and Bethge, *The Fifth Gospel: The Gospel of Thomas Comes of Age*, 42. Quispel, who is a supporter of Thomas' independence in that the Thomas text has a marked affinity with the Jewish-Christian gospels, also supports the Judaic-Christian origins of Thomas. Quispel, '"The Gospel of Thomas" and "Gospel of the Hebrews"', 371–382. Ibid., 'The Gospel of Thomas and the Trial of Jesus', 193–9.

79   For the historical figures of the community of Thomas in relation to the Q community, see Kim, 'What Shall We Do?: The Community Rules of Thomas in the "Fifth Gospel"', 393–414. Mack, *Who Wrote the New Testament?: The Making of the Christian Myth*, 60–4.

80   This tradition, mentioned by Koester, refers to Christian activities in Galilean cities as coming from a Judaean Christian community (Q 10.13–15). Koester, *Ancient Christian Gospels: Their History and Development*, 164.

81   Burkett, 176.

82   ⲮⲚⲦⲰⲦⲚ̄ Ⲇⲉ ⲱⲱⲡⲉ ⲘⲫⲢⲞⲚⲒⲚⲘⲞⲤ Ⲛ̄Ⲑⲉ Ⲛ̄Ⲛ2Ⲟⳓ` ⲀⲨⲰ Ⲛ̄ⲀⲔⲉⲢⲀⲒⲞⲤ Ⲛ̄Ⲑⲉ Ⲛ̄Ⲛ̄ 6ⲢⲞⲘ`ⲡⲉ (you, however, be as wise as serpents and as innocent as doves). NHC II, 2.40: 11–13.

83   See Kim, 'What Shall We Do?', 393–414. Burkett, 176.

84   Riley places the Pauline, Matthean and Johannine communities as brother communities of Thomas, though the historical order of origin is still controversial. Riley, 'Influence of Thomas Christianity on Luke 12.14 and 5.39', 229–35. Moule, *The Birth of the New Testament*, 153–77. Spivey and Smith, 57–65.

85   'Pilate had a notice prepared and fastened to the cross. It read: JESUS OF NAZARETH, THE KING OF JEWS. Many of the Jews read this sign, for the place where Jesus was crucified was near the city, and the sign was written in Aramaic, Latin, and Greek' (*Jn.* 19.19–20).

86   Brock, 'Greek and Syriac in Latin Antique Syria', 149–60.

87   Brock, 149–50. An anonymous person, *Aramaic Language*. Available from http://en.wikipedia.org/wiki/Aramaic (accessed 20 September 2004). Greenlee, *Introduction to New Testament Textual Criticism. (Revised Edition)*, 38–9.

88 ⲮⲈⲒⲤϨⲎⲎⲦⲈ` ⲀϥⲈⲒ ⲈⲂⲞⲖ ⲚϬⲒⲠⲈⲦ`ⲤⲒⲦⲈ ⲀϥⲘⲈϨ ⲦⲞⲞⲦϥ̄ ⲀϥⲚⲞⲨⲬⲈ ⲀϨⲞⲈⲒⲚⲈ ⲘⲈⲚ ϨⲈ ⲈⲬⲚ̄ ⲦⲈϨⲒⲎ` ⲀⲨⲈⲒ Ⲛ̄ϬⲒ Ⲛ̄ϨⲀⲖⲀⲦⲈ (See the sower went out, he filled his hand, he threw. Some fell *on* the road, the birds came, they gathered them.)'

89 Quispel completely separates the two groups of the Jewish-Christians and Gentile Christians by their language. Quispel, 'The Gospel of Thomas and the Trial of Jesus', 193–199. Ibid., 'Some Remarks on the Gospel of Thomas', 276–90. Baarda, 'The Cornerstone: An Aramaism in the Diatessaron and the Gospel of Thomas?', 285–300.

90 Frend, 13–26. Morrice, 63–5.

91 Yamauchi, 90–91. Davies' concept of Syria as the geographical location of Thomas resulted in Syriac being claimed as the origin of the Thomas language. Davies, *The Gospel of Thomas: Annotated and Explained*, xvii–xxi.

92 Perrin's theory is not completely discussed in this part. For the complete theory see Perrin, *Thomas and Tatian: The Relationship between the Gospel of Thomas and the Diatessaron*, Ibid., 'NHC II, 2 and the Oxyrhynchus Fragments (*P. Oxy.* 1, 654, 655): Overlooked Evidence For A Syriac Gospel of Thomas', 2004, 138–44.

93 Logia 3, 6, 27, 28, 30 of the Greek and Coptic texts are used 'to posit a Syriac subtext behind both the Greek and Coptic'. Perrin, 2004, 144–51.

94 Since the language was a dialect of Aramaic, the claim that Syriac itself has a pure origin is a weaker view. Greenlee, 39–40.

95 The analysis of Logia 2 and 5 is clearly discussed in Cullmann, 'The Gospel of Thomas and the Problem of the Age of the Tradition Contained Therein', 418–38.

96 Barrera, *The Jewish Bible and the Christian Bible: An Introduction to the History of the Bible*, 68–73.

97 See Kloppenborg, *The Formation of Q: Trajectories in Ancient Wisdom Collections*, 1987.

98 Helms, *Who Wrote the Gospels?*, 100–8.

99 Murray, *Elementary Coptic (Sahidic) Grammar*, 1–4.

100 Greenlee, *Revised Edition*, 20–2.

101 This article only discusses the linguistic aspect of the Thomas name, not the personal character of Thomas. Harding, 'Making Old Things New: Prayer Texts in Josephus' Antiquities, 1–11; A Study in the Transmission of Tradition', in *Ancient History in a Modern University (Volume 2: Early Christianity, Late Antiquity and Beyond)*, 1–14.

102 Cullmann, 418–38.

103 Wilson, 56–67.

104 There were many God-worshippers in the regions of the Empire. Luke depicts *Cornelius* with his household in Caesarea (*Ac.* 10.1–8) and Lydia in Philipp. (*Ac.* 16.11–15) as God-worshippers.

105 Crossan, *Four Other Gospels: Shadows on the Contours of Canon*, 9.

106 The overall context of ⲆⲓⲆⲨⲘⲟⲤ ⲒⲟⲨⲆⲀⲤ ⲐⲰⲘⲀⲤ in the *Gos. Thom.* emphasizes the direct blood line relationship with Jesus. This is such a tempting notion that many people want to sample it in different ways. Hoberman, *How Did the Gospel of Thomas Get Its Name?*, 10–11.

107 Because Mani founded the individual religious movement under the influence of *baptist* Christianity. Review some translated writings of Manicheans in Gardner and Lieu, *Manichaean Texts from the Roman Empire*, 158–9.

108 *Mt.* 10.3; *Mk.* 3.18; *Lk.* 6.15; *Ac.* 1.13.

109 *Jn.* 20.28. Wilson, 58–60.

110 Cameron, 'The Gospel of Thomas and Christian Origins', in *The Future of Early Christianity: Essays in Honor of Helmut Koester*, 387.

111 Imagining Thomas within a Syriac context could be another theory, but given that readers do not currently possess the Syriac *Gos. Thom*, the premise should merely remain in the sense that the Syriac regions of the first couple of centuries A.D. at some stage were, as their major mission field, strongly influenced by the Christian missionaries of the Thomasine community.

112 Meanwhile, the rest of the Greek Logion *7* is not changed, even in the Coptic text.

113 According to the existing part of the Greek Logion 24, the Coptic version has not been changed. If it is correct, the lost part of the Greek text could be understood like the beginning of the Coptic saying: 'His disciples said, "Show us the place …" He said to them, "whoever has ears, let him hear"' (NHC II, 2 38.03–07).

114 The beginning part of the Coptic version is the same as the Greek text (*P. Oxy.* 1). One can then consider the lost (end) part of the Greek text like the Coptic section: 'for empty they came into the world, and empty too they seek to leave the world. But for the moment they are intoxicated. When they shake off their wine, then they will repent' (NHC II, 2 38.27–31).

115 For the Greek text, see Attridge, 'Appendix: The Greek Fragments', in *The Coptic Gnostic Library; Nag Hammadi Codex II, 2–7 (with XII,2, BRIT. LIB. OR. 4926(1), and P.OXY. 1, 654, 655)*, 95–128.

116 For the Coptic text, see Lambdin, 'The Gospel of Thomas (II, 2)', in *The Nag Hammadi Library in English*, 124–38.

117 Even if the Coptic translator did not add any artificial concept on top of the Greek texts of *P. Oxy.* 1 and 655, the Coptic text, for the Greek part of *P. Oxy.* 654, has been altered, providing additional explanations for its modernity. Mueller, 'Kingdom of Heaven or Kingdom of God?', 266–76. Liebenberg, *The Language of the Kingdom and Jesus: Parable, Aphorism, and Metaphor in the Sayings Material Common to the Synoptic Tradition and the Gospel of Thomas*, 490–1.

118 In the case of *P. Oxy.* 1 (Logia 26–33), five of the eight Logia are partly unclear (Logia 26, 28, 29, 30, 33). In the case of *P. Oxy.* 655 (Prologue-Logia 7), two of the five Logia have been lost (Logia 24, 37). However, *P. Oxy.* 654 (Logion 24 and

Logia 37–39) is in the best condition as only one of the eight Logia is damaged (Logion 7).

119 'Verso' text means that one of the writings was recorded on the vertical fibres of a papyrus. 'Recto' is the other side of verso on a papyrus. Fitzmyer, *Essays on the Semitic Background of the New Testament*, 387–404.

120 Yamauchi, 89–90. Koester, 'The Gospel of Thomas (II, 2)', in *The Coptic Gnostic Library; Nag Hammadi Codex II, 2-7*, 124–6.

121 There are few articles written on their spirituality so far, since the majority of readers continue to attempt to place the text in the context of Syriac influence. The identity of the Egyptian Christian community was disregarded due to the concept of a gnostic group. See Parrott, 'Gnosticism and Egyptian Religion', 73–93.

122 Koester initially analysed the fragments of the Greek and Coptic texts in 1989, but these data unveil more previously unknown details. See Layton, 38–49, 96–102.

123 The rest of them are the same even in the Coptic version of Thomas, but there is no certain theory for the lost parts of Logia 7, 24 and 28. They simply cannot be compared.

124 Logia 2, 3, 6, 26, 29, 30, 31, 32, 33, 36, 37, 38, 39. It is a common principle that when a translator tries to deliver a sentence of a language into another language, he, according to the culture or custom of the new readers, might rearrange the sentence.

125 Mueller also points out the scribal errors of the Coptic translator through the case of Logion 3. The phrase 'then you will become known, and' is also considered as a secondary addition. Mueller, *Kingdom of Heaven or Kingdom of God?*, 267–9.

126 Such parts of the Greek Logia 4 and 5 are ignored, but the Coptic translator did not create any words or phrases for its improvement.

127 Such locational and structural changes in Thomas, according to Tuckett, are understood to have occurred no earlier than the time when the text was translated into Coptic. Logion 36 is also one of the cases in which a huge part of the Greek text was cut in the process of translation. As the three parts, 'neither', 'your food and what you will eat, nor about your clothing and', and 'you are far better than the lilies ... He it is who will give you your cloak' are eliminated in the Coptic text, one can perceive the effort of the translator in terms of her/his own socio-religious concept or something else. Tuckett, 'Thomas and the Synoptics', 132–57.

128 The reduction of 'and once he has ruled, he will attain rest' into 'over the all' seems to imply that the Coptic translator, while keeping the main context, discarded the original Greek text.

129 The view that the adverb 'rather' from the Coptic version seems to be more advanced than the Greek conjunction 'and' also supports the primitive figure of the Greek Logion 3.

130 It is the same question, but the Coptic translator seems to have approached the question from a different linguistic angle, while the following question style is the same as the Greek text. The Greek and Coptic texts are all like 'How shall we pray? … What diet shall we observe?' (*P. Oxy.* 654 and NHC II, 2 33.16–18).

131 A large (beginning) part of the Greek text (*P. Oxy.* 1) is missing, but if one were to reconstruct it, the phrase might be similar to the Coptic version: 'Jesus said, "You (sg.) see the mote in your brother's eye, but you do not see the beam in your own eye … cast the beam out of your own eye"' (NHC II, 2 38.12–16).

132 The damage rate of the Greek Logion 29 is very critical, but if one tries to reconstruct the lost (beginning) part from the Coptic version, it might read: 'Jesus said, "If the flesh came into being because of spirit, it is a wonder … Indeed, I am amazed at how this great wealth …"' (NHC II, 2 38.31–29:02).

133 The Greek Logion 33 is not clear in terms of meaning and the damaged section (the final part) has also been changed in the Coptic version. However, the lost part of the Greek text could be similar to the Coptic version of 'for no one lights a lamp and puts it … but rather he sets it on a lampstand so that everyone who enters and leaves will see its light' (NHC II, 2 39:13–18).

134 The beginning part of the Coptic version is similar to the Greek text. One can then hypothesize the missing (last) part of the Greek text from the Coptic version (NHC II, 2 39.31–40.02).

135 Koester confesses that 'the only surviving manuscript evidence for the *Gos. Thom.* is either Greek or translated from the Greek'. There is no evidence, but one still cannot exclude the possibility that the Coptic version could be derived from one of the three Greek texts. Koester, *The Gospel of Thomas (II, 2)*, 40.

136 One can guess that some copies of the original text would be informally preserved in an isolated place or private collection, since today we have three Greek fragments of Thomas.

References

Akagi, Tai. The Literary Development of the Coptic Gospel of Thomas (PhD Dissertation). Western Reserve University, 1965.

Attridge, Harold W. 'Appendix: The Greek Fragments'. In *The Coptic Gnostic Library; Nag Hammadi Codex II, 2-7 (with XII,2, BRIT. LIB. OR. 4926(1), and P. Oxy. 1, 654, 655)*, by Bentley Layton. Leiden, New York, København and Köln: E. J. Brill, 1989, pp. 95–128.

Ayer, Joseph Cullen. *A Source Book for Ancient Church History: From the Apostolic Age to the Close of the Conciliar Period.* New York: Ams Press, 1913.

Baarda, Tjitze. 'The Cornerstone' An Aramaism in the Diatessaron and the Gospel of Thomas?' *Novum Testamentum*, July 1995: 285–300.

Barnes, Arthur Stepylton. *St Peter in Rome and His Tomb on the Vatican Hill.* London: Swan Sonnenschein & Co. Ltd, 1900.

Barrera, Julio Trebolle (translated by Wilfred G. E. Watson). *The Jewish Bible and the Christian Bible: An Introduction to the History of the Bible.* Leiden, New York and Köln, and Grand Rapids, Michigan and Cambridge: E. J. Brill, and William B. Eerdmans Publishing Company, 1998.

Barrett, C. K. *The New Testament Background: Selected Documents.* London: SPCK, 1987.

Brandon, S. G. F. *The Fall of Jerusalem and the Christian Church: A Study of the Effects of the Jewish Overthrow of A.D. 70 on Christianity.* London: SPCK, 1978.

Brock, Sebastian P. 'Greek and Syriac in Latin Antique Syria'. In *Literary and Power in the Ancient World,* by Alan K. Bowman and Greg Woolf. Cambridge: Cambridge University Press, 1994, pp. 149–150.

Brown, Raymond E. and Meier, John P. *Antioch and Rome: New Testament Cradles of Catholic Christianity.* New York and Ramsey: Paulist Press, 1983.

Bruce, F. F. *Jesus and Christian Origins Outside the New Testament.* London: Hodder & Stoughton, 1974.

Bull, Norman J. *The Rise of the Church.* London: Heinemann, 1967.

Burkett, Delbert. *An Introduction to the New Testament and the Origins of Christianity.* Cambridge: Cambridge University Press, 2002.

Burkitt, F. Crawford. *Early Christianity Outside the Roman Empire.* Piscataway: Gorgias Press, 2002.

Cameron, Ron. 'The Gospel of Thomas and Christian Origins'. In *The Future of Early Christianity: Essays in Honor of Helmut Koester,* by Birger A. Pearson. Minneapolis: Fortress Press, 1991, p. 387.

—*The Other Gospels: Non-Canonical Gospel Texts.* Philadelphia, PA: The Westminster Press, 1982.

Cary, Earnest. *Dio's Roman History.* London and Cambridge: William Heinemann and Harvard University Press, 1961.

Catchpole, David R. 'Tradition History'. In *New Testament Interpretation: Essays on Principles and Methods,* by I. Howard Marshall. Exeter: The Paternoster Press, 1977, pp. 165–79.

Clark, Francis. *The Rise of Christianity.* Milton Keynes: The Open University Press, 1974.

Conzelmann, Hans. *History of Primitive Christianity.* Nashville: Abingdon, 1979.

Crossan, John Dominic. *Four Other Gospels: Shadows on the Contours of Canon.* Sonoma, California: Polebridge Press, 1992.

Cullmann, Oscar. 'The Gospel of Thomas and the Problem of the Age of the Tradition Contained Therein'. *Interpretation,* 1962: 418–38.

Davies, Stevan L. *The Gospel of Thomas: Annotated & Explained.* London: Darton, Longman and Todd, 2003.

De Ste Croix, G. E. M. 'Early Christian Attitudes to Property and Slavery'. In *Church Society and Politics: Papers Read at the Thirteenth Summer Meeting and Fourteenth*

Winter Meeting of the Ecclesiastical History Society, by Derek Baker. Oxford: Blackwell and The Ecclesiastical Society, 1975, pp. 1–38.

Diema, David Van and Armstrong, Karen. 'Jerusalem at the Time of Jesus'. *Time*, 2001: 46–56.

Dunderberg, Ismo. 'Thomas' I-Sayings and the Gospel of John'. In *Thomas at the Crossroads: Essays on the Gospel of Thomas*, by Risto Uro. Edinburgh: T & T Clark, 1989, pp. 33–64.

Edwards, David L. *Christianity: The First Two Thousand Years*. London: Cassell, 1998.

Eisenman, Robert. *James the Brother of Jesus*. London: Watkins Publishing, 2002.

Elliott-Binns, L. E. *The Beginnings of Western Christendom*. London and Redhill: Lutterworth Press, 1948.

Ellis, E. Earle. 'New Directions in the History of Early Christianity'. In *Ancient History in a Modern University (Volume 2: Early Christianity, Late Antiquity and Beyond)*, by R. A. Kearsley, C. E. V. Nixon and A. M. Nobbs, edited by T.W. Hillard. Sydney, Grand Rapids, Michigan and Cambridge: William B. Eerdmans, 1998, pp. 71–92.

Esler, F. Philip. *The First Christians in Their Social Worlds: Social-Scientific Approaches to New Testament Interpretation*. London and New York: Routledge, 1994.

Eusebius, Pamphilus (translated by C. F. Cruse). *Ecclesiastical History*. Peabody, MA: Hendrickson Publishers, 1998.

Everitt, Charles *et al. Part III: The Christian Testament Since the Bible*. Harmondsworth, Middlesex: Penguin Books, 1985.

Ferguson, Everett. *Backgrounds of Early Christianity (Third Edition)*. Grand Rapids, MI: William B. Eerdmans, 2003.

Fitzmyer, Joseph A. *Essays on the Semitic Background of the New Testament*. London: Geoffrey Chapman, 1971.

Freeman, Charles. *Egypt, Greece and Rome: Civilizations of the Ancient Mediterranean*. Oxford: Oxford University Press, 1999.

Frend, W. H. C. 'The Archaeologist and Church History'. In *Town and Country in the Early Christian Centuries*, by W. H. C. Frend. London: Variorum Reprints, 1980, pp. 259–265.

—'The Gospel of Thomas: Is Rehabilitation Possible?' *Journal of Theological Studies*, 1967: 13–26.

Gardner, Iain and Lieu, Samuel N.C. *Manichaean Texts from the Roman Empire*. Cambridge: Cambridge University Press, 2004.

Grant, Robert M. and Freedman, David Noel. *The Secret Sayings of Jesus: According to the Gospel of Thomas*. London and Glasgow: Collins, 1960.

Greenlee, J. Harold. *Introduction to New Testament Textual Criticism. (Revised Edition)*. Peabody, MA: Hendrickson Publishers, 1995.

Gwatkin, Henry Melvill. *Early Church History to A.D. 313 (Volume 2)*. London: Macmillan and Co., 1912.

Harding, Mark. 'Making Old Things New: Prayer Texts in Josephus' Antiquities, 1–11; A Study in the Transmission of Tradition'. In *Ancient History in a Modern University*

(Volume 2: Early Christianity, Late Antiquity and Beyond), by R. A. Kearsley, C. E. V. Nixon, and A. M. Nobbs, edited by T.W. Hillard, Sydney, Michigan and Cambridge: William B. Eerdmans, 1998, pp. 1–14.

Helms, Randel McCraw. *Who Wrote the Gospels?* Altadena: Millennium Press, 1997.

Hoberman, Barry. 'How Did the Gospel of Thomas Get Its Name?' *Biblical Archaeologist*, 1983: 10–11.

Hurtado, Larry W. *Lord Jesus Christ: Devotion to Jesus in Earliest Christianity.* Grand Rapids, MI, and Cambridge: William B. Eerdmans, 2003.

Ivor, J. *The Birth of the Church: From Jesus to Constantine AD 30–312.* Oxford, and Grand Rapids, MI: Monarch Books, 2005.

Jeremias, Joachim (translated by Reginald H. Fuller). *Unknown Sayings of Jesus.* London: SPCK, 1957 (1964).

Johnson, Luke Timothy. *The Writings of the New Testament. Revised Edition.* London: SCM Press, 1999.

Kim, David W. *Revival Awaken Generations: A History of Church Revival.* Sydney: DKM Press, 2006.

—'What Shall We do?: The Community Rules of Thomas in the "Fifth Gospel"'. *Biblica*, 2007: 393–414.

Klauck, Hans-Josef (translated by Brian McNeil). *The Religious Context of Early Christianity: A Guide to Graeco-Roman Religions.* Edinburgh: T & T Clark, 2000.

Klijn, A. E. *The Acts of Thomas.* Leiden: E. J. Brill, 1962.

Kloppenborg, John S. *The Formation of Q: Trajectories in Ancient Wisdom Collections.* Philadelphia, PA: Fortress Press, 1987.

Koester, Helmut. *Ancient Christian Gospels: Their History and Development.* London: SCM Press, 1990.

—'GNOMAI DIAPHOROI: The Origin and Nature of Diversification in the History of Early Christianity'. In *Trajectories Through Early Christianity*, by James M. Robinson and Helmut Koester, 126–132. Philadelphia, PA: Fortress Press, 1971, pp. 126–32.

—'The Gospel of Thomas (II, 2)'. In *The Coptic Gnostic Library; Nag Hammadi Codex II, 2–7*, by Bentley Layton. Leiden, New York, København and Köln: E. J. Brill, 1989, pp. 124–6.

—'The Text of the Synoptic Gospels in the Second Century'. In *Gospel Traditions in the Second Century: Origins, Recensions, Text and Transmission*, by William L. Petersen. Nortre Dame and London: University of Notre Dame Press, 1989, pp. 19–37.

Labubna, Bar Sennak (translated by George Howard). *The Teaching of Addai.* Chico: Scholars Press, 1981.

Lambdin, Thomas O. 'The Gospel of Thomas (II, 2)'. In *The Nag Hammadi Library in English*, by James M. Robinson. Leiden, New York and Köln: E. J. Brill, 1996, pp. 124–138.

Lapham, F. *An Introduction to the New Testament Apocrypha.* London and New York: T & T Clark, 2003.

Layton, Bentley. *The Coptic Gnostic Library; Nag Hammadi Codex II, 2–7 (with XII,2, BRIT. LIB. OR. 4926(1), and P. Oxy. 1, 654, 655)*. Leiden, New York, København and Köln: E. J. Brill, 1989.

Liebenberg, Jacobus. *The Language of the Kingdom and Jesus: Parable, Aphorism, and Metaphor in the Sayings Material Common to the Synoptic Tradition and the Gospel of Thomas*. Berlin and New York: Walter de Gruyter, 2001.

Liebeschuetz, W. 'Problems Arising from the Conversion of Syria'. In *The Church in Town and Countryside*, by Derek Baker. Oxford: Blackwell and The Ecclesiastical History Society, 1979, pp. 17–24.

Lincoln, Bruce. 'Thomas-Gospel and Thomas-Community: A New Approach to a Familiar Text'. *Novum Testamentum*, 1977: 65–76.

Lüdemann, Gerd. 'The Successors of Pre–70 Jerusalem Christianity'. In *Jewish and Christian Self-Definition: Volume One The Shaping of Christianity in the Second and Third Centuries*, by E.P. Sanders. London: SCM Press, 1980, p. 161.

Mack, Burton L. *Who Wrote the New Testament?: The Making of the Christian Myth*. New York: HarperSanFrancisco, 1989.

McLaren, J. S. 'Christians and the Jewish Revolt, 66–70 A.D'. In *Ancient History in a Modern University (Volume 2: Early Christianity, Late Antiquity and Beyond)*, by R. A. Kearsley, C.E.V. Nixon and A.M. Nobbs, edited by T. W. Hillard. Sydney, Michigan and Cambridge: William B. Eerdmans, 1998, pp. 53–60.

Merrill, Elmer Truesdell. *Essays in Early Christian History*. London: Macmillan and Co., 1924.

Metzger, Bruce M. *The Text of the New Testament: Its Transmission, Corruption, and Restoration*. New York and Oxford: Oxford University Press, 1977.

Meyer, Marvin. *Secret Gospels: Essays on Thomas and the Secret Gospel of Mark*. Harrisburg, London and New York: Trinity Press International (A Continuum Imprint), 2003.

Miller, N. P. *Tacitus Annals 15: Annalivm Liber XV*. Basingstoke and London: St Martin's Press, 1973.

Morrice, G. William. *Hidden Sayings of Jesus: Words Attributed to Jesus Outside the Four Gospels*. London: SPCK, 1997.

Moule, C. F. D. *The Birth of the New Testament*. London: Adam & Charles Black, 1962.

Mueller, Dieter. 'Kingdom of Heaven or Kingdom of God?' *Vigiliae Christianae*, 1973: 266–76.

Murray, Alice. *Elementary Coptic (Sahidic) Grammar*. London: Bernard Quaritch, 1911.

Museum, The British. *The New Gospel Fragments with one Plate*. London: Cambridge University Press, 1951.

Nock, Arthur Darby. *Early Gentile Christianity and Its Hellenistic Background*. New York, Evanston and London: Harper Torchbooks, 1964.

Parrott, Douglas M. 'Gnosticism and Egyptian Religion'. *Novum Testamentum*, 1987: 73–93.

Patterson, Stephen J. *The Gospel of Thomas and Jesus*. Sonoma: Polebridge Press, 1993.

—Robinson, James M. and Bethge, Hans-Gebhard. *The Fifth Gospel: The Gospel of Thomas Comes of Age*. Harrisburg, PA: Trinity Press International, 1998.

Perrin, Nicholas. 'NHC II, 2 and the Oxyrhynchus Fragments (*P. Oxy.* 1, 654, 655): Overlooked Evidence For A Syriac Gospel of Thomas'. *Vivarium*, 2004: 138–44.

—*Thomas and Tatian: The Relationship between the Gospel of Thomas and the Diatessaron*. Leiden, Boston, MA, and Köln: E. J. Brill, 2002.

Phillips, George. *The Doctrine of Addai the Apostle*. London: Trubner, 1876.

Pliny, The Younger (edited by Helen H. Tanzer). *The Letters of Pliny*. New York, Leipzig, London and Paris: G.E. Stechert & Co., 1936.

Pritz, Ray A. *Nazarene Jewish Christianity*. Jerusalem and Leiden: The Magnes Press and E. J. Brill, 1988.

Quispel, Gilles. ' "The Gospel of Thomas" and "Gospel of the Hebrews" '. *New Testament Studies*, 1966: 371–82.

—'Some Remarks on the Gospel of Thomas'. *New Testament Studies*, 1959: 276–290.

—*Tatian and the Gospel of Thomas: Studies in the History of the Western Diatessaron*. Leiden: E. J. Brill, 1975.

—'The Gospel of Thomas and the Trial of Jesus'. In *Text and Testimony: Essays on New Testament and Apocryphal Literature in Honour of A. F. J. Klijn*, edited by T. Baarda, A. Hilhorst, G. P. Luttikhuizen and A. S, Van Der Wonde. Kampen: Vitgeversmaatschappij. J.H. Kok, 1988, pp. 193–9.

Richardson, Peter. *Israel in the Apostolic Church*. Cambridge: Cambridge University Press, 1969.

Riley, Gregory J. 'Influence of Thomas Christianity on Luke 12.14 and 5.39'. *Harvard Theological Review*, 1995: 229–35.

Robinson, James M. and the Department of Antiquities of the Arab Republic of Egypt. *The Facsimile Edition of the Nag Hammadi Codices: Codex II*. Leiden: E. J. Brill, 1974.

Robinson, John A. *Reading the New Testament*. London: SCM Press, 1976.

Sher Win-White, A. N. *Fifty-Letters of Pliny*. Oxford: Oxford University Press, 1969.

Spence, H. Donald M. *Early Christianity and Paganism: A.D. 64 to the Peace of the Church in the Fourth Century*. London, Paris, New York and Melbourne: Cassell and Co., Ltd, 1902.

Spivey, Robert A. and Smith, Jr. D. Moody. *Anatomy of the New Testament: A Guide to its Structure and Meaning*. New York and London: Macmillan Publishing Co. and Collier Macmillan Publishers, 1974.

Stancliff, Clare. *St. Martin and His Hagiographer: History and Miracle in Sulpicus Serverus*. Oxford: Clarendon Press, 1983.

Symes, John Elliotson. *The Evolution of the New Testament*. London: John Murray, 1921.

Tuckett, Christopher. 'Thomas and the Synoptics'. *Novum Testamentum*, 1988: 132–57.

Valantasis, Richard. *The Gospel of Thomas*. London and New York: Routledge, 1997.

Van, G. K. *The Christian Concept of History in the Chronicle of Sulpicius Severus*. Amsterdam: Adolf M. Hakkert, 1976.

Vööbus, Arthur. *Early Versions of the New Testament: Manuscript Studies.* Stockholm: Estonian Theological Society in Exile, 1954.

William, Neville. *Chronology of the Ancient World: 10,000 B.C. to A.D. 799.* London: Barrie & Jenkins, 1976.

Williams, Frank. *The Panarion of Epiphanius of Salamis Book I (sects 1–46).* Leiden and New York: E. J. Brill, 1997.

Wilson, Ian. *Are These the Words of Jesus?: Dramatic Evidence from Beyond the New Testament.* Oxford: Lennard Publishing, 1990.

Wilson, R. McL. *Studies in the Gospel of Thomas.* London: A. R. Mowbray, 1960.

Yamauchi, Edwin M. *Pre-Christian Gnosticism.* London: Tyndale Press, 1973.

2

St Michael of Chonai and the Tenacity of Paganism

Alan H. Cadwallader

For myself the conversion of the orbis terrarum, the first overthrow of paganism, is to me the most supernatural event in the history of Christianity.[1]

The story of The Miracle of St Michael of Chonai was remarkably popular in the Byzantine world, spawning at least three versions of the story and numerous iconographic retellings that extend from Moscow to Mt Sinai. The ubiquity of representation reflects how important the city of Chonai (ancient Colossae) had become in the early medieval period. It was one of the major healing springs attracting a stream of pilgrims. It was an acclaimed locus of the success of Christianity against external competitors and internal fratricides. An array of these forces finds a narrative presence in the story, especially in its vernacular (anonymous) form, the oldest of the versions of the story. The battles with Greek idolatry, inter-city rivalry with Laodiceia and more nebulous pagan protagonists are related with increasing show-casing of the figure of St Michael, the archangel, the archistrategos.

The story of St Michael of Chonai

The vernacular version of the story has traditionally been seen as an awkward amalgam of two stories. The first supplies an apostolic testimony to the foundation of a miraculous healing spring through the beneficence of the archangel Michael (Chapters 1–2); the second unfolds the even more dramatic miracle of the rescue of this hagiasma, of the guardian Archippos who had come to tend the sacred site, and of the surrounding region (Chapters 5–12).

The healing spring is declared to be the miraculous provision of the archangel Michael by the apostles John and Philip after they have cleansed the region around Hierapolis (Chonai's western neighbouring city) of its idols. The bridge from this story to the weightier miracle story comes with a demonstration of the therapeutic power of the waters. The mute daughter of a pagan from Laodiceia is healed by the waters, proclaiming in her first utterance the triune God (Chapter 3). Her father's euergetism in the building of a shrine at the sacred site is followed by the arrival of young Archippos from Hierapolis (Chapter 4). Archippos' exemplary custody of the shrine and the fame of the Christian curative spring are woven together to the point where both are marked for destruction by followers of the still-influential gods of the pagans, evil-doers who have fallen under the sinister direction of the devil. An initial attempt to pollute the waters of the spring and ruin Archippos' reputation fails but is succeeded by a more elaborate conspiracy to unleash a catastrophic flood intended to sweep away the spring, its keeper and those who have gathered in the surrounding region. The undaunted and prayerful custodian is joined by the awesome appearance of St Michael. The archistrategos of the heavenly host splits an impenetrable monolith, shafts an evacuation well to receive the waters and petrifies the enemies of the shrine. As a result, the fame and authority of the healing spring and its attendant are confirmed and Michael is acclaimed as its formidable patron under the triune God.

Paganism and Christianity in the story of St Michael of Chonai

The spread, vindication and triumph of Christianity was, from the time of the writings of Eusebius of Caesarea (*c.* AD 263–339), celebrated as a victory over pagan religious practice and theology.[2] The history came to be written as a demonstration of the truth of the theological apologetic mounted by Christian writers before the Constantinian imperialization of Christianity. Apologetic had become prophecy had become history.[3] But this was no mere literary artifice. The assertive confidence of avaricious monastics rampaged through the empire, laying claim to pagan sanctuaries, either by wholesale demolition or graffitied imposition of their names.[4] The walls, pillars and pediments of a Klaros or a Didyma – legendary pilgrimage points on the Aegean – are saturated with parenthetical crosses marking the boundary of a name inscribed in the genitive, thereby claiming not only ownership but, so bounded by the now ubiquitous

Christian symbol *par excellence*, providing the justification for the often slovenly epigraphical incision.

In spite of the rationalization and apparent imperial sanction of the destructive toppling of the pagan inheritance, a plethora of contemporary scholars have argued that the rhetoric of annihilation was in great measure a masquerade. This was evident in the obvious attention addressed to pre-Christian writers and myths; there was even a begrudging acceptance of the laudatory virtues occasionally portrayed therein, albeit sanitized by other sleights of hand, such as the claim that these positive examples were hewn from a Jewish bedrock or that pagan forebears had themselves witnessed the triumph of Christianity.[5] More importantly however, the official endorsement of Christian faith could only achieve mundane and localized adherence (with all its political and ecclesial benefits) if it retained significant elements from the previous hegemonic sacrality. Some commentators have regarded such survivals as an 'excrescence'.[6] Others have recognized that the Christianization of local heroes, sites and cults was critical to the establishment of a measure of unity and continuity.[7]

One story gathers together the tensions and demonstration of these general elements and provides a particular insight into some neglected mechanisms in the survival of the pagan heritage in Christian garb. That story is the Miracle of St Michael the archistrategos of Chonai. I present the evidence which shows that the figure of Michael the archangel is imbued with elements of the pre-Christian pagan deities. These male deities (especially Zeus) are enabled to survive in their colouring of the central hero of the story, precisely because paganism is identified with feminine gods that are vanquished at the beginning of the story. The expiation is assisted by ill-fitting incorporations of Christian scriptural typologies that help to veil what has occurred and by Michael's orthodox acknowledgement of the (male) triune God, an acknowledgement that carries Zeus' presence into its confession.

The available critical edition of the popular version of the story used in this chapter is that of Max Bonnet, and references are to his page and line numbers.[8]

Chonai in the Byzantine Empire

Chonai gives its name to the title of the story, as the identifying place for the archangel Michael. It was the major strategic fortress city of the Thrakesion theme in the mid-to late Byzantine period, located on the rise of towering Mt Cadmus (modern Honazdağ) in south west Turkey. It held sweeping views of the latitudinal line of the Lycus Valley and the pass through the Tauros mountains to the south. Even before its resurgent military significance, it had been established as one of the most important pilgrimage centres on the west-east passage from Ephesus to the Holy Land.[9] Exactly when the name Chonai (meaning 'funnels') came into existence is disputed but a weight of ancient attestation and importance adhered to it by collation with the Persian and Greek city of Colossae. As Constantine Porphyrogenitos expressed it in his tenth-century overview of Byzantine administration: Κολοσσαὶ αἱ νῦν λεγόμεναι Χῶναι, οὗ ἐστι ναὸς διαβόητος τοῦ ἀρχαγγέλου Μιχαήλ ('Colossae the place now called Chonai, where there is a famous shrine of the archangel Michael').[10] Nicetas Choniates was one of a pair of renowned educated brothers who adopted Choniates either directly from the city's name or in imitation of the innovation in making it the epithet of the city's patron archangel.[11] Nicetas was forthright in claiming the ancient heritage by working the language of Xenophon into his description of the city: πόλιν εὐδαίμονα καὶ μεγάλην ('a prosperous and grand city').[12] By the time of Nicetas, and his brother Michael, the battle with Hellenism was long over; its surviving texts provided rich pickings for the embellishments of Byzantine literateurs.[13]

In the popular story of St Michael neither the name Colossae nor Chonai occurs, though a number of manuscripts of the story and the summary headings in early menologia remedy the deficiency with one or both names.[14] However, the finale of the climactic miracle that is engineered by the archangel and rehearsed in numerous iconographic retellings – the diversion of a dangerous flood into a subterranean cavern – is expressed in language that deliberately and sonorously summons a resonance of the Byzantine city.[15]

ἀκοντίσθητε ὑμεῖς ἐν τῇ χώνῃ ταύτῃ καὶ ἔστε χωνευόμενοι ἐν τῷ χάσματι τούτῳ. (19.5–6)
Be flung into this funnel; you are to be funneled into this vault.[16]

There is a reason for the avoidance of an overt naming of Chonai. Nowhere in the popular story is the site of the healing shrine of Michael situated by connection with a city. The initial location of the spring is, early on in the story, named as Chairetopa (2.17), a naming that has long distracted scholars intent on tying the place to the city of the same name to the southwest, an episcopal see that was later subject to the Metropolitan of Chonai.[17] Such a name is a commonplace in Turkey, built on the notion of greeting (cf. *Lk.* 1.28).[18] In fact two manuscripts of the popular story read χαῖρε τόπε.[19] Even allowing that this reading is secondary, it coheres with the emphasis in the story that the site of the healing spring, the shrine and the miraculous rescue are only referred to as a 'place', 'site' or 'sacred grove', but never as a city.[20] The 'cities' in the story are Hierapolis and Laodiceia, a contrasting pair – the former a cleansed city replete with apostolic presence, grace and blessing; the latter the source of idolatry, opposition and evil.

Chonai and the healing shrine of St Michael in its regional context

The sanctuary of St Michael is therefore a *rural* sanctuary in the story. It is a context that appears at odds with the city of Colossae-Chonai as it actually operated in medieval times at the peak of its ecclesial influence and may reveal a trace of the ancient (Graeco-Roman and Christian) unease between city hegemony and country resistance.[21] The story participates in the wider dynamic of battles between cities for influence, but it transposes the suspicion of heterodoxy associated with rural sanctuaries to the menacing city.[22] In the story, the antagonism towards the healing site is expressly located at the city of Laodiceia, which is uncompromisingly painted in pagan colours. Again this is apparently at odds with the actual case, where Laodiceia was early on a Metropolitanate, with Colossae an ecclesial satellite (until Chonai secured metropolitical status in the mid-tenth century).[23]

The competition between cities that was cultivated under the early principate remained unabated in Byzantine complexities. Laodiceian efforts to diminish Colossae's growing significance through repudiation (indeed anathematization) of the invocation of angels seem to have met with a powerful rejoinder, even if employing a different mode of attack. Laodiceia harnessed the political power of a synod (held around AD 360) and condemned the εἰδωλολατρεία ('idolatry') of the practice. Colossae was not mentioned explicitly but, about 70 years later, Theodoret of Cyrrhus triangulated the synodal canon, the Pauline text of Colossians 2.18 (which criticized the worship of angels) and the sanctuary of St Michael at Colossae.[24] One scholiast ignored the synod's veneer of reticence to the naming of Colossae and identified it explicitly in the margin to Canon 35.[25]

Colossae could not mount a *synodal* counter-attack but seems to have opted for the cultivation of sympathetic populist resistance through a story in the vernacular (itself an interesting study of modes of political engagement within the Byzantine Church).[26] The damning expression twice underscored in the anathema of Canon 35 of the Synod of Laodiceia (εἰδωλολατρεία) is transformed in the popular text into the key descriptor, not of Colossae/Chonai but of Laodiceia. Εἰδωλοθύτης is the narrative's preferred characterization of Laodiceia (3.15, 9.9–10, 11.4, 13.4), though some manuscripts revert to the exact wording of the Laodiciean canon. The story expands the semantic field of vocabulary to hammer home the portrait of the city, describing both its inhabitants and those who muster there for the attacks (upon Archippos, the shrine and the region) as ἀσεβής ('ungodly') (3.15, 11.9) and τῆς ἀληθείας ἐχθροί ('enemies of truth') (11.9; cf. 18.17).[27] Perhaps the most powerful, confrontational maligning of Laodiceia comes in the transparent play on the city's name in 11.10: ἦλθεν εἰς Λαοδικίαν ὁ λαὸς τῆς ἀδικίας ('the lawless mob came to Laodiceia').[28] In fact, this section implies that Laodiceia is the centre of an assembly (note συναχθέντες immediately preceding this defamatory phrase) of cities opposing the Michael hagiasma. This suggests that the popular story of St Michael the archangel of Chonai functioned, at least in part, as a means of resistance to the Synod of Laodiceia, its proponents and its reiterators.

Positing the complexities of paganism in the story

When this literary retaliation originated cannot be determined precisely but an earlier rather than a later date is attractive, even though some of the language is coeval with the vehement polemics of the iconoclast controversies.[29] It is likely that the popular story passed through a number of revisions according to a succession of concerns over time.[30] One particular clue relevant to this discussion of a preoccupation with the pagan is the shift of the dominant description of the opponents from Ἕλληνες ('Greeks'). This naming is last attested in chapter 5, where they are described as idolatrous (9.9–10). The same general group then becomes the ἀσεβεῖς ('heathen'), and the various antagonists remain the ἀσεβεῖς ('heathen') as they continue their unrelenting opposition through to the final unleashing of the flood in chapter 10 (13.16).[31] All this indicates that the semantic field of the debate between Colossae and Laodiceia is paganism,[32] initially identified as 'Greek'. The story as we have it probably witnesses to the triumph of the Church over Hellenism (with consequent pillaging of its remains), a triumph signalled in the story by the change of identifier. The issue then is to explore how paganism, especially in its Greek expression, is deployed in the story.

It needs to be underscored that paganism in the story is not to be anchored to an elaborate slanging match between neighbouring cities even though accusations of idolatry do appear to be part of the contest between Laodiceia and Colossae. The ubiquity of paganism in the conflicts in the story, rather than, say, the ongoing conflict with Judaism, suggests that this is a real battle that both cities are turning to their advantage in an infra-ecclesial stoush. In other words, the overt battle with paganism is also a covert battle between Christian centres for the spoils of paganism.

It has been a regular surmise of commentators on the story that the healing spring pre-existed Christian exultation of the divinely inspired therapeutic qualities of the centre.[33] Accordingly, the Christian take-over (and sometimes destruction) of pagan temples was part of a larger expropriation that extended to sacred groves and springs. The miraculous spring of St Michael at Chonai is far from a unique combination of healing waters and angelic or divine beneficence.[34] The usual Christian rationalization was that such providence had been inaugurated under the true dispensation. However, while the story of St Michael pits idolaters against the shrine, its guardian and the waters, there are indications in the text of a prior existence of the spring. In spite of the words of the apostles that Michael would bring about a wonder at a particular site, the spring erupts without any archangelic epiphany (3.6–7). In fact, in a minor contradiction in the following chapter, the story speaks of the 'discovery' (εὕρεσις) of the seemingly pre-existent spring (3.10).[35] When Michael appears in a dream to the Laodiceian father of a mute daughter to instruct him for her healing, the healing spring is not tied directly to Michael's initiative; Michael speaks of it simply as ἔνθα τὸ ἅγιον ὕδωρ πεφανέρωται ('where the holy water has appeared') (4.4). Accordingly, the implication behind key elements in the story – the attacks on Archippos the guardian of the shrine (8.16–9.1), the emphasis on the invocation of the divine name in relation to bathing in the waters (4.9–10, 11–12), the explicit acclamation (by a female child) of the God of the Christians (4.15) and the acknowledgement that many 'Greeks' attended the waters, some of whom were converted (3.13–14, 8.9–10) – is that ownership of the site was viciously contested. The place was tied to constructions of identity that were strenuously asserted by opposing groups in terms of religious adherence and symbolic imagination.[36]

This is why the climax of the story needs to be interrogated. The construction and reconstruction of place out of primeval space is the backbone of the story. Michael's orchestrated crescendo of a refashioning of the created order is demonstrated in the eruption of fire from water (9.3), in the changing of the course of the river Chruses to prevent pollution of the sanctuary waters

(10.1–4), and in the splintering of a monolith that had stood impregnable from eternity (18.1–4) which effortlessly yielded the puncturing of a cavity into a subterranean cavern (18.8, 19.5–7). This sculpturing of space for the assertion of Christian place confronts the destructive manipulation of pre-existing natural alignments by the enemies of Christian faith who similarly endeavour to claim their place in and upon the landscape, even if, in this narrative, it is intent upon carnage. The culmination of the actions of the devotees of the gods is portrayed as the engineering of a weir holding back an immense volume of water with the intent of discharging a destructive deluge (chapter 8). All these actions upon the landscape, whether from Christian or pagan, are as fantastic as they are imaginative. However, they are not novel. The metaphor of 'flood' for a destructive invasion of one force unleashed upon another was precisely that used by the urbane, pagan philosopher Libanius in the late fourth century. In his protest to the Emperor Theodosios against Christian incursions upon ancient rural religious foundations, Libanius drew upon the Homeric and Demosthean storehouse: χωροῦσι τοίνυν διὰ τῶν ἀγρῶν ὥσπερ χείμαρροι κατασύροντες διὰ τῶν ἱερῶν τοὺς ἀγρούς ('So now they gorge through the country like torrents, devastating sacred estates').[37] The lexical choice may be different in the St Michael story but the metaphor is from a common inheritance which was accessed by both groups to describe a sacrilegious take-over (from the pagan perspective) or a blasphemous attempt at reinstatement (from the Christian point of view). Oratorical imagery has been forged into an expansive, highly tensile narrative episode, this time with the battered characters reversed.

Tracing a pagan background

I posit therefore that paganism is used both as a negative backdrop and as an unacknowledged positive contribution in the story, most especially to the portrayal of the main figure Michael, the archistrategos of the heavenly host of God. The wider Asia Minor context may have already produced the conjunction of a divine angel with and/or in service of familiar members of the Graeco-Roman pantheon.[38] Certainly, Michael's characterization retains sufficient marks of the pagan context as to be recognized in terms of the old deities. Christian expropriation is therefore not just of temples or even sacred groves; it is of language, ideas and imagery.

Many commentators have suspected what Frank Trombley calls the 'synoikism' of the cult at Chonai, whereby a Christian saint assumes the characteristics of the local deity in an area to enable an ease and comfort in the transfer of allegiance in worship, avoiding too many demands of a change in religious practice. Trombley believed that Michael had acquired the healing attributes of the chthonic deity Attis, a Phrygian god attested in the region as late as the third century AD.[39] Others have claimed the Phrygian Mên Karou as the assimilated god, again on the basis of a neighbouring healing sanctuary.[40] The ubiquitous Zeus and Apollo are favoured by some.[41] Dionysos and Herakles have also been proffered.[42] One or two have been content with Jewish speculation about Michael for the characterization and have therefore bypassed the pagan analogies.[43] Some of the impressionistic alignments offered up until now have been based on an author's privileging of one particular local sacred context over another – Hill favouring Hierapolis, Marten opting for Keretapa, for example. The sheer range of suggested inspirations points to a lack of detailed sifting of the text for the analogies that may strengthen an argument for genealogy. Moreover, the search for a single, discrete option tends to conflict with religious texts and images from the region, which show a remarkable ability to blend and absorb features that, formally, are separated.[44] An assembly of all features is required.

Apart from the desire for some definite results from the array of secondary interpretations, there is an added impulse for the enquiry from the primary source. The text of the story itself has Michael speak in the language that evokes divinity – of himself. In chapter 3, the idolater from Laodiceia, who has a mute daughter, is confronted by the archangel in a night vision, directing him to venture with his child to the holy water. The text of the narrative introduction to the angelic voice of this dream epiphany is disputed but was probably the simple ὁ ταξιάρχης Μιχαὴλ ('the taxiarch Michael') rather than the fuller ταξιάρχης κυρίου Μιχαὴλ ὁ ἀρχιστράτηγος ('the taxiarch of the Lord, Michael the archistrategos') (4.2–3). The absence of a reference to God is, however, more definitive in Michael's instructions. He reassures the father:

μὰ τὸ ὄνομά μου, ἐὰν πιστεύσῃς, οὐ μὴ ἐξέλθῃς λυπούμενος.
Mark my name; if you believe, you will in no way leave disappointed. (4.5)

The expression, μὰ τὸ ὄνομά μου, recurs at the end of the story but, significantly, in the form μὰ τὸ τοῦ θεοῦ ὄνομά καὶ τὸ ἐμόν (18.14–15). The insertion of God in the combination, with Michael occupying a secondary position, highlights the absence of 'God' in the first occurrence. The phrase is extremely rare in Christian literature of any sort. By contrast it is a commonplace in classical literature. The reason for the disparity is easy to find. Even when no name was attached to the ejaculation, it was taken as an oath drawing on the power of (pagan) divinity for its weight. As the Byzantine lexicographer Suidas noted:

> Μὰ τόν. ἐλλειπτικῶς ὀμνύει. καὶ οὕτως ἔθος ἐστὶ τοῖς ἀρχαίοις ἐνίοτε μὴ προστιθέναι τὸν θεόν. εἰώθεισαν γὰρ τοῖς τοιούτοις ὅρκοις χρῆσθαι ἐνευφημιζόμενοι, ὥστε εἰπεῖν μὲν μὰ τόν, ὄνομα δὲ μηκέτι προσθεῖναι.
>
> Μὰ τόν. An incomplete oath. The convention of speaking thus is from the ancients, sometimes without being offered to God. For they were accustomed, in their desire to enquire of a god, to speak auspiciously using such oaths so as to speak 'μὰ τόν' without adding the name [but implying the god].[45]

A sweep of classical literature is sufficient to confirm the general summation (though allowing that μά can occasionally be used as a mundane expletive), although one might quibble with the frequency of the specific god to be named. Without a full quantitative survey, it is nevertheless clear that the god most often called upon in this 'μά' oath (either for affirmation or negation) was Zeus. Others do occur, such as Apollo, Athena, Poseidon, Dionysos, even the Muses. At times a non-defined reference to 'god' is found; presumably this means that the particular focus was understood in the mind of the speaker and/or hearer or it was a simple appeal to the supreme (pagan) god. The generic plural also occurs.[46]

Some scribes transmitting the St Michael story were nervous about the usage and its connotations, and adjusted the text.[47] This corroborates the suggestion that the oath was consciously disavowed for Christian usage, along similar lines as the rabbis warned, that in speaking for God, 'do not call upon Michael or Gabriel, but call upon me'.[48] The refined versions of the story, that of Simeon Metaphrastes and of Sisinnius, drop the expression altogether. Its appearance here in the mouth of Michael the archangel shows the survival in a popular hagiography of a pagan oath formula invoking a god or the gods. Its application to Michael indicates the proximation of the archangel to the gods, sufficient to draw the oath. Whether the oath reflects part of the ritual of a prayer for healing or a semi-graffito testimony that existed at the sacred spring before the Christian take-over can only be speculated. However, this examination establishes a *prima facie* case for the appropriation of pagan formulae in the story; it also predisposes the enquiry to a particular set of deities, most especially Zeus. Female deities, for the reasons given below, can be excluded. Lexical comparison will be helpful to the task but motifs will also be important.

The attributes of the Archangel Michael Choniates

One of the requirements for a more probing examination of the survival of pagan elements in the characterization of Michael the archistrategos of Chonai is to harvest all the features of Michael provided by the popular story. Table 2.1 presents this collation, again with reference to the page and line number in Bonnet's 1890 edition.

Table 2.1 Table of attributes of St Michael the Archangel of Chonai.

Description of Michael the Archangel	Reference
provider of favour (χάρις), beneficence (δωρεά) and wonders (τὰ θαύματα)	2.17–3.1, 5
mighty (μέγας) taxiarch and archistrategos	3.3–4, 4.3 …
dispenser of power (δύναμις)	3.4, 4.16, 16.7
associated with a healing spring (ὕδωρ ἐπιτελῶν ἰάματα) / holy water (ἅγιον ὕδωρ) / hagiasma / sanctuary (ναός) / sacred house (ἅγιος αὐτοῦ ὅικος), where rivers, mountain (ὄρος μεγάς) are present	3.6–7, 10, 4.4 9.12, 15, 10.8–9, 12.7, 13.14,…
draws pilgrims to his place of healing, a sanctuary	
appears in a dream (ὅραμα) (at night)	3.10–12, 18.12
bears a powerful name (μὰ τὸ ὄνομά μου)	4.2–3
offers intercessions (πρεσβεῖα) before God	4.5, 17–5.1, 18.14–15
receives structures (εὐκτήριον, θυσιαστήριον), with furnishings (σταυροί, ἅγια τράπεζη) in his honour	4.12, 6.13
has (an ascetic) sanctuary custodian (προσμονάριος), known as a slave of God (δοῦλος τοῦ θεου), (perhaps) hermit (κασουδάριος)	4.17, 8.17, 9.13, 15.9… 5.9, 6.10, 9.6 …
manipulates nature: fire? (φλόξ πῦρος), river courses, rock (πέτρα στερεά), earth (γη), subterranean world (χάσμα)	9.3, 10.2–3,
incorporeal (ἀσώματος)	18.1–4, 19.5–6
descends with massive thunder (βροντὴ μεγάλη σφόδρα … κατελθών)	11.11, 13.13 14.16–17
stands (ἐπίσταμαι, ἵστημι), before God (παρεστηκὼς ἐνώπιον τοῦ θεου) with fear (μετὰ τρόμου)	4.2, 14.17, 16.8, 14
has a booming voice (φωνή μεγάλη)	14.19
appears as a blazing vision of glory (ἀπαστράπουσα θέα τῆς δόξης) / pillar of fire from earth to heaven (στῦλος πυρὸς ἀπὸ τῆς γῆς ἕως τοῦ οὐρανου), induces fear	15.2, 6, 16.3–4
is addressed as 'Lord' (κύριος)	15.5 …
makes a mark (of the cross) (σφραγίζω)	17.7, 18.7
petrifies (ἀπολιθόω) enemies	19.1
bears witness to the Trinity	18.13–14

Of the 20 or more features of Michael listed here, some are clearly Christian or Jewish; others however are far less so, even allowing for mere intimations of a Judaeo-Christian background. The combination of allusive features from disparate sources is also part of the literary ploy of retaining pagan references but with just enough orthodox additives to deflect reproach. Examples of this occur below. I will concentrate here on the impact that Michael makes in his appearance, both visually and upon nature.

The fullest panorama for Michael in the story sets the archistrategos into a natural environment of rivers, mountains, springs and countryside. Michael's appearing directly impacts upon, even as it is coloured by, these forces of nature. It is a noisy and spectacular appearance. The earth shakes, rocks are split, thunder cracks, light blazes out as heaven and earth seem joined by a blinding column; all this heralds or results from the descent of the great taxiarch. The claim of Glenn Peers that the descriptions are deliberately imprecise so as to convey the intangible quality of the asomatic hyper-being may be true as a general perception but it cannot overcome the lack of fit with the biblical evidence that he claims provokes an imaginative visualization.[49] Nowhere in the biblical material does the pillar of fire, for example, stretch from heaven to earth; rather it is frequently the night-time inner glow of the same cloud that had hovered above the tabernacle directing traffic by day (Ex 40.38, Num 9.15, but without reference to heaven). By contrast, the heaven–earth shaft of light is known in Greek mythology.[50]

Thunder and lightning sometimes appear in the Hebrew Scriptures but these are tied to a theophany (Deut 4.11–12, 5.22–25) not an angelophany and certainly are not connected with a descent that could invite a human being to stand at the left and then the right hand (16.2, 19.3). Rather these features indicate those places (and people) where, in a previous dispensation, Zeus Katabaites and/or Zeus Brontes had marked his presence, booming through the land with earthquakes and thunderclaps and/or descending in the blinding lightning strike that frequently earmarked a place for the development of a sacred site. Shrines at such sites were the focal point for the local community, the place where healings of individuals were sought and prayers for the well-being of an entire community were offered (cf. 4.9–10, 5.8–10, 13.14, 18.8–15),[51] and gifts were left on the holy *trapeza* (cf. 15.9).[52] Important in this regard is that one of the earliest known coins from the Colossae mint features the blazing thunderbolt of Zeus, nature's flamboyant demonstration of the connection of heaven and earth and the descent of the god.[53] Other deities are of course featured on Colossae's coins, notably Artemis and Serapis, but it is the features of Zeus tantalisingly attested at Colossae but evidenced clearly in other parts of Phrygia that seem to resonate most closely with some of the emphatic lines in the portrait of Michael in the popular story.

Accommodating the resilience of paganism in the Michael story

Stephen Mitchell writes that 'Imperial legislation and Christian fundamentalism, the least savoury legacy of the Constantinian revolution, sharpened the divide between religious groups in the fourth and fifth centuries' but goes on to allow that in country communities the alienation was far from complete.[54] In the popular story of the Archangel Michael Choniates, there are three devices that rhetorically deflect a reader/hearer from imitating the aggressive scruples about the presence of paganism.

The first is the use of direct and indirect references to the Judaeo-Christian scriptures even when they are ill-fitting to an episode in the story. Thus, in the defeat of the first inimical attempt against the site, a fiery flame (φλόγα πυρός) launches from the water, slamming into the faces of the idolatrous attackers (9.3–4). Even though the surrounding context is dissimilar, the key phrase directly recalls the transformational qualities of angels given in the Christian Bible (Psalm 103:4 LXX and Hebrews 1.7). Again, in a curious inversion of a biblical story, Michael's rupture of the impregnable monolith that had stood before the sacred shrine (a rupture which leads to the funnelling evacuation of the watery inundation) is likened to Moses dividing the sea with his rod so that the people might pass through it (17.13–18.2; cf. Ex 14.16). One might have expected the story of Moses' striking the rock to yield water (Ex 17.5–6) and to construct a contrasting inversion. Alternately the vernacular version may have applied the sea-crossing story to the first attack on the site, previously mentioned, where Michael causes the torrent of waters to mount up like a wall – the very intertextual connection that Sisinnius made in his retelling.[55] The most (only?) apt application of Scripture comes in the song of Archippos from Psalm 93.3–5 LXX. These uses of Scripture from allusion to reference to quotation are not designed, it would appear, to present clarifying typological parallels. Rather, they add a scriptural polish to the popular text, a sheen that reflects the light of orthodoxy, even as it blinds the inquisitorial reader to the presence of pagan elements.

The second device used in the story is a strident affirmation of the ineffable otherness of the triune God, a lengthy declaration that stalls the narrative flow of the story and thereby focuses attention on it. Michael confesses himself as terrified in the presence of God as Archippos is before the archistrategos. Key features that have been used to describe Michael – the brilliance of glory and fire – are now applied to God in terms that far surpass what have been used of Michael (16.8–14). This archangelic deference to the ultimate divinity indicates that whatever of the pagan gods remains is now standing (subsumed to the form of Michael) in the service of the triune God. The ultimate act of humiliation of this Zeus-hued taxiarch is then to call himself a slave (16.12), the very language constantly applied to Archippos as custodian of the Michael shrine.[56]

The third, most subtle and powerful device in the rhetoric of the story is to ground the entire narrative in a demonstration of the vanquishing of pagan idolatry. Here paganism is carved sharply with a horrendously ugly and threatening *feminine* face in the opening two chapters. Most commentators see these chapters as an odd prelude to the story, borrowed from the *Acts of Philip* to provide little more than an apostolic contextual authorization for the sacred healing spring.[57] However, the apostolic confrontation with the female anti-Trinity (Artemis, Echidna and the Great Goddess [Cybele] in 1.9–2.8) sates the call for the obliteration of paganism. But no male gods are named or destroyed. Male-framed paganism is absorbed by a named male defender of the necessarily masculine Trinity. The surviving female voice of the story is that of the mute girl brought by a pagan from Laodiceia. When her tongue is released, it is to acclaim that God is truly of the Christians (the one named as Father, Son and Holy Spirit by her father) and that the power of Michael his archistrategos is indeed great (4.15–16). Conversely, when the enemies of the shrine – and its custodian and the God whom he serves – are defeated at the end of the story, along with their destructive plans (chapter 12), they are conquered as followers of gods (note 9.7, 11.15) that have already been identified as female, inextricably connected with the devil. Here is the dark quaternity that weakly mirrors the quaternity of light.

The ultimate punishment that the hostile onlookers receive is petrification (19.1), presumably turning back upon them the power of the gods they have served (Medusa was closely allied with one of those named at the beginning – Echidna).[58] The irony is that here occurs a fissure in the construction of the defeat of paganism – Michael the archistrategos is revealed as concealing in his powerful arsenal the feminine power to petrify. Prior to this finale however, the full array of masculine pagan characteristics has been able to be harnessed. A subterfuge has occurred, one that allows the male divinities of the pagan (Greek) world to remain in the story now enhancing the portrait and actions of the Archangel Michael. The means by which this has been achieved and the masking of the pagan borrowings that have been made is achieved precisely because the goddesses have been sacrificed. Christian lust for the defeat of paganism has been satisfied by the expulsion of the female deities. Christian determination to survive has pragmatically assimilated the male deities.

Conclusion

The popular story of St Michael of Chonai has a complex transmission history, one which reflects various revisions that address different stages in the developing life of the Byzantine Church in a particular location. The story, in the core of its development, provided a large body of devotees with a narrative rebuff to efforts to curtail the cult of the Archangel Michael Choniates, directed against the encroachments of the powerful metropolitan church of Laodiceia. The cult itself stretched back into pagan times but survived with a powerful following because a negotiated settlement with paganism had been reached. Sufficient lines of cultural continuity were retained to ensure that the site could still be patronized, even with the adoption of a development in religious expression. The exchange exacted in the negotiations was the repudiation of the female element in paganism, represented by the figures of Artemis, Echidna and the Great Mother. Zeus and probably other male gods were thereby deftly able to survive, albeit through their key characteristics being subsumed under the name of Michael, taxiarch and archistrategos.

Notes

1   John Henry Newman to Ulric Charlton, 2 October 1883 (C. S. Dessain and T. Gornall (eds), *The Letters and Diaries of John Henry Newman: Volume XXX: A Cardinal's Apostolate* (Oxford: Clarendon Press, 1976), p. 259).

2   Eusebius *Praep Ev.* In his *Dem. Ev* 114c 'pagan' embraces Roman, Greek and Egyptian gods and ideas.

3   See, generally, R. P. C. Hanson, *Studies in Christian Antiquity* (Edinburgh: T & T Clark, 1985), pp. 144–229.

4   See J. Moralee, 'The Stones of St Theodore: Disfiguring the Pagan Past in Christian Gerasa'. *Journal of Early Christian Studies* 14 (2006): 183–215; P. Brown, *The Cult of the Saints* (London: SCM Press, 1981), pp. 106–27.

5   A. Kaldellis, *Hellenism in Byzantium* (Cambridge: Cambridge University Press, 2007), 162–4; R.L. Fox, *Pagans and Christians* (Harmondsworth: Penguin, 1986), 678–81.

6   W. M. Ramsay, *The Church in the Roman Empire* (London: Hodder & Stoughton, 1903), p. 465.

7   S. Vryonis, *The Decline of Medieval Hellenism in Asia Minor and the Process of Islamization from the Eleventh to the Fifteenth Century* (Berkeley: University of California Press, 1971), pp. 36–7; A. Kaldellis, *The Christian Parthenon: Classicism*

and Pilgrimage in Byzantine Athens* (Cambridge: Cambridge University Press, 2009), p. 44.

8   M. Bonnet, *Narratio de Miraculo a Michaele Archangelo Chonis Patrato* (Paris: Librairie Hachette, 1890). Bonnet included two of the three Greek versions of the story, the popular anonymous narrative and the refined offering of Simeon Metaphrastes. Another high literary rendition is connected with the name Sisinnius and belongs, like that of Metaphrastes' work, to the tenth century. The only available edition is that of J. Stiltingo, C. Suyskeno, J. Periero and J. Cleo (eds), *Acta Sanctorum: September* (Paris/Rome: Victor Palmé, 1869 [1762]), Vol. 8, 41C–47C). F. Nau made minor adjustments to Bonnet's edition (not always to be left uncontested however): 'Le Miracle de Saint Michel a Colosses'. *Patrologia Orientalis* 4 (1908): 542–62. A French translation, based on Nau's text, was provided by B. Bouvier and F. Amsler, 'Le Miracle de l'Archange Michel à Chonai: Introduction, Traduction, et Notes', in D.H. Warren, A.G. Brock and D.W. Pao (eds), *Early Christian Voices: In Texts, Traditions and Symbols: Essays in Honor of François Bovon* (Boston/Leiden: Brill Academic Publishers, 2003), pp. 395–407. My English translation of the popular version of the story appears in A. H. Cadwallader and M. Trainor (eds), *Colossae in Space and Time: Linking with an Ancient City* (Göttingen: Vandenhoeck & Ruprecht, 2011), pp. 323–30. The translations of texts in this chapter are my own unless otherwise stated.

9   B. Kötting, *Peregrinatio religiosa: Wallfahrten in der Antike und das Pilgerwesen in der alten Kirche* (Munster: Antiquariat Th. Stenderhoff, 1980), pp. 166–171; C. Foss, 'Pilgrimage in Medieval Asia Minor'. *Dumbarton Oaks Papers* 56 (2002): 129–151; M. Kaplan, 'Les saints en pèlerinage al'époque mésobyzantine (7e–12e siècles)'. *Dumbarton Oaks Papers* 56 (2002): 121–4.

10   *De Them* 3.24 (edition: A. Pertusi, *De thematibus Introductione, testo critico, commento* (Città del Vaticano, Biblioteca apostolica vaticana, 1952), 68.32–40).

11   Three eleventh-century lead seals provide the addition ὁ Χονιατῆς to the name of Archangel Michael: see J. Cotsonis, 'The Contribution of Byzantine Lead Seals to the Study of the Cult of the Saints (6th–12th Cent)'. *Byzantion* 75 (2005): 440. The Choniates brothers were born in the mid-twelfth century.

12   Nicetas Choniates, *Chronicon* 178.19 (edition: Jan-Louis van Dieten ed., *Nicetae Choniatae Historia* (Berlin: Walter de Gruyter, 1975); cf. Xenophon, *Anabasis* 1.2.8.

13   See, generally, H. Hunger, 'On the Imitation (ΜΙΜΗΣΙΣ) of Antiquity in Byzantine Literature'. *Dumbarton Oaks Papers* 23 (1969–1970): 15–38.

14   See the Menologion of Basil II: *PG* 117.33CD.

15   For a discussion of various icons of the miracle at Chonai, see S. Gabelic, 'The Iconography of the Miracle at Chonae: An Unusual Example from Cyprus'. *Zograf* 20 (1989): 95–103; C. Joliver-Lévy, 'Culte et iconographie de l'Archange Michel

dans l'Orient Byzantin: le Témoignage de quelques monuments de Cappadoce'. *Les Cahiers de Saint-Michel de Cuixà* 28 (1997): 187–98.

16 The translation has been deliberately adjusted to match the assonance of the Greek. The allusive alliteration is played even more heavily in Metaphrastes' version (Bonnet 27.24). Sisinnius adjusts the pun in the drama of the final rescue (§17 AS 47A) but has probably accented the reversal wrought by St Michael through the use of κατανχώννυμι, an expression for one idolater's design upon the site earlier in the story (AS 43B); see further below.

17 M. Martens, 'L'Archange Michel et l'héritage eschatologique Pré-Chrétien', in A. Abel and A. Destrée (eds), *Mélanges Armand Abel*, Vol. 3 (Leiden: Brill, 1974), pp. 148–51; Ramsay, *Church in the Roman Empire*, pp. 468, 479. See the criticism of Louis Robert, *Villes d'Asie Mineure: Études de géographie antique* (Paris: Boccard, 1935), p. 105 n4.

18 See O. Meinhardus, 'St Michael's Miracle of Khonae and its Geographical Setting'. *Ekklesia kai Theologia* 1 (1980): 462; G. Peers, *Subtle Bodies: Representing Angels in Byzantium* (Berkeley: University of California Press, 2001), p. 161.

19 Bonnet, p. 2 n6.

20 3.6 *et al.*; cf. Metaphrastes 22.3, Sisinnius 5 (*AS* 43A).

21 See M. Ricl, 'Society and Economy of Rural Sanctuaries in Roman Lydia and Phrygia'. *Epigraphica Anatolica* 35 (2003): 77–101.

22 In this case, the story of St Michael is a counterpoint to the general concern (such as we see in the *Life of Saint Hypatia*) that country areas were barely Christian. See F. R. Trombley, 'Paganism in the Greek World at the End of Antiquity: The Case of Rural Anatolia and Greece'. *Harvard Theological Review* 78 (1985): 327–52. It should be noted that Archippos, the one most qualified to fulfil the witness to Christian verities in the countryside, only comes to his role of custodian of the shrine (ch. 4ff.) after the healing site has been established for some time.

23 See A. Darrouzès, *Notitiae episcopatum ecclesiae Constantinopolitanae* (*Géographie ecclésiastique de l'empire byzantin 1*) (Paris: Institut Français d'Études Byzantines, 1981), p. 150; K. Belke and N. Merisch, *Phrygien und Pisidien* (Vienna: Österreichischen Akademie der Wissenschaft, 1990), p. 133.

24 G. D. Mansi, *Sacrorum Concilium Nova et Amplissima Collectio* (Florence: 31 volumes, 1759–1998), Vol. 2, p. 569. Theodoret, *Comm. ad Col.* (PG 82.613B, 620D–621A). Theodoret's impressionistic and anachronistic mode of exegesis has been repeated through to the present generation of New Testament commentators.

25 See W. Lueken, *Michael: Eine Darstellung und Vergleichung der jüdischen und der morgenländisch-christlichen Tradition vom Erzengel Michael* (Göttingen: Vanderhoeck & Ruprecht, 1898), p. 75.

26 For another example of the use of literary fiction as a weapon against ecclesial marginalization, see R. N. Slater, 'An Inquiry into the Relationship between

Community and Text: The Apocryphal Acts of Philip 1 and the Encratites of Asia Minor', in F. Bovon, A. G. Brock and C. R. Matthews (eds), *The Apocryphal Acts of the Apostles* (Cambridge, MA: Harvard University Press, 1999), pp. 295–6.

27   In Sissinius' retelling of the story, even the idolatrous father of the daughter brought for healing at St Michael's spring was initially intent on 'burying' the sacred flow (AS 43B: καταχώννυμι – possibly an additional, ironic pun on the name Chonai).

28   Some scribes (as in manuscripts D, V, A) were either dissatisfied with the pun or thought a mistake had been made. They turned the lawless mob into ὁ δὲ λαὸς τῆς Λαοδικίας ('the people of Laodiceia') who were joined at Laodiceia by other aggressors.

29   Hence, contra Foss, 'Pilgrimage', 137 who argues for a ninth-century date, I would argue for a fifth- or sixth-century date, without requiring that the story exist at that time in the form we now have; cf. Bonnet, pp. xxxviii–xix, Bouvier and Amsler, p. 398.

30   See A. Cadwallader, 'The Stratigraphy of an Ancient City Through its Key Story: The Archistrategos of Chonai', in Cadwallader and Trainor, *Colossae in Space and Time*, pp. 282–98.

31   On the distinction between Greek and pagan see Kaldellis, *Hellenism in Byzantium*, p. 327. The distinction arose early in the Byzantine period: see J. W. McCrindle ed., *The Christian Topography of Cosmas, an Egyptian Monk* (New York: Burt Franklin, 1897), p. xi.

32   Even though some have sought the origins of angel worship in Jewish progenitors, there is no anti-Jewish sentiment in the story, even though the Synod of Laodiceia directed a number of its canons (29, 37, 38) to such concerns; see Lueken, *Michael*, p. 80.

33   See, for example, E. Lucius, *Die Anfänge des Heiligenkults in der christlichen Kirche* (Tübingen: JCB Mohr, 1904), p. 268.

34   See F. R. Trombley, *Hellenic Religion and Christianization* (Leiden: Brill, 2 vols, 2001), Vol. 2, p. 115.

35   One scribe perceived the anomaly and adroitly modified the word to ῥεῦσις ('gushing') (Codex A).

36   See J. Lieu, *Christian Identity in the Jewish and Graeco-Roman World* (Oxford: Oxford University Press, 2004), pp. 211–12.

37   Libanius *Or 30.9* (*Pro templis*) Homer *Il* 4.452; Demosthenes *Or* 18.152.

38   S. Mitchell, 'The Cult of Theos Hypsistos between Pagans, Jews and Christians', in P. Athanassiadi and M. Frede (eds), *Pagan Monotheism in Late Antiquity* (Oxford: Clarendon Press, 1999), pp. 102–4. R. M. M. Tuschling, *Angels and Orthodoxy: A Study in their Development in Syria and Palestine* (Tübingen: Mohr Siebeck, 2007), p. 52.

39 Trombley, *Hellenic Religion*, Vol. 2, p. 101.

40 Lucius, 268, Meinardus, 'St Michael's Miracle', 466, A. L. Williams, 'The Cult of the Angels at Colossae'. *Journal of Theological Studies* 10 (1909): 437.

41 For Zeus: Ramsay, *Church in the Roman Empire, 477; Pauline and other Studies in Early Christian History* (London: Hodder & Stoughton, 1906), p. 183 (he apparently changed from his first preference for Mên, though he sought to combine the two in his *Letters to the Seven Churches of Asia* (London: Hodder & Stoughton, 1904), pp. 417–18); for Apollo: G. F. Hill, 'Apollo and St Michael: Some Analogies'. *Journal of Hellenic Studies* 36 (1916): 134–62; cf. M. Simon, *Verus Israel: Étude sur les relations entre chrétiens et juifs dans l'empire romain (135–425 ap. J-C.)* (Paris: Boccard, 1948), p. 430.

42 For Dionysos: A. B. Cook, *Zeus: A Study in Ancient Religion* (Cambridge: Cambridge University Press, 1940), Vol. 2, pt. 1, pp. 114–15; for Herakles: Marten, 'L'Archange Michel', pp. 151–3, 157–8.

43 G. Peers, 'Apprehending the Archangel Michael: Hagiographic Methods' *Byzantine and Modern Greek Studies* 20 (1996): 110–13.

44 See, for a specific example of the combining of different gods, L.L. Thompson, 'ISmyrna 753: Gods and the One God', in D. E. Aune and R. D. Young (eds), *Reading Religions in the Ancient World* (Leiden: Brill, 2007), pp. 101–22.

45 Suidas §292.

46 See LSJ sv; for further examples see Aesop, *Fab* 297 (1), Aristophanes *Archarn* 88, Plato, Gorgias 489e, Vit Aes (G) 8.4, Xenophon, *Mem* 4.6.9.

47 Μά is softened to μετά, an associational sense, in ch. 3 (4.5) in Codex A (see H. W. Smythe, *Greek Grammar* (Cambridge, MA: Harvard University Press, 1976), §1691); in ch. 12, the same codex reveals particular scruples, engaging in wholesale erasure; see Bonnet, p. 18 n69.

48 Jerusalem Talmud, *Ber* 9.13a.

49 Peers, 'Apprehending the Archangel Michael', pp. 110–11, 115. He is correct however in drawing attention to the repetitious use of ὡς and its cognates (e.g. 4.2, 17.16.). Not all of these pick up biblical allusions however and even those that do may be the requisite compensation for the retention of pagan features in the same episode. See further below.

50 Cook, *Zeus*, Vol. 2, pp. 114–15. Cook sees a direct reminiscence of this in the Michael Choniates story.

51 Ricl, 'Society and Economy', pp. 78, 84.

52 The *trapeza* was a particular item of sacred furniture of both Mên and Zeus: Thompson, 'Ismyrna 753', p. 106.

53 H. von Aulock, *Münzen und Städte Phrygiens* (Tübingen: Ernst Wasmuth Verlag, 1980, 1987), Vol. 2, p. 83, §§443–446.

54 Mitchell, 'Cult of Theos Hypsistos', p. 124.

55   *AS* 46F.

56   See A. Cadwallader, 'The Inversion of Slavery: The Ascetic and the Archistrategos
      at Chonai', in G. D. Dunn, D. Luckensmeyer and L. Cross (eds), *Prayer and
      Spirituality in the Early Church Volume 5: Poverty and Riches* (Strathfield: St Pauls
      Publications, 2009), pp. 215–36.

57   *Acts of Philip*, pp. 107–30; see, generally, Bonnet xviii–xx, p. 97; J. P. Rohland, *Der
      Erzengel Michael: Arzt und Feldherr* (Leiden: Brill, 1977), p. 97. Similar motifs and
      settings of the apostolic battle with the evil forces of goddesses are also found in
      the story of the icon of Maria Romaia: see E. von Dobschütz, 'Maria Romaia: Zwei
      unbekannte Texte'. *Byzantische Zeitschrift* 12 (1903): 193–5.

58   Bonnet's footnote cross-reference to Exodus 15:16 LXX (where the same verb,
      ἀπολιθόω, is used) is pertinent but not decisive, though a blend of Scripture
      and classical allusions is possible. The Egyptians are held in *temporary* abeyance
      and while it might be argued that the writer is presenting an *a fortiori* argument,
      nevertheless the story has already been coloured by the associations with the
      goddesses in the opening chapter. Medusa was frequently blended with Echidna
      (Nonnus, *Dionysiaca* 30.267), owing to the common dominance of snakes. See Y.
      Ustinova, *The Supreme Gods of the Bosporan Kingdom: Celestial Aphrodite and the
      Most High God* (Leiden: Brill, 1999), p. 94. Most significantly, the turning to stone
      is tied to staring bystanders (οἱ ἑστῶτες καὶ βλέποντες, 18.17–19.1), a clear
      signal of the Medusa myth and an element absent from the Red Sea passage. There
      may be a derived aetiology operating here as well, given the renowned petrifying
      quality of the heavily mineralized waters of one of Colossae's streams, the Ak-su,
      noted by Pliny the Elder (*NH* 31.2: see E. le Camus, 'Colosses' in F. Vigouroux ed.,
      Dictionnaire de la Bible (Paris: Letouzey et Ané, 1899), Vol. 2, p. 865.

References

von Aulock, H. *Münzen und Städte Phrygiens.* Tübingen: Ernst Wasmuth Verlag, 2 vols,
      1980, 1987.

Belke, K. and N. Merisch. *Phrygien und Pisidien.* Vienna: Österreichischen Akademie
      der Wissenschaft. 1990.

Bonnet, M. *Narratio de Miraculo a Michaele Archangelo Chonis Patrato.* Paris: Librairie
      Hachette, 1890.

Bouvier, B. and F. Amsler. 'Le Miracle de l'Archange Michel à Chonai: Introduction,
      Traduction, et Notes', in D.H. Warren, A.G. Brock and D.W. Pao (eds), *Early
      Christian Voices: In Texts, Traditions and Symbols: Essays in Honor of François
      Bovon.* Boston/Leiden: Brill Academic, 2003, pp. 395–407.

Cadwallader, A. H. 'The Inversion of Slavery: The Ascetic and the Archistrategos at
      Chonai', in G. D. Dunn, D. Luckensmeyer and L. Cross (eds), *Prayer and Spirituality*

in the Early Church Volume 5: Poverty and Riches. Strathfield: St Pauls Publications, 2009, pp. 215–36.

—'The Stratigraphy of an Ancient City Through its Key Story: The Archistrategos of Chonai', in A. H. Cadwallader and M. Trainor (eds), *Colossae in Space and Time: Linking with an Ancient City*. Forthcoming.

—'The Story of the Archistrategos, St. Michael of Chonai', in A. H. Cadwallader and M. Trainor (eds), *Colossae in Space and Time: Linking with an Ancient City*. forthcoming.

le Camus, E. 'Colosses', in F. Vigouroux ed., *Dictionnaire de la Bible*. Paris: Letouzey et Ané, 1899, Vol. 2, 860–6.

Cook, A. B. *Zeus: A Study in Ancient Religion*. Cambridge: Cambridge University Press, 1940.

Cotsonis, J. 'The Contribution of Byzantine Lead Seals to the Study of the Cult of the Saints (6th–12th Cent)'. *Byzantion* 75 (2005): 383–498.

Darrouzès, A. *Notitiae episcopatum ecclesiae Constantinopolitanae (Géographie ecclésiastique de l'empire byzantin 1)*. Paris: Institut Français d'Études Byzantines, 1981.

Dessain, C. S. and T. Gornall (eds). *The Letters and Diaries of John Henry Newman: Volume XXX: A Cardinal's Apostolate*. Oxford: Clarendon Press, 1976.

Dieten, J-L. van ed.. *Nicetae Choniatae Historia*. Berlin: Walter de Gruyter, 1975.

Dobschütz, E. von. 'Maria Romaia: Zwei unbekannte Texte'. *Byzantische Zeitschrift* 12 (1903): 173–214.

Foss, C. 'Pilgrimage in Medieval Asia Minor'. *Dumbarton Oaks Papers* 56 (2002): 129–51.

Fox, R. L. *Pagans and Christians*. Harmondsworth: Penguin, 1986.

Gabelic, S. 'The Iconography of the Miracle at Chonae: An Unusual Example from Cyprus'. *Zograf* 20 (1989): 95–103.

Hanson, R. P. C. *Studies in Christian Antiquity*. Edinburgh: T & T Clark, 1985.

Hill, G. F. 'Apollo and St Michael: Some Analogies'. *Journal of Hellenic Studies* 36 (1916): 134–162.

Hunger, H. 'On the Imitation (MIMHΣIΣ) of Antiquity in Byzantine Literature'. *Dumbarton Oaks Papers* 23 (1969–1970): 15–38.

Joliver-Lévy, C. 'Culte et iconographie de l'Archange Michel dans l'Orient Byzantin: le Témoignage de quelques monuments de Cappadoce'. *Les Cahiers de Saint-Michel de Cuixà* 28 (1997): 187–98.

Kaldellis, A. *Hellenism in Byzantium*. Cambridge: Cambridge University Press, 2007.

—*The Christian Parthenon: Classicism and Pilgrimage in Byzantine Athens*. Cambridge: Cambridge University Press, 2009.

Kaplan, M. 'Les saints en pèlerinage al'époque mésobyzantine (7e–12e siècles)'. *Dumbarton Oaks Papers* 56 (2002): 109–27.

Kötting, K. *Peregrinatio religiosa: Wallfahrten in der Antike und das Pilgerwesen in der alten Kirche*. Munster: Antiquariat Th. Stenderhoff, 1980.

Lieu, J. *Christian Identity in the Jewish and Graeco-Roman World*. Oxford: Oxford University Press, 2004.

Lucius, E. *Die Anfänge des Heiligenkults in der christlichen Kirche*. Tübingen: JCB Mohr, 1904.

Lueken, W. *Michael: Eine Darstellung und Vergleichung der jüdischen und der morgenländisch-christlichen Tradition vom Erzengel Michael*. Göttingen: Vanderhoeck & Ruprecht, 1898.

McCrindle, J. W. ed.. *The Christian Topography of Cosmas, an Egyptian Monk*. New York: Burt Franklin, 1897.

Martens, 'L'Archange Michel et l'héritage eschatologique Pré-Chrétien'. in A. Abel and A. Destrée (eds), *Mélanges Armand* Abel, Vol. 3. Leiden: Brill, 1974, pp. 141–159.

Mansi, G. D. *Sacrorum Concilium Nova et Amplissima Collectio*. Florence: 31 volumes, 1759–98.

Meinhardus, O. 'St Michael's Miracle of Khonae and its Geographical Setting'. *Ekklesia kai Theologia* 1 (1980): 459–69.

Mitchell, S. 'The Cult of Theos Hypsistos between Pagans, Jews and Christians', in P. Athanassiadi and M. Frede (eds), *Pagan Monotheism in Late Antiquity*. Oxford: Clarendon Press, 1999, pp. 81–148.

Moralee, J. 'The Stones of St Theodore: Disfiguring the Pagan Past in Christian Gerasa'. *Journal of Early Christian Studies* 14 (2006): 183–215.

Nau, F. 'Le Miracle de Saint Michel a Colosses'. *Patrologia Orientalis* 4 (1908): 542–562.

Peers, G. 'Apprehending the Archangel Michael: Hagiographic Methods'. *Byzantine and Modern Greek Studies* 20 (1996): 100–21.

—*Subtle Bodies: Representing Angels in Byzantium*. Berkeley: University of California Press, 2001.

Pertusi, A. *De thematibus Introductione, testo critico, commento*. Città del Vaticano, Biblioteca apostolica vaticana, 1952.

Ramsay, W. M. *The Church in the Roman Empire*. London: Hodder & Stoughton, 1903.

—*Pauline and Other Studies in Early Christian History*. London: Hodder & Stoughton, 1906.

Ricl, M. 'Society and Economy of Rural Sanctuaries in Roman Lydia and Phrygia'. *Epigraphica Anatolica* 35 (2003): 77–101.

Robert, L. *Villes d'Asie Mineure: Études de géographie antique*. Paris: Boccard, 1935.

Rohland, J. P. *Der Erzengel Michael: Arzt und Feldherr*. Leiden: Brill, 1977.

Simon, M. *Verus Israel: Étude sur les relations entre chrétiens et juifs dans l'empire romain (135–425 ap. J-C.)*. Paris: Boccard, 1948.

Slater, R. N. 'An Inquiry into the Relationship between Community and Text: The Apocryphal Acts of Philip 1 and the Encratites of Asia Minor', in F. Bovon, A. G. Brock and C. R. Matthews (eds), *The Apocryphal Acts of the Apostles*. Cambridge, MA: Harvard University Press, 1999, pp. 281–306.

Smythe, H. W. *Greek Grammar*. Cambridge, MA: Harvard University Press, 1976.

Stiltingo, J., C. Suyskeno, J. Periero and J. Cleo (eds). *Acta Sanctorum: September*. Paris/ Rome: Victor Palmé, 1869 [1762].

Thompson, L. L. 'ISmyrna 753: Gods and the One God', in D.E. Aune and R. D. Young (eds), *Reading Religions in the Ancient World*. Leiden: Brill, 2007, 101–122.

Trombley, F. R. 'Paganism in the Greek World at the End of Antiquity: The Case of Rural Anatolia and Greece'. *Harvard Theological Review* 78 (1985): 327–52.

—*Hellenic Religion and Christianization*. Leiden: Brill, 2 vols, 2001.

Tuschling, R. M. M. *Angels and Orthodoxy: A Study in their Development in Syria and Palestine*. Tübingen: Mohr Siebeck, 2007.

Ustinova, Y. *The Supreme Gods of the Bosporan Kingdom: Celestial Aphrodite and the Most High God*. Leiden: Brill, 1999.

Vryonis, S. *The Decline of Medieval Hellenism in Asia Minor and the Process of Islamization from the Eleventh to the Fifteenth Century*. Berkeley: University of California Press, 1971.

Williams, A. L. 'The Cult of the Angels at Colossae'. *Journal of Theological Studies* 10 (1909): 413–38.

Part 2

Chivalry

3

The Cultural Repository of Persian Sufism: Medieval Chivalry and Mysticism in Iran

Milad Milani

Whoever enters this house, give him bread, [and] ask not of his faith. For whoever is worthy of a Soul granted by the Almighty, is certainly worthy of Bol-Hasan's bread.

(Kharaqani; Bastani-Parizi, 'Khaniqah', 71)

The Sufis are inheritors of both Iran's rich cultural heritage and its mystical legacy. Although this is true of the culture of Sufism in general, since Persia was once a dominant cultural and linguistic force throughout the East, such a claim, however, applies directly to the Sufis of Iran. It would appear that Sufism has its roots in a pre-Islamic age, a hypothesis which asserts the existence of a Persianate Sufism that is highlighted by the distinct presence of Iranian identity and cultural products. Iranian Sufism may therefore display a measure of Mithraic, Zoroastrian or Firdausian influence. Particularly important is the chivalric ideal that is found at the heart of Sufism, which is readily noted across the board, but given greater emphasis among the Iranians especially. What is unique about the chivalric component within Sufi practice is that through it the Sufis found a more practical approach to spirituality, giving their tenets greater weight in the daily life of the Muslim. Sufism and chivalry have always been closely connected, and it is often difficult to discern which had first influenced the other, in particular in terms of how the connection was lived in the Iranian Middle Ages as well as the way it is perceived today.[1]

Introduction

Chivalry may have its origins in the ancient world of the nomadic tribes of the Steppes. It is in this far-off and forgotten world that Western Europe and the

Arab world may discover the foundations for a common origin in their chivalric ideals. The Aryans, whose historical detail remains unknown to us in full, are the likely ancestors of the peoples ranging from Western Europe to the Indus Valley, also known as the Indo-Europeans.[2] Among them is one of the oldest civilizations, the Iranians – a name that clearly bears their Aryan heritage.[3] The Iranians, or 'Persians', as the Greeks called them, dominated the Middle East region for centuries, stretching their boundaries time and again westward, rousing the Greeks and later the Romans to war.

The Persians were certainly not the sole originators of things, but they were great innovators. The Iranians asserted their influence over the regions of Near and Middle East, Asia Minor, Egypt and Southern Asia for almost 1,100 years; their culture and language still bears its mark on the Turkish- and Indic-speaking world. Even the periodic conquerors of this once mighty empire – such as Alexander the Great, the Muslim Arabs or even the Mongol hordes – were eventually made patrons to Iran's cultural legacy. Persia retained its 'mystical' quality and its uniqueness to become a 'melting-pot' of culture, language and religion; and, more importantly, of ideas. In so doing, Persia has celebrated several revivals in its long-standing history. Following the example of the ancient Persians, the Abbasids (AD 750–1258), upon seizing power from the Umayyads, revived the spirit of a truly universal civilization, thus giving way to the Golden Age of Islam. The Persian system of governance, language and culture was the chief influence of the day under the Abbasids.

It is interesting to note, then, that chivalry is a continuing aspect of Iranian culture to this day, and it is from the Persians that the Arabs allegedly derived their concept of *fûtûwwat* (chivalry). We know that chivalry did not exist as an identifiable institution during the lifetime of Mohammed;[4] and the term was only used within a social and organizational setting outside of the Arabian Peninsula, in Iraq and Iran, where such organizations have their roots in pre-Islamic times.[5] The Iranians then transferred their institutions to Turkish Anatolia and from there it spread into the Balkans under the Ottomans.[6]

On the other hand, in the Occident, the seed of Western chivalry originates in Celtic and Teutonic culture.[7] From here, swept up by the Britons and other European cultures that came into contact with it, it resulted in the famed legends and romance of chivalry so recounted in the French and Germanic imagination. It is also interesting to note that the first Orders of Western chivalry, for example, the Knights Templar and the Teutonic Knights, were founded in the Middle East. This is not to assert an Eastern or Persian origin for Western chivalry, merely to note the broad influence the Persio-Arab world had had on the receptive cultures of twelfth-century Western Europe. Worthy of note is the fact that chivalry came to prominence synonymously in the twelfth century, across both Europe and the Orient. In both cultures a similar chronology may be observed, and from there, chivalry progressed through stages of fusion with religious and secular idealisms, and finally was made the subject of romance literature.

Primal notions of chivalry may well have been inclined towards battle-hardened knights, but the evolution of its history suggests a gradual refinement that infuses the sophistications of the social codes of gentility and gallantry. In addition, chivalry is given a third and most crucial attribute: that of the spiritual component, which created a mutual bond across the ages on the common ground of sacrifice and selfless service. Regardless of how such virtue was used or under whose patronage chivalry was directed, all three aspects – martial, ethical and spiritual – were interconnected and interweaved in making up the reality of the code and practice of chivalry in the Middle Ages.

Iranian chivalry

The Iranian world has a rich cultural heritage, with chivalry deeply entrenched in both its social and religious domain. Chivalry has in fact been a significant contributor to Iranian identities.[8] The Iranian ideal of chivalry is very much founded in its nation's distant past, and although the 'old' and 'new' (pre- and post-Islamic) era of Iranian history appears to be mutually exclusive, they are indeed connected in an intimate way. That is, the Iranian ideals of old are as much a part of the Iranian lifestyle and cognition, just as they are a real part of the Iranian religious consciousness today, and it is oftentimes difficult to speak of the one without the other. This has, of course, led to some debate over the proper analysis of Iran's history.

The most recent study on the subject of Iranian chivalry is Lloyd Ridgeon's *Morals and Mysticism in Persian Sufism*. This timely work elucidates the social realities of Sufism more broadly, while offering a necessary chronological account of chivalry in Persian Sufism specifically. Ridgeon rightly cautions against patriotic, nationalist Iranians who present an ethic of chivalry in an unbroken chain that pre-dates the Islamic conquest of Iran.[9] He suggests that the history of chivalry in Iran involves contributions from both periods, and the Iranian medieval era is unique in the merging of the pre-Islamic and Islamic cultures.[10] This, in turn, gives birth to a special perspective on the notion of the

'Persian' and its influence as an amalgamation of two remarkable cultures: the Iranian and Arab. In this way, Ridgeon points out that 'Persian' is not limited to the chauvinistic ideals of either the 'Iranian, Persian, Sasanian, Islamic or Arab',[11] a view that reflects the contemporary character of modern-day Iran. Nevertheless, those proponents of Iranian chivalry that Ridgeon critiques, we must be reminded, are not academics. In the first instance their works are highly nuanced, and second, they must be understood in proper context. This requires closer attention. For instance, Karim Zayyani's claim to a 3,000-year history of Sufi chivalry, which pre-dates Islam, is actually grounded in the view that both *fûtûwwat* (chivalry) and *tasawwuf* (Sufism) originate in the Khurasan province.[12] Zayyani's view is, in fact, based on the hypothesis of Javad Nurbakhsh, who proposed that it was the chevaliers who founded the creed of Sufism 'on the basis of both Islam and chivalry'.[13]

Indeed, the province of Khurasan and the role of the chevaliers are crucial to the history of Sufism and chivalry in Iran, as will be elaborated on later. Ridgeon does not deny this, but points out that the challenge remains in the correct assessment of this fact. To their credit, advocates of Iranian chivalry generally write from a repository of cultural imagination – thanks to Firdausi's resurrection of Persian history, language and culture – and from the core of their collective national memory – a skill of which only Iranians are masters, since the Persians – wilfully illiterate for the most part of their early history – were the great champions of oral diffusion.[14] In short, it will not do to reduce the Iranian claim for a pre-Islamic tradition of mysticism and chivalry to nationalistic or patriotic dogma. There is still much to be said for Persian Sufism as a corollary for the pre-Islamic heritage of Iran.[15] What is more, the Persian influence was not only greatly significant to the culture of the Islamic Middle East, but also through it, effective in permeating the European cultures that were in contact with the growing Arab Empire, also under Persian influence.

Iranian culture has a distinct word for chivalry, *javânmardî* (or its Arabic equivalent, *fûtûwwat*), which signifies not only the 'strong man' aspect of chivalry, celebrated by the Persians prior to the Arab conquests, but also the more important facet of gentility and ethics that is accompanied by the term. The word *fûtûwwat* fundamentally translates as 'chivalry', but is taken from the Arabic root f.t.a., which yields the noun *fatâ* (young man). Although it remains a matter of dispute, it is more than likely that *javânmardî* (literally, 'young-manliness') is unique to Iran and stands in contrast to the Arab notion of *mûruwwat* ('manliness'). The former harbours a unique ideal that is alien to Arabia. The Sufi adaptation of *fûtûwwat* makes a provocative statement:

'"Manliness" is to be feminine and receptive towards God's command and so properly masculine and active in the world.'[16] This is because the Sufis radically envisaged the qualities of kindness and selfless service as the feminine attributes of God, and therefore, for the Sufis, *fûtûwwat* defined the proper synchronicity of the masculine and feminine in the individual; but more than that it defined the balance between the spiritual and the worldly. Thus the *fûtûwwat* movement during the Middle Ages welcomed both men and women in the struggle to serve their companions selflessly.[17] Admittedly, the Arabs had always held a basic notion of 'manliness' and 'virtue' (*mûruwwat*) promoting courage and valour in their dealings with rival tribes in pre-Islamic Arabia; but this is a notion far removed from a refined concept of chivalry (encompassing an ethical and spiritual code) found within the Persio-Mesopotamian domain. A parallel development in the Christian West is seen in the 'Truce of God' anticipating the rise of chivalry. Apropos, the Arab understanding of chivalry is greatly challenged, and affected, by the new Koranic references to *fûtûwwat* in the time of Mohammed.[18] Although no institution of chivalry was yet in place in Arabia, the Koranic ideals of chivalry, which were foreign to the Arabs of the Hijaz, were further developed by the Sufis and increasingly spiritualized by them, the practical aspect of which remained well grounded in the social fabric of their time.

Persian Sufism and chivalry

The true mystery of Sufism is the fact that scholars fail to openly recognize a more than accidental role of Iran's past in the identity and practice of Persian Sufism. In effect, for as much as the Iranians are involved, 'Sufism' is the name given to the mysticism that has in one way or another featured throughout the history of Iranian spirituality. Sufism was born in the Islamic era but it does not stray far from its Iranian heritage among the Persian Sufis. In a sense, Persian Sufism is rather intimately linked with the culture of *javânmardî*, and has been so for the past 1,000 years. Such is the distinctive character of Persian Sufism, which sprang out of Khurasan, the northeastern province of Iran that resisted Arab cultural dominance to the last – but it is also a region where many intriguing syntheses between Persian and Arab models appeared. Many Sufis, however, congregated in Basra and/or Baghdad, the capital of the Abbasid dynasty, where a great deal of theological and philosophical debate and development was underway during the ninth through to the thirteenth centuries.

Although it is difficult to impart definite dates, it would seem that connections between Sufism and chivalry are first attested to in early twelfth-century Khurasan. It is here that the Sufis encounter the chevaliers, or frontier warriors (pl. *gâziân*) recruited for the expansion of Muslim territories. The assimilation of these mercenaries looks to be no different to that of the integration of 'rough' warriors by clergy during European feudal times to defend the helpless and the Church. What is peculiar about the *gâziân*, however, is that they were already immersed in altruistic practices prior to their interactions with those Muslims who were mystically inclined; that is, their chivalry was already refined beyond a base warrior attitude. Stretching across Khurasan, Transoxiana and Sistan, in these lands the conventions of the chevaliers plainly emphasized piety, steadfastness, self-sacrifice, courage and fortitude[19] – indeed, suggesting a likely pre-Islamic (Iranian) origin. It is possible that the Sufis and chevaliers met on the common grounds of the Koran, and in particular, the Apostolic tradition that distinguished between the lesser and greater struggle (*jihad*) – the former imploring battle with enemies of the faith; the latter, with the internal sinful tendencies of the soul. The Sufis consistently employed material from Koran and *hadith*, but this was mainly to deploy their mystical narrative. Their legacy was unique in giving a multi-layered meaning to Islam's sacred text, and which typically remained absent in a literal reading of it by orthodox Muslims.

A distinct and developing characteristic of Sufism was an emphasis on the transformation of the soul (*nafs*), rather than the struggle (*jihad*) against it.[20] This was an idea that Henry Corbin rightly identified in the fusion of chivalry and Sufism as the transition of chivalry from 'chivalerie militaire' to 'chivalerie spirituelle'. Corbin correctly noted this correlation with the shift in Persian literature from the heroic epic written by Firdausi to the mystical epic proposed by Suhrawardi maqtul.[21] The celebrated mystic martyr (*al-maqtul*), Shahab al-Din Yahya al-Suhrawardi (d. AD 1191), formulated the origin of spiritual wisdom to arise out of four cultural wellsprings: the Hermetic, Greek, Indian and Persian. Accordingly, in the case of Persia, Islam was seen as the new face of Iran's ancient spiritual tradition.

To clarify, there are three main archetypal identities associated with Sufi chivalry that should be mentioned: the Shi'ite, nationalist and Sufi. The Shi'ite is modelled around the chivalry of Imam Ali; and the nationalist is centred on Firdausi's champion, Rustam, a mythical figure of the *Shâhnâmeh*; as for the Sufis, although incorporating the two aforementioned, a model *par excellence* specific to Sufism was missing, often reflected in their reference to the mystical green saint, al-Khidhr, as the model Sufi chevalier. The Sufi tradition lacked an apparent Sufi chevalier model for good reason, since theirs was based on the abstract ideal of the Perfect Man (*al-insan al-kamil*). The Sufis understood chivalry to be an inward self-reflective process that was part of their personal relationship with God, which was originally based on the Sufi teachings of Abu'l Hassan-e Kharaqani (d. AD 1033), a distinguished figure in Sufism who understood *javânmardî* in the terms of an interiorized 'spiritual' chivalry.[22] Not only was Kharaqani placed as the chief recipient of Persia's sacred wisdom by Suhrawardi maqtul,[23] but his nonconformist Sufi attitude continued to inspire the antinomian strand of Sufism right up to the modern era.

In connection to this theme, the late *pir* (master) of the Nimatullahi Khaniqahi Sufi Order, Javad Nurbakhsh, wrote of the ideal Sufi chevalier: 'In all his labours, he acts by love. And from love come all his manners',[24] a verse that sums up the kind of antinomian character of Sufi chivalry so typical of Kharaqani. In this verse, there is an unmistakable impression that all of Sufism can be summed up in *javânmardî* (chivalry) and *adâb* (moral etiquette) in order to define a practical Sufism.[25] The Nimatullahi Order, of whom Leonard Lewisohn has made a thorough study, is one of the fastest-growing Sufi orders in the West, with its headquarters in London.[26] The Order prescribes to a form of Sufism that is based on an idealization of the early Sufi masters, Bayazid-e Bistami (d. AD 874) and Mansour Hallaj (d. AD 922), not to mention adopting a Suhrawardian approach in placing themselves as Sufi heirs of the ancient wisdom of Persia.[27] Regardless of this order's unique expression of Sufism, we can, nevertheless, say that Sufi doctrine is – generally speaking –firmly grounded in points of chivalry and etiquette. The Sufis of the Middle Ages were certainly not recluses; instead they were actively involved in the social workings of their time.[28]

The heritage of etiquette and chivalry in Iran

The ideas of chivalry and etiquette are well entrenched in pre-Islamic Iran. In its earliest form, chivalry and etiquette dealt with the categorization and formulation of individual conduct and behaviour, and was concerned with its proper measure of restraint. Etiquette is difficult to trace on its own, since it permeates a vast proportion of human interaction from the personal to the divine. Chivalry, on the other hand, is easier to define due to its strong association with the virtue of warfare. Indeed, chivalry was from its beginning an *ideal* that characterized the proper behaviour and conduct of the 'warrior'.

Unique to Iranian chivalry and etiquette is the fact that these were not an exclusive right of any particular class or privilege. Even when fraternities and organizations eventually came into existence attempting to standardize chivalry through membership and codes, they were not prejudiced to social rank, racial or even religious origin. Throughout medieval times members included Muslims and non-Muslims, and there were a variety of backgrounds from artisans to slaves.[29] Within Persia, the oldest reference can probably be traced to the Achamaeanid period and the legends that surround the virtue of Cyrus the Great (*kurosh-e kabir*).[30] Cyrus the Great is the archetypal 'Eastern Knight', foreshadowing the figure of Salahaddin Ayubi, and whose Western parallel is found in the legends of King Arthur and his knights. Persian cavalrymen and knights were a prominent feature of warfare in the ancient world. According to Heredotus, Persian boys were taught three things: to shoot a bow, ride a horse and tell the truth. Since formal manhood in ancient Persian culture has been associated with horses and the wearing of pants (*shalwar*) and belt, these components have become iconic symbols of the later *fûtûwwat* organizations and the *javânmardân*. Although little investigated, the life of Cyrus the Great is still very much a pillar for chivalry and moral etiquette in Persian culture – in addition to which it is believed that the legendary figure of Firdausi's Rustam was modelled.

The Persians did not possess a written culture; they adhered to an oral tradition, and, as a result, any record of Persia's chivalric and moral tradition had to be reconstructed by post-Sassanid authors, the most famous of whom was Firdausi.[31] Subsequently, when the Persians did use writing, they did so by borrowing an existing system, such as the Babylonian Cuneiform, the Aramaic and later the Arabic script in the ninth century. Despite the increasing presence of Arabian loan words in the Persian language and literature of the Islamic period, the Iranian origin of the chivalric motifs cited there remain undisputed.[32] It is also commonly thought that the strong tradition of pre-Islamic Arab story-tellers and poets influenced Persian literary efforts, whereas we can read in Ibn an-Nadim that the first story-tellers were the early inhabitants of Fars: 'After the stories of the early Persians had passed to the Arsacids and the Sasanians, the Arabs translated them into their own language and then began to compose similar stories themselves.'[33] The origins of the Persian–Arab interaction can actually be traced back to the Achaemenid period, but was especially prominent under the Sasanians when there was an opening up of a great cultural exchange between the two peoples. During this time, the Arabs of the Levant were vassal kingdoms to the ruling powers of the time: the Lakhmids served the Sasanians;

the Ghassanids were in the service of the Byzantines. The Islamic conquest, then, presented a role reversal with the balance of power falling to the Arabs.

The virtue of *adab* [pl. *âdâb*] in the Arabic denotes 'learning of the exercises of the carnal soul (*nafs*), the betterment of morals'.[34] Outside of the religious context, it defines 'habit, hereditary norm of conduct, [and] custom'. The Middle Persian equivalent is *frahang*, New Persian *farhang*.[35] This term has a correlation with another Pahlavi word, *êwên* or Persian *âyîn*, which means education, culture, good behaviour, politeness and proper demeanour, as closely linked with the concept of ethics.[36] The most ancient reference to etiquette is found in Mithra, the Old Iranian divinity who was the overseer of the ethics and moral conduct of the individual.[37] Firdausi's *Shâhnâmeh* (The Book of Kings) carries the ideal of *adab* to its peak. He presents etiquette as the refinement of thought, word and deed, and as proportion (*andâza*) and moderation (*miânaravi*) in one's conduct.[38] Firdausi explained etiquette with respect to the manner of one's speech and generosity, which he colourfully portrayed in the *Shâhnâmeh* through the conduct of its heroes. Take, for example, 'soft-spokenness' (*narm-guyi*) as a constant, whereby Firdausi reminds his readers that one should never 'tear anyone's skin with words'.[39] Moreover, in the face of insult 'silence' is prescribed, and should insult persist, a reply should be made with 'smooth' and 'fresh', i.e. vigorous, but moderate language.[40] Most importantly, the refinement of generosity is marked by the giver's indebtedness to the receiver, since it is in the act of the receiver's acceptance that peace and serenity of soul are bought with the gift.[41]

The term *fûtûwwat* was first used in the eighth century to denote the qualities of the ideal *fatâ*, pl. *fityân* (young man). From the twelfth to the fourteenth centuries *fûtûwwat* organizations were flourishing throughout the Islamic Empire: Iran, Asia Minor and the Fertile Crescent. It was during the same time that chivalry was being popularized in Europe. The late date of the institutionalization is suggestive of its borrowing from earlier versions of men's groups that were still functioning in the Middle East in both Byzantine and Sassanid fraternities.[42] Among the Persians *fûtûwwat* was commonly translated by *javânmardî*, spelt out literally as *javân* (young) *mardî* (manliness). For the Persians, however, *javânmardî* emphasized the specifically Iranian character as defined by the adherents of the *zurkhâneh* ('House of Strength'), 'the gymnasium where the so-called "ancient exercises" (*varzish-e bâstânî*) are performed'.[43] The ideals of chivalry can also be made to connect with Mithra, yet again, since this was also the divinity that functioned as both an emissary between heaven and earth, as well as between parties. Such a connection is significant because Mithra possessed a dual function that epitomized both the ethical staple of society and its heroic cornerstone.[44] *Javânmardî* is easily linked with Mithraic morality and heroism through a distinctive social sense that gives rise to the practice of 'service' (*khidmat*) in Persian Sufism.[45] Likely in imitation of the chevaliers, the concept of social exertion (*kasb* and *amal*) was adapted by Sufis of Transoxania and Khorasan and by the *akhis* of Turkic regions into the mystical stream. In these lands it took on an esoteric meaning for the purification of the soul. Surely it would not be far-fetched to think of *javânmardî* as indicating the 'young man' as a code for the 'renewed man', 'refreshed man', a person very much 'born again', i.e. 'reborn' into the world of spirituality and gnosis.

The fusion of *adab* and *javânmardî* during the Islamic Middle Ages is very much owed to two outstanding figures: Ibn al-Muqaffa (d. AD 756)[46] and Firdausi (d. AD 1020).[47] The former was born in Fars (later Firuzabad), of a noble Iranian family. The latter, according to the oldest source, was born at Baz, a village in the Tabaran quarter of Tus, and he came from a family of *dihqans* (landowners) and was a man of influence in his village and of independent means due to the revenues from his lands. Both al-Muqaffa and Firdausi were of the *Shu'ubiyya*, a Persian movement within the early Muslim society, which denied any privileged position of the Arabs.[48] Usually of the well-to-do class, the *Shu'ubiyya* were basically a non-extremist, revivalist group who opted for an internal revolution without dramatic structural change.[49] They were particularly characterized by their strong attachment to Iranian culture and a superficial Islamic faith – not surprisingly a typical attitude among the majority of Persian *mawali* (clients) in the early Islamic period.[50]

Al-Muqaffa was a prominent adherent of the *Shu'ubiyya* movement. He was an Arabic author and translator of Persian origin and introduced many notable works of foreign, but particularly Iranian, origin to the Arab world.[51] The more famous of the two, Firdausi is remembered for his monumental work the *Shâhnâmeh*, which channelled material from Persia's past into the literary consciousness of the Islamic Middle Ages. His great nationalist epic in fact secretly told the history of Persia through mythical figures and colourful allegories, though he was not alone in the attempt to revive Persian culture and language.[52]

In this way, the development of *fûtûwwat* contained elements of racial rivalry, in particular between the newly risen Arab Islamic Empire and its non-Arab subjects (*mawali*). The Abbasid era was a crucial time for the *mawali*, especially since it gave the Persians a chance to counteract the long-term subjugation endured under the tribal chauvinism of Arab (Umayyad) rule. Thereby, the

Shu'ubiyya, the administrative elite who served the Islamic community in the previously owned Sasanian lands, deliberately framed their identity, behaviour and heritage as distinctly different to that of the Arabs. They did this above all by promoting *futûwwat* as something indelibly Iranian, and something of which 'the Arab' was inevitably devoid. The efforts of the *Shu'ubiyya* would become significant to the Sufis who embraced Persian as the language of mysticism.[53]

The institutionalization of Sufi chivalry

The period of institutionalization is preceded by earlier efforts to standardize Sufism in the works of two Sufis: Uthman al-Jullabi al-Hujwiri (d. AD 1077) and Abu Hamid al-Ghazali (d. AD 1111). Hujwiri's *Kashf al-Mahjub* (Revelation of the Veiled) is one the first attempts to produce a standard for Sufism. From his work it is clear that by the eleventh century Sufism had become an integral aspect of Persian society. Al-Ghazali is perhaps the best known for his efforts to homogenize Sufism, and whose works had a considerable impact on the development of later Sufism. In the first half of the twelfth century al-Ghazali moved to reconcile a disjointed Sufism with Islamic orthodoxy. Al-Ghazali was not only enthused to reciprocate the saving hand of Sufism in his own life, but he was also convinced that Sufism would do the same in reviving the essential message of Islam, which he believed was being lost to intellectual and libertine movements. Prior to al-Ghazali's time, Sufism had ventured dangerously close to heresy – the Sufism of Mansour ibn al-Hallaj (d. AD 922) is a case in point.[54] Hallaj was martyred on the grounds of openly declaring God-consciousness (*anna'l haqq*), as well as suspected of being a non-Muslim passing as Sufi.[55] Hallaj was the first to talk about chivalry in the context of Sufism,[56] but it was not until the second half of the twelfth century that Sufism and chivalry were officially fused through institutionalization.

The first Sufi to write a substantial work on chivalry was Abd al-Rahman al-Sulami (d. AD 1021), who wished to place Sufi chivalry on a par with other Islamic sciences. Sulami's work was fully endorsed by his pupil Abu Qasim al-Qushayri (d. AD 1074), who condensed his master's work on Sufi chivalry. Yet it is with Kharaqani that the Sufi appropriation of chivalry is taken beyond (the erudite plane) to its spiritual height. Already, among the Sufis cited, two very different attitudes emerge: the 'sober' and the 'intoxicated' – both being markers of the two prominent schools of Sufi thought; the former advocating a coherent relationship with orthodoxy, the latter defined by a character of nonconformity.

All in all, the Sufis made prolific use of chevalier terminology and customs, which gave a distinctive moral stimulus to their spiritual teachings. Conversely, Sufism was also affected by the chevalier mercenary attitude, through which Sufism came to be defined as a 'passive movement' in the face of orthodoxy.[57] It would not be strange to assert Persian Sufism as the product of early *fûtûwwat* and *tasawwuf* trends, a fusion that first occurs in Khurasan. This would certainly explain the strong antinomian attitudes of Persian Sufism, but even so the liberal outlook of later Sufism quite generally.

In time, chevalier fringe groups would eventually be viewed as a threat to caliphal powers; the evasive mystic orders were no exception. Rather than oppose these movements, the caliph made a bid to make himself the chief authority over them, merging the chevaliers, strongmen fraternities, guilds and Sufi orders. The director of this fusion was the Abbasid caliph al-Nasir al-din Allah (AD 1181–1223) and its architect, Umar al-Suhrawardi (d. AD 1234). At first, al-Nasir joined one of the *fûtûwwat* groups and then outlawed all others. In league with Suhrawardi, he made himself master of a Sufi chivalric order, inviting all others to join him, thereby becoming the spiritual as well as the political authority.[58] In so doing, al-Nasir neutralized chevalier influence along with any future military threat and competition, and gained relative control over the Sufis. Al-Nasir capitalized on the formalities of membership, adaptation of genealogy, rites and ritual by modifying these to suit.[59]

Umar al-Suhrawardi, as the spiritual adviser to caliph al-Nasir, led the campaign to promote the homogeneity of Sufi chivalry within the mainstream, forcing loyalty to the caliph. Suhrawardi was the first of a series of writers in Persian who inaugurated a literary category that in Irano-Turkish territories (and also in Egypt during the Ottoman period) was to continue until the beginning of modern times.[60] Suhrawardi founded his own order of Sufis and promoted the caliph's significance as its head.[61] Noticeable is their attempt to fabricate *isnads* ('spiritual chains') to Sufism in their claim to ancestry;[62] for instance, in Iran these chains most often returned to Ali ibn Abi Talib as the *fatā* exemplar and then to Salman the Persian, the patron of Irano-Mesopotamian artisan guilds. To Ali is attributed the phrase *la fata illa Ali/la sayf illa dhu'l fiqar* ('There is no *fata* but Ali and no sword but Dhu'l-Fiqar [Ali's sword])'. As for Salman, Caliph Umar made him governor of Ctesiphon after the Arabs took the city, even while Salman continued to maintain a modest living for himself as an artisan.[63]

Al-Nasir's institutionalization is a good example of how ancient cultures were assimilated into standard orthodoxies, since chivalric rituals and codes of honour represented small pockets of historical continuity. The independent chivalric orders harboured centuries of subterranean 'culturo-religious resilience',[64] in particular the Persian, defined by the *fûtûwwat* trousers and belt of honour.[65] The result, none the less, was that al-Nasir secured complete hegemony, or so, at least, in name.

An important figure involved in the production of books for al-Nasir's 'aristocratic chivalry'[66] is Abd Allah Mohammed al-Sharim, known as Ibn al-Memar (d. AD 1244). He was a *fûtûwwat* scholar and author of the most factual book on the subject available at the time. Ibn al-Memar's *Kitab al-Fûtûwwa* presented a strictly Islamic agenda, which aimed at incorporating *fûtûwwat* into the *sharia* (Islamic Law) restricting the identity of the *fatâ* to only true believers.[67] The book affords considerable insight into the hierarchical structure, initiation ceremonies and the terminology used by al-Nasir's organization.[68] Al-Nasir's legacy was to have a lasting effect even beyond the Mongols' invasion of Baghdad. Even Suhrawardi's Sufi chivalry order persisted in the post-Mongol era. Note the Persian text *Fûtûwwat namah* of Najm al-din Zarkub (Kubra, d. AD 1221?), which explains *fûtûwwat* as vital to the three stages of religious knowledge: *shariat, tariqat, haqqiqat*.[69] The book again offers a great deal of information on the rites of initiation and its significance. For instance, the book explains how the initiatic trousers symbolize 'chastity' (*'iffat*) and the belt is a symbol of 'bravery' (*shuja'at*); the water drunk in the initiatic ceremony is a symbol of 'wisdom' (*khirad*); and the salt mixed into it symbolizes 'justice' (*'adâlat*).[70] Al-Nasir's trajectory of Sufi chivalry had a notable effect on two later Kubrawis: Semnani (d. AD 1336) and Hamadani (d. AD 1384).[71] The success of blending *tasawwuf* (mysticism) with *fûtûwwat* (chivalry) is especially celebrated in the work of the Naqshbandi Sufi Waiz Kashifi (d. AD 1505). His handbook of spiritual chivalry, *Fûtûwwat namah-i Sultani*, is testament to the fact that Sufi chivalry had a far-reaching influence in fifteenth-century Iran. Indeed, the Sufi chevaliers kept to a code of honour that incorporated the virtues of generosity, courage and hospitality right through to the modern period.

Al-Nasir is certainly due credit for the magnitude of his project, but the details of achieving the Sufi chivalry synthesis are somewhat gruelling. Al-Nasir's efforts brought dissident chevaliers and Sufis into a manageable social sphere, but it reflected a somewhat paranoid establishment. Integrating Sufism and chivalry into the broader stream of social consciousness was a gradual but forceful process, chiefly owing to differences between the establishment and fringe groups. A repeat of this was seen with the Safavids (AD 1502–1736), under whom the institutionalization of Sufism met its peak in the sixteenth century – the Safavids imposed their own version of Sufism, stamping out all others. The strict differentiation between mainstream and esoteric forms of Sufism is made obvious at this time – based on the degree of their apparent appeal to the Islamic establishment.

The spiritualization of chivalry in Persian Sufism

The Sufis pioneered a 'spiritual innovation' in their own unique fusion of moral etiquette (*adab*) and chivalry (*javânmardî*) into the one tradition of mystical thought. The Sufis also adapted these and other Persian elements to the Islamic sphere in such a way that they appeared almost indefinitely as permanent fixtures of the Islamic ideal and spirituality. Over time, the Sufis would transform the traditions of chivalry and moral etiquette into a more profound 'para-Islamic' theosophy, explained by the prolific notions of 'love' and 'death' – two consistent notions found in the vast ocean of Sufi mystical literature. For Sufism, then, the points of etiquette and chivalry are no longer significant in and of themselves; that is, as cultural ornaments and ideals that cling to a decadent past. Instead, they became integral to the spiritual practice of Sufism epitomized in the Sufi doctrine of 'annihilation' and 'subsistence' in God (*fana wa baqa*).

The way in which the Sufis used etiquette and chivalry, however, differed considerably from its use among the chevaliers and the elite social classes. As defined by al-Sulami (d. AD 1021), Sufi chivalry consisted of such fervent selflessness that the Sufi was bereft of recognition for his good deeds. Sulami's ideas may have been analogous with the *malâmatiyâ* Sufi movement ('People of Blame').[72] Taking a contemporary example from an alleged *malâmatî*, Javad Nurbakhsh (d. AD 2008) exclaims: 'abandon the observance of manners; the people of the heart are beyond mere manners', and again it is paradoxically prescribed: 'While you are travelling the Path you must have manners; but when you reach God it is unbelief to observe manners.'[73]

Also from Nurbakhsh is an anecdote from Attar's *Tadhkirat al-Auliya* ('Memorial of the Saints'), paraphrased here, to illustrate the point:

> A great Sufi master attended the speech of another respectable saint who was speaking about chivalry at a gathering. The saint said that chivalry consisted of serving others and giving of oneself without expectation of reward. The master agreed to himself, sitting silently amid the gathering. Then a beggar entered and asked that someone offer him their shirt since he had none and was cold.

The saint immediately jumped to his feet, took off his shirt and gave it to the old beggar. Suddenly the Sufi master shouted, 'Hypocrite! You said chivalry is in serving others and giving of oneself?' 'Yes'. Replied the saint, 'What have I done wrong?' 'You,' retorted the master 'could not even contain yourself long enough to give another a chance to offer their shirt. Instead, you selfishly rush to do a chivalrous act without consideration of others'. The master then got up and left the gathering.[74]

From the above, it was incumbent upon the Sufi not to be too hasty in acts of chivalry and etiquette and certainly never to practise these for the satisfaction of the ego. Indeed, what is detected here is an echo of Sufi modifications made to the concept of *javânmardî*, which may be categorized as 'meta-chivalry' from my point of view.

The great Sheikh Abu Sa'id Abul Khayr (d. AD 1049) frequently incited *malâmat* (blame) in order to elucidate the subtleties of Sufi etiquette and chivalry for his students. He was asked, 'What is evil and what is the worst evil?' He replied, 'Evil is "thou;" and the worst evil is "thou," when thou knowest it not.'[75] Another time he recalls an episode from his youth saying, 'I opened the Koran, and my eye fell on the verse, *We will prove you with evil and with good, to try you; and unto Us shall ye return.*'[76] He then explains the verse: 'All this which I put in thy way is a trial. If it is good, it is a trial, and if it is evil, it is a trial. Do not stoop to good or to evil, but dwell with Me!' There are many dramatic anecdotes citing Abu Sa'id's practice of *malâmat*. For instance, when engaged in strict austerities during his early years, villagers perceived the dung from his horse as an object of veneration, whereby in later years, the same folk saw Abu Sa'id to be worth no more than that object! A preliminary lesson in the practice of 'blame' allowing the sheikh to realize the transitoriness of both, and thereby to attain the proper state of unity, as dependent on neither the aspiration nor anxiety for 'good' or for 'evil'.[77] So Abu Sa'id concludes, 'Once more my "self" vanished, and His grace was all in all.'[78]

Another occasion has Abu Sa'id apparently indulging in luxuries, but his inner state of contemplation of divine unity is hidden from onlookers.[79] Of course, 'blame' was used by the Sufis to eradicate all trace of vanity when performing good deeds, which also reinforced the idea that the Sufi was merely the vehicle of divine intervention and not the source of grace. This was particularly the practice of two other noted *malâmatis*: Bayazid e-Bistami and Mansour al-Hallaj.[80] In practice, going beyond the self, and self-interest, allowed for a kind of 'disinterested love' as the spiritual staple of the Sufis. Abu Sa'id learned from a very young age that all acts of piety are 'to serve God' and 'to love God', which one could do through the kindness shown to His creation, saying, 'there is no better and easier means of attaining to God than by bringing joy to the heart of a Muslim [i.e. brother].'[81] Even Hasan al-Basri found supporting evidence to this effect in the Koran: 'Surely God bids to justice and good-doing and giving to kinsmen; and He forbids indecency, dishonour, and insolence, admonishing you, so that happly you will remember [K 16:90]'.[82]

Concluding remarks

The Sufis were instrumental to the development and refinement of the chivalric ideal in medieval Iran. They were among the first to record and examine the concept as well as to incorporate its conventions into their spiritual discipline. Slowly, there emerged a fusion of the two movements that gave new impetus to the social dynamic of the Islamic Middle Ages. By this time, Sufism had espoused a practical philosophy for the everyday, and was fully integrated into society where the Sufis imparted moral guidance on all matter of worldly concerns. The principles of chivalry were the practical means through which the deeper meanings of spiritual truths were communicated to the disciple, and the worldly, who sought the wisdom of the Sufis. However, there was a special part of this Sufi chivalry, which echoed Persia's distant past. Chivalry, a well-entrenched aspect of Iranian culture, had its roots in deep antiquity. Yet the constant theme in Sufi chivalry, namely selfless service and the practice of giving precedence to others over oneself, was not only a consistent aspect of Iranian culture from the pre- to post-Islamic period, but that it was most importantly a fundamental humane quality transcending social and geographical boundaries.

Notes

1   I am particularly grateful to Terry Graham for his generous insight on the subject of Sufism and chivalry, a subject which I believe is still ongoing and requiring much further elaboration and scholarly attention. I also appreciate Lloyd Ridgeon's latest book *Morals and Mysticism in Persian Sufism*, which, as made evident through my numerous citations to it, has had a profound impact on the research of the current work.

2   Dillan, *Celts and Aryans*; Childe, *The Aryans*; Taylor, *The Origin of the Aryans*.

3   Bailey, 'Arya'.

4   Cahen, *Mouvements populaires*, pp. 32–4.

5   Baldick, 'The Iranian Origin of the *Fûtûwwa*', pp. 352–61.

6   Zakeri, 'Javânmardî'.

7   Moncrieff, *Romance and Legend of Chivalry*, p. 5.

8   Ridgeon, *Morals and Mysticism*, p. 1.

9   Ridgeon, *Morals and Mysticism*, p. 5.

10   Ibid.

11   Ibid.

12   Lewisohn, 'Persian Sufism in the Contemporary West', p. 59; Ridgeon, *Morals and Mysticism*, pp. 5, 22 n1.

13   Nurbakhsh, *Discourses*, p. 13.

14   Consider the macrohistorical attitude of Garry W. Trompf in this regard. Trompf, 'Macrohistory'.

15   Milani, *Secret Persia*.

16   Silvers, 'Representations: Sufi Literature'.

17   Ibid.

18   Ibid.

19   Zakeri, 'Javânmardî'.

20   Milani, 'Sufism and the Subtle Body'.

21   Sarraf, *Rasael-e javanmardan*, pp. 6–7; Zakeri, 'Javânmardî'.

22   Ridgeon, *Morals and Mysticism*, pp. 29, 46.

23   Ziai, 'al-Suhrawardi's Illuminationist Political Doctrine', pp. 326–7; Ridgeon, *Morals and Mysticism*, p. 46.

24   Nurbakhsh, *The Truths of Love*, p. 21.

25   Nurbakhsh, *Javânmardî*.

26   Lewisohn, 'Persian Sufism in the Contemporary West'. p. 51.

27   Milani, *Secret Persia*.

28   Kashifi, *fûtûwwat namah*; Ridgeon, *Morals and Mysticism*, p. 3.

29   Simon, 'Fûtûwwa', p. 263.

30   Dandamayev, 'Cyrus II the Great'.

31   Cf. e.g. the works of masters of Persian literature, such as Rudaki (d. *c.* 941), who is considered the founder of Persian classical literature and is the first to compose poetry in the New Persian language that combined Persian and Arabic script, and Nezami (d. 1209) who wrote the great romance epics of 'Khosrow and Shirin' and 'Leyli and Majnun' – the tales of star-crossed lovers – in his famed *Panj Ganj* [Five Jewels]. These and many others, the most famed in the West being Firdausi's *Shâhnâmeh*, were involved in the monumental task of reviving Persian culture and language, and instilled the wisdom of the Persians in their works.

32   Hosri, *Ketâb zahr al-âdâb*.

33   an-Nadim, *fehrest*; Khaleghi-Motlagh, 'Adab', p. 434a.

34   an-Nadim, *fehrest*; Khaleghi-Motlagh, 'Adab', p. 434a.

35   Nöldeke, 'Geschichte', p. 38; Nyberg, *Hilfsbuch*, p. 70.

36   Khalighi-Motlagh, 'Adab', p. 432.

37   Imoto, 'Mithra, The Mediator', p. 299.

38   Khaleghi-Motlagh, 'Adab', p. 432a.

39   Firdausi, *Shâhnâmeh*, vol. 6, p. 270; Khaleghi-Motlagh, 'Adab', p. 432a–b.

40   Firdausi, *Shâhnâmeh*, vol. 6, p. 506; Khaleghi-Motlagh, 'Adab', p. 432a–b.

41   Firdausi, *Shâhnâmeh*, vol. 6, p. 260; Khaleghi-Motlagh, 'Adab', p. 432b.

42   Simon, 'Fûtûwwa', p. 263.

43   Ridgeon, *Morals and Mysticism*, p. 166.

44   Imoto, 'Mithra'.

45   Milani, *Secret Persia*.

46   Gabrieli, 'Ibn Al-Mukaffa'.

47   Huart, 'Firdawsi'.

48   Enderwitz, 'al-Shu'ubiyya'.

49   Hamzehee, *Land of Revolutions*, p. 51.

50   Khaleghi-Motlagh, 'Adab', pp. 438a–439a.

51   Gabrieli, 'Ibn al-Mukaffa'.

52   Huart, 'Firdawsi'.

53   Montgomery Watt, *The Majesty that was Islam*, p. 76.

54   Massignon, 'The Juridical Consequences of the Doctrines of al-Hallaj'.

55   Nicholson, *Studies*, p. 80; Glasse, 'Some Notes on Manicheism, Islam, the Essenes'.

56   Ridgeon, *Morals and Mysticism*, p. 29.

57   Hamzehee, *Land of Revolutions*, p. 50ff.

58   Zakeri, *Javânmardî*.

59   Simon, 'Fûtûwwa', pp. 264–265; Cahen, 'Fûtûwwa', p. 964ff.

60   Cahen, 'Fûtûwwa', p. 964a–b.

61   Ibid.

62   Cahen, 'Fûtûwwa', p. 964b.

63   Zarrinkub, 'The Arab Conquest of Iran', p. 13.

64   Milani, *Secret Persia*.

65   Loewen, 'Proper Conduct (*Adab*) is Everything', pp. 557–562.

66   Zakeri, *Javânmardî*.

67   Simon, 'Fûtûwwa', p. 264b.

68   Zakeri, *Javânmardi*.

69   Ibid.

70   Ibid.

71   Ibid.

72   Ibid.

73 Nurbakhsh, 'Silence and Etiquette of the Sufis', pp. 24–5.

74 Nurbakhsh, 'Guiding Others', p. 42.

75 Asrar, 403, 3; Nicholson, *Studies*, p. 53.

76 Koran 21:36; Nicholson, *Studies*, p. 17.

77 *Halat*, 19, 6; *Asrar*, 37, 8; Nicholson, *Studies*, pp. 16–17.

78 *Asrar*, 37, 8; Nicholson, *Studies*, p. 17.

79 Hujwiri, *Kashf*, p. 346.

80 Arberry, *Muslim Saints*; Massignon, *The Passion of Hallaj*.

81 *Asrar*, 380, 11; Nicholson, *Studies*, p. 55.

82 Arberry, *The Koran Interpreted*; Simon, 'Fûtûwwa', p. 12.

References

Arberry, A. J. *The Koran Interpreted*. London: Oxford University Press, 1982.

—*Muslim Saints and Mystics: Episodes from the Tadhkirat al-Auliya (Memorial of the Saints) by Farid al-Din Attar*. London: Routledge, 1983.

Bailey, H. W. 'Arya'. In *Encyclopaedia Iranica*, Vol. 2. New York: Routledge & Kegan Paul, 1987, pp. 681–3.

Baldick, J. 'The Iranian Origin of the *Fûtûwwa*'. *Istituto Universitario Orientale di Napoli* 50 (1990): 345–361.

Bastani-Parizi, M. E. 'Khaniqah: A Phenomenon in the Social History of Iran'. In *Mehregan in Sydney: Proceedings of the Seminar in Persian Studies during the Mehregan Persian Cultural Festival Sydney, Australia, 28 October 6 November 1994* ed. Garry W. Trompf Morteza Honari (Sydney Studies in Religion, 1). Sydney, 1998, pp. 71–8.

Cahen, C. *Mouvements populaires et autonomisme urbain dans l'Asie Musulmane du Moyen Age*. Leiden, 1959.

—'Fûtûwwa'. In *Encyclopedia of Islam*, Vol. 2, s.v.

Childe, V. G. *The Aryans: A Study of Indo-European Origins*. New York: Dorset Press, 1987.

Crook, J. R. *The Royal Book of Spiritual Chivalry (Futuwat nama-yi Sultani)*. Chicago, IL: KAZI Publications, 2000.

Dandamayev, M. A. 'Cyrus'; 'iii. Cyrus II the Great'. In *Encyclopaedia Iranica*, Vol. 6. Costa Mesa, 1993, pp. 516–21.

Dillan, M. *Celts and Aryans: Survivals of Indo-European Speech and Society*. Simla: Indian Institute of Advanced Study, 1975.

Enderwitz, S. 'al-Shu'ubiyya'. In *Encyclopaedia of Islam*, Vol. 9, s.v.

Firdausi. *Shâhnâmeh*, edited and translated by J. Mohl, Vol. 6. Paris, 1838–78 (7 vols).

Gabrieli, F. 'Ibn Al-Mukaffa'. In *Encyclopaedia of Islam*, s.v.

Hamzehee, R. *Land of Revolutions*. Göttingen: Edition Re, 1991.

Hosri, A. I. *Ketâb zahr al-âdâb* (ed. Z. Mobarak), Vol. 1. Cairo, 1925.

Imoto, E. 'Mithra, The Mediator', in *Acta Iranica*, Vol. 7, 299–307. Leiden: E. J. Brill, 1974–1984.

Kashifi, H. V. *Fûtûwwat -namah-i Sultani* (ed. M.J. Mahjub). Tehran, 1971.

Khaleghi-Motlagh, D.J. 'Adab'. In *Encyclopaedia Iranica*, Vol. 1, pp. 433b–4a. London, 1985.

Lewisohn, L. 'Persian Sufism in the Contemporary West: Reflections on the Ni'matullahi Diaspora'. In *Sufism in the West*, edited by Jamal Malik and John Hinnells. London: Routledge, 2006, pp. 49–70.

Loewen, A. 'Proper Conduct (*Adab*) is Everything: The *Fûtûwwat -namah-i Sultani* of Husayn Va'izi-i Kashifi'. *Iranian Studies* 36 (2003): 557–62.

Mahjub, M. J. 'Chivalry and Early Persian Sufism'. In *The Heritage of Persian Sufism*, translated by L. Lewisohn, Vol. 1. Oxford: Oneworld, 1999, pp. 579–580.

Massignon, L. 'The Juridical Consequences of the Doctrines of al-Hallaj'. In *Studies on Islam*, edited by M. Swartz. Oxford: Oxford University Press, 1981.

—*The Passion of al-Hallaj: Mystic and Martyr of Islam*, translated, edited and abridged by Herbert Mason. Princeton: Princeton University Press, 1982.

Milani, M. *Secret Persia: From Deep Antiquity to the Sufis*. London: Equinox-Acumen Publishing, (forthcoming).

—'Sufism and the Subtle Body'. In *Between Mind and Body: Subtle Body Practices in Asia and the West*, edited by G. Samuel and J. Johnston. London: Routledge, forthcoming.

Mohammed ibn Monawwar. *Asraru'l-tawhid fi maqamati'l Shaykh Abi Sa'id*, edited by Zhukovski. Petrograd, 1899.

Moncrieff, A. R. H. *Romance and Legend of Chivalry*. London: Guernsey Press, 1994.

(al-)Nadim. *Ketab al-Fehrist*, translated by B. Dodge as *The Fihrist of al-Nadim*. New York, 1970 (2 vols).

Nicholson, R. A. *Studies in Islamic Mysticism*. Cambridge: Cambridge University Press, 1921.

Nöldeke, T. 'Geschichte des Artaschir-i Papakan aus dem Pahlevi übersetzt mit Erläuterungegn und einer Einleitung versehen'. *Bazzenberger's Beiträge zur Kunde der indogermanischen Sprache* 4 (1879): 38.

Nurbakhsh, J. Tehran: Khaneqahi Nematollahi Publications, 1385/2007.

—*Discourses on the Path*. London: KNP, 1996.

—*The Truths of Love: Sufi Poetry*. New York: KNP, 1982.

—'Silence and Etiquette of the Sufis' [Poem]. *Sufi* 9 (1991): 24–5.

—'Guiding Others'. *Sufi* 53 (2002): 42.

Nyberg, H. S. *Hilfsbuch des Pehlevi*, Vol. 2. Uppsala: Almqvist & Wicksell, 1931.

Ridgeon, L. *Morals and Mysticism in Persian Sufism*. New York: Routledge, 2010.

Rumi, J. *Koliyateh Shams-e Tabrizi*, edited by Badi al-Zaman Forouzanfar. Tehran, 1382/2003.

Sarraf, M. ed.. *Rasael-e javanmardan moshtamel bar haft fotowwat-nama/Traités des compagnons-chevaliers*. Tehran and Paris, 1973, Introduction by Henry Corbin, 1–109.

Silvers, L. 'Representations: Sufi Literature'. In *Encyclopaedia of Women and Islamic Cultures*, edited by S. Joseph, Vol. 5, s.v.

Simon, R. S. 'Fûtûwwa'. In *Encyclopedia of Islam and the Muslim World*, edited by R. C. Martin, Vol. 1, 263–264. New York: Macmillan, 2004.

Taeschner, F. 'As-Sulami's *Kitab al-Fûtûwwa*'. In *Studia Orientalia Ioanni Pedersen Septuagenario*, edited by F. Hvidberg, Copenhagen, 1953, pp. 340–51.

Taylor, I. *The Origin of the Aryans*. New York: Scribner and Welford, 1890.

Trompf, G. W. 'Macrohistory'. In *Dictionary of Gnosis and Esotericism*, edited by W.J. Hanegraaff *et al.*, Vol. 2, Leiden: Brill, 2005, pp. 701a–716a.

Watt, M. W. *The Majesty that was Islam*. London: Sidgwick & Jackson, 1974.

(al-)Zabidi. Mohammed ibn Mohammed. *Taj al-'aruz*, Vol. 2. Kuwait, 1974.

Zakeri, M. 'Javânmardî'. In *Encyclopaedia Iranica*, s.v.

Zarrinkub, A. H. 'The Arab Conquest of Iran and its Aftermath'. In *Cambridge History of Iran*, edited by R. N. Frye, Vol. 4. Cambridge: Cambridge University Press, 1975, pp. 1–56.

Ziai, H. 'The Source and Nature of Authority: A Study of al-Suhrawardi's Illuminationist Political Doctrine'. In C.E. Butterworth, *The Political Aspects of Islamic Philosophy*, 326–7. Cambridge, MA: Harvard University Press, 1992, pp. 326–7.

4

From Knight to Chevalier

Chivalry in the *chanson de geste* Material from Aquitaine to Germany

Stephanie L. Hathaway

When we think of the ideal thirteenth-century knight, we think of someone who is exemplary in strength, courage and spirit. He is a defender of the weak, a courtier of ladies, a champion of justice. What he is not is a clumsy, coarse-mannered, club-wielding Saracen giant and kitchen slave. However, it was this very giant in the figure of Rainouart of *chanson de geste* fame who Wolfram von Eschenbach used for the creation of his own chivalric hero, Rennewart. In Rennewart, Wolfram would take the giant Rainouart and transform him from an underdeveloped buffoon into an instrumental defender of Christian Aquitaine.

Chivalry was an important part of medieval Europe's vernacular literature. As a social institution with a strict moral code and structured orders, chivalry was also instrumental in developing the ideal of the warrior-knight. This happened over a span of approximately 100 years, from the twelfth to the thirteenth centuries. During that time it came to incorporate features with which it would be ever synonymous: investiture that carried symbols of service and loyalty, a self-reflective moral and spiritual integrity, and the practice of a courtly code including service to ladies. These cornerstones of European chivalry illustrate the intertwining of spirituality with knighthood that was influenced by the intermingling of cultures from the Mediterranean Rim, including Arabia.

Through the formation of these three features of chivalry, we can observe the transformation of knighthood in literature over the same period of time. One of the most famous Saracens in medieval epic, Rainouart, features in the story of the *La Bataille d'Aliscans* in the Old French *chansons de geste* of twelfth-century Aquitaine, and as Rennewart in Wolfram's thirteenth-century Middle High German courtly epic, *Willehalm*. *Willehalm* and *Aliscans* represent the development of the story of the battles of Guillaume d'Orange at Aliscans over more than a century, traversing the Pyrenees and the Rhine. The connection between service, spirituality, love and knighthood that influenced the refinement of the chivalric ideal in medieval Europe is mirrored in the depictions of the figure of Rennewart and his evolution from buffoon to chevalier.

Rennewart and his transformation

The story of Rainouart/Rennewart's transformation from a comical, albeit endearing giant to a knight takes us from its *chanson de geste* origins in Provence to Northern Europe and across the Rhine, where the epic romance *Willehalm* was composed. Affected by its own cultural–historical setting and themes of European romance, the idea of chivalry is further refined to what may perhaps be termed a more spiritual form of its practice. The author of *Willehalm*, Wolfram von Eschenbach, was far from unknown. He was the famous author of the Arthurian romance *Parzival*. Perhaps the pinnacle of Middle High German verse, *Parzival* told the story of the renowned knight on his quest to find Grail Castle and inner perfection in chivalry. The self-reflective quality in Wolfram's works gives us an impression of the courtly idea of knighthood and chivalry that had developed by the thirteenth century in European literature: Parzival's terrestrial and spiritual journey to find the Grail allows him to realize that chivalry, guided by love, brings humans closer together, and ultimately closer to God. In *Parzival* Wolfram sharpens the perception of chivalry, explores its strengths and weaknesses, and expands its spiritual significance. The refining traits of chivalry reveal themselves in the spiritual and religious significance of the duty to service, an adherence to the courtly code, and in heightened poetic expression.

Wolfram exploits the inherent morals and values of chivalry in their spiritual sense and applies them to the fallible, human world of the thirteenth century, with all its contradictions, philosophies and conflicting senses of propriety. Wolfram uses chivalry as a tool to convey a philosophical message that his thirteenth-century audience would have understood as being consistent with its medieval worldview: that the value of chivalry was in the journey to attain its perfection. However, the chivalry of the romance *Parzival* is not the same chivalry we see in the epic material of *Willehalm*. This text was written by Wolfram after the romances were well known, and incorporated that familiarity into the earlier, heroic-epic material of the *chansons de geste*.

If we take a retrospective view from *Willehalm* to its sources, we see that knighthood and chivalry as they appear in courtly literature are imbued with undertones of service, conscience and spirituality, coupled with suffering and fate. We also find that the source of these concepts in a post-Roman, Carolingian Europe – the Europe in which the epic material takes place – lies outside the conventional boundaries of the vernacular texts in which they appear. The refining influences on chivalry resulted from the intermingling of cultures around the Mediterranean.

One of the groups of *chansons de geste*, the *Geste de Garin de Monglane*, comprises a smaller group, the *Cycle de Guillaume d'Orange*, most of it composed in the latter half of the twelfth century in Old French.[1] These relate the deeds of Charlemagne's nephew, Count William of Toulouse, who, historically, defeated the Arabs when they invaded the Spanish March in 793 at a legendary battle on the River Orbieu between Narbonne and Carcassonne. Wolfram tells his audience that it was this *chanson de geste, Aliscans*, that served as the source for his fragment *Willehalm*.[2]

The plot of the two texts remains mostly analogous. *Willehalm* and *Aliscans* open just as the hero, Guillaume/Willehalm, loses the battle on the field. He must defend himself against the retaliation of the defeated Saracen King Terramer, who has come with his son-in-law to reclaim his lost territory and its queen. The Narbonnais Christians face devastating defeat, and William fights a retreat back to the fortress at Orange, which is surrounded. He consults with his wife Gyburg, the converted Saracen queen, and they decide that William must make his way to Montlaon to secure the support of the imperial forces of France under Louis the Pious. At court, he meets the young Saracen giant Rainouart/ Rennewart, who is given to him by Louis, and who is the long-lost son of King Terramer. Rainouart/Rennewart provides humour for the story through his almost childlike actions, misunderstanding of propriety and untested strength. He later develops into William's loyal companion, serving heroically, motivating the reluctant French reinforcements and saving the day.

Willehalm breaks off just after the second battle. In *Aliscans*, Rainouart is baptized, marries the French princess Aélis and receives a fief from Guillaume. Wolfram's innovations to this material include the more focused development of characters who influence the action and thoughts of the hero, Willehalm. His adversaries, the Saracen knights, and a reflection on the nature of chivalry in the face of reality, are brought to the foreground in *Willehalm*.

As the texts themselves span a period of about 100 years, and the material more than 400 years, the prevalence of Saracens in important roles reflects the continuous interaction with, and confrontation of the Muslim world with a Europe whose political borders were frequently shifting. The identification of Saracens with the 'other' is evident in medieval literature, both in fiction and non-fiction. It is a complex role, as the Saracen took on a somewhat varied identity, appearing as an enemy as well as a fellow knight, as an invader as well as one conquered, and as an ally as well as a traitor. This reflects the challenge presented by a vast and different culture – one that did not hold the same religious beliefs as those of Christian Europe and therefore was not subject to a Roman pontiff – among the many differences medieval Christian Europe faced when confronting the Muslim world. The means and manner of interaction between Christian and Saracen knights in these texts is chivalry.

Rennewart, although he is a Saracen, perhaps even because he is one, proves to be one of the figures most capable of representing Wolfram's chivalric ideal, and this representation is accomplished by Rennewart's individual development. He begins as a captured prisoner: he is a kitchen-slave, brutish and ridiculed. But by the start of the second battle he has excelled as the noble leader he was born to be, and he plays an instrumental role in the Christian victory.[3] Rainouart does not develop in *Aliscans*: he remains violent, impetuous and naïve. Rennewart, in contrast, learns to control his temper, is motivated by love for Alyze, and is employed in the service of ladies to defend Christendom.[4] Rennewart's pivotal role, his contradictory elements and personal realization, centre on his anticipated investiture, baptism and marriage to King Louis' daughter Alyze, making possible reconciliation between kinsmen and adversaries in battle. For Wolfram, this is achievable only with God's grace; for him, spirituality must be linked with chivalry and sanctified by God. Rennewart, the captured Saracen prince, beloved kinsman of Gyburg and brother-in-law to Willehalm, seems the character best suited to traverse the cleft between spiritual chivalry and temporal knighthood.

In *Aliscans* Rainouart is introduced as a comical, God-fearing Saracen, destined to marry Aélis, to be baptized, and to feature in *La Bataille Loquifer* and the *Moniage Rainoart*. His portrayal borders on the absurd, and presents a parody of other *chansons de geste*. His beloved *tinel*, a weapon fashioned from a tree large enough to shade 100 knights, becomes his hallmark;[5] preposterous in its size, Ranouart is strong enough to wield it easily, and prefers it to the sword of a knight. He is ignorant in the ways of gentility and etiquette, and his conduct throughout the second battle and during his baptism shows that there is no development or improvement in his behaviour. Rainouart remains a strong warrior; he is rough around the edges, a source of buffoonery as well as impressive heroics, and he is steadfast in his Christian persuasion, even if he does not always understand Christian values.

Despite his Saracen background and humble origins as a kitchen slave, Rainouart proves himself as one of the most capable and fervent Christians in the story. Wolfram, known for his at times wry sense of humour, must have enjoyed this aspect of his character, and also seen in it something that could set Rainouart apart, and demonstrate the refining power of thirteenth-century chivalry. It was from this Saracen giant, then, that Rennewart was fashioned: under Wolfram's pen he becomes a diamond-in-the-rough recognized for his true value, a coarse gem who is allowed to develop and strive for chivalric goals, and who helps bring about a complete Christian victory. Wolfram's 'Christian victory' is one that would encompass more than a military success; it would also achieve peace and concord between kinsmen and knights, and between people of different religions, cultures and political motives. To accomplish this, Wolfram would require a knight who was tied to both sides, while also being free from the cycle of vengeance that bound the opposing kinsmen and characters;[6] he needed a character whose humility could be realized spiritually, and whose noble background predestined him for chivalry and leadership.

Rennewart would have to develop from a kitchen-slave into a knight, and more, a chevalier, in the eyes of the audience. This being so, Wolfram supplies him with calculated opportunities, allowing him to cultivate the kinds of innate chivalric ideals that his audience would recognize as visible symbols of a knightly status. Rennewart's chivalry surfaces in his inspiration to the courtly code of love, his ability to reflect inwardly on his spiritual and moral state, signalling his readiness to serve, and in public symbols of investiture, which enable him to be seen and respected as a chevalier by friend and foe.

Investiture, service and symbol

The visible emblem of a knight, his status and his loyalties in service lay in his accoutrements just as much as in his heroic bearing. Evidence of this may be seen in the *chansons de geste. Aliscans*, faithful to its genre, features knights that conform to a heroic-epic warrior code, even before knightly orders were widely in practice. Its subject matter is influenced by the socio-political environment of the Capetian period during which it was composed, and an emphasis is placed on vassalage and loyalty in the feudal order. The hero is characterized by physical strength, loyalty and courage. Conflict is a prevailing theme, and the superiority of family solidarity to feudal obligation is underscored. In *Aliscans*, the emerging European ideal of chivalric introspection does not make an appearance; what it *does* offer, however, is the foundation for the development of this ideal.

The search for the origin of the ideal of chivalry in medieval Europe inevitably leads to France:

> Von dort kam mit der höfischen Kultur und den höfischen Romanen das Wort *chevalier*, in dem fast alles das vorgeprägt ist, was dann den adligen Ritterbegriff in Deutschland auszeichnet.
> (Courtly culture came from there and the courtly romance word *chevalier*, which held all the connotations that would distinguish chivalry for Germany's nobility.)[7]

France, and indeed Europe, had long enjoyed the institution of knighthood for warriors; it held a place in a feudal system that depended upon loyalty and vassalage for its survival. This feudal system, which evolved and rescued Europe following the death of Charlemagne and his empire,[8] made use of the knights of warrior societies; these had been part of European culture for a long time, pre-dating the Roman conquest. As the use of the horse was improved and mounted armies came into prominence, so too did the cultural image and ideal of a knight.

Chivalry placed a high value on characteristics such as those described by Wacyf Boutros Ghali: humanity in combat, generosity after victory, the quest for moral perfection, and a concept of love that became refined, exalted and mystical, the foremost motivator of manly action.[9] He sees chivalry as an inherent tendency in human nature: the desire for glory, passion and love, and for rules and governances fashioned from a strict moral system.[10] However, Ghali discounts that either the Germanic tribes or classical antiquity had much influence over this development in European chivalry.[11] While a recognition of warrior codes existed in Europe prior to the twelfth century, with importance placed upon loyalty and vassalage, the refinement of these values came not from the world of classical antiquity, from mounted eastern invaders, or from any ethics inherent in the tribes of Europe; rather, it developed in Europe with the benefit of influence from the Islamic Mediterranean, at an opportune time when the cultures of Europe were ready for it.

From France, where chivalry may be seen to have been firmly established in one form or another in the literature of the thirteenth century, and in Provence in the twelfth century, we look back towards Spain and the Islamic world for the influences that further refined the code of chivalry already forming in Europe under the established feudal regime. This regime was largely for the benefit of the nobility, and formed a uniform institution exalting the warrior, his horse and his moral perfection. Although France is accepted as the cradle of European chivalry, the influence of centuries-old cultures from the Islamic Mediterranean during the Middle Ages should not be overlooked,[12] and it is this influence that will be integrated into this study.

During this time of heightened contact between the Islamic and European worlds, there was naturally a cross-over of influences, elements that would merge with one another. Rather than one culture influencing the other exclusively, both East and West transformed as a consequence of their contact. It is practical to think of the Eastern influence on medieval European chivalry as a balancing blend of effective concepts, evolving in much the same way that George Makdisi showed the European university to have evolved:

> The University, at first, was strictly European; and the college, strictly Islamic. But as the university absorbed the functions of the college, it took on characteristics which had their origins in Islam [...] In this fusion of the elements, the medieval West benefited greatly by marrying the corporation to the charitable trust [...] it was the combination of both concepts that gave the composite institution the stability and flexibility it needed. Its remarkable longevity is due in great measure to a marriage of the two concepts.[13]

Likewise, the institution of chivalry as it came to exist in medieval Europe was a synthesis of ideals, both spiritual and ethical, from Europe's own history, the influences of Classical Mediterranean literature and philosophy, and the refining concepts adopted and adapted from contact with the Islamic Mediterranean. This was a development from which both major cultures benefited, and that transcended nationality, political ties, and sometimes even religious prescripts.

The maturing of the warrior society was also marked by the formation of orders of knighthood, a concept that had a profound impact on the development of chivalry. Arabic chivalry itself did not appear definitively as an institution or order until the twelfth century, but seems to have been a part of life that was closely tied to religion for the Arabic world before the Crusades. Though war was not a career, there was an aspiration towards glory and a sense of dignity in bearing arms; during the months of the Truce of God, a harmony of perfection was also sought, and virtues such as moral beauty and poetry were pursued.[14] Saracen knights did not form into strict orders, however, until after contact with European knights around the twelfth century, when increased conflict and the exchange of ideas and philosophies brought about the armaments and organization that sustained the noble traditions of the Arabic knights.[15] Christian knightly orders first appeared at this time as well, as Mahmud Shelton writes, the first ones 'along the marches of the same Muslim-European frontier, bringing together religious inspiration and knightly vocation.'[16]

There was another purpose discernible in the institution of knightly orders in both Europe and the Orient. The far-reaching ideals of ethics and spirituality emerge in all of the cultures that had contact with Arabia in the twelfth century, including European Christendom, and underpinned the formation of chivalric orders as well as politics.[17] The many diplomatic correspondences show a desire to find a universal belief formula, or to come to a diplomatic agreement, such as was sought between rulers exemplifying chivalric ethics (Richard the Lionheart, Saladin, Emperor Frederick II and Al Kamil, Saladin's nephew). With this in mind, it is possible to view chivalry as that sought-after point of unity that would bring disparate cultures and peoples together.[18] If it was not in fact pursued relentlessly, the sentiment of respect for peers in the institution of knighthood and chivalry was certainly present among its practitioners.

The search for unity was a significant occupation of the twelfth century. Perhaps it was the achievements of Caliph al-Nasir li-Din Allah and his minister al-Suhrawardi that appealed to Christian knights, employing *adab*[19] as a means of strengthening the caliph's power by enforcing behavioural practice and investiture. Shelton writes, 'not surprisingly, the Christian West found in the spiritual chivalry of Islam a model in its efforts to establish this "true power" of a united head of spiritual authority and temporal power.'[20] However, as the Arabic world contended with its enemies by exploiting spiritual chivalry, it sought the same answers for unity and harmony that the European West aspired to in a post-Roman feudal age in which the rift between Byzantium and Rome was felt more profoundly, politically as well as religiously. Oleg Grabar writes:

> similar concerns and similar needs lead to an almost automatic transfer of information [...] The Christian West turned to Islamic ideas and interpretations because the same issues of faith and reason had been posed, not because of a precise influence of Islamic thought on the West.[21]

Central to this chivalry was investiture into the order by the grand master, a caliph in the Arabic world, with symbols of pre-eminence, and the code of behaviour with its deep spiritual underpinning. Investiture was to play a key role not only in centralising the power of the caliphate, but also in the relations between Saracen and Christian nobility during the period of the Crusades, profoundly influencing Christian knightly orders and their values. It was the Abbasid caliphate of Baghdad after al-Nasir that invested Malek al-Adel Nur ad-Din Mahmûd (AD 1117–1173),[22] who in 1145 succeeded his father as ruler of Northern Syria and defeated the crusaders, capturing Tripoli, Antioch and Damascus. He was later defeated by his nephew Saladin, his successor who completed the conquest of Egypt. It is Saladin who is remembered as 'that paragon of medieval chivalry'[23] and who himself, it is said, was dubbed a knight in Alexandria in 1174 by Humphrey of Toron, a Templar master.[24]

Girding and its significance in European knightly orders may be described as a 'statement of spiritual reality and a public commitment by the initiated individual to practice that reality through proper conduct'; a girded or belted waist was a symbol of a man's service to his patron.[25] It was not only the symbols and code of etiquette required in investiture that were so important, but also the patron. By the thirteenth century, the activity of the Crusades and the enthusiasm for following chivalric ideals saw the caliphs of the Arab world and the Seljuks of the Anatolian frontier invested by the nobility of the Christian West, demonstrating a common respect for a knightly code and loyalty to an ideal that would seem to transcend political ties.[26]

Wolfram employs this developed ideal of symbol and loyal service to illustrate Rennewart's chivalry to his audience. In *Willehalm*, Gyburg bestows upon Rennewart the armour and sword of King Sinagun, won as a prize by Willehalm; it is costly, beautiful and very strong.[27] Though Rennewart is reluctant at first and even casts the sword aside, he at last accepts the gift: he is helped into his armour, and the sword is fastened around his waist.[28] By the beginning of the second battle, Rennewart is visibly in service to Willehalm, who is loyal to God and to Gyburg, and he has acquired a suit of armour and a sword. With these symbolic as well as practical accoutrements, he is now by all appearances a knight.

However, Rennewart still does not entirely embrace chivalry, and this is reflected in his determination to use his *tinel* in the coming battle. While Rainouart's *tinel* is a source of humour in *Aliscans* (he forgets it owing to drunkenness the night before, and holds up the army in order to retrieve it), Wolfram uses Rennewart's *tinel* and his forgetfulness to signal developmental steps in his chivalric character. If he is to become a knight, Rennewart must learn from his mistakes and take responsibility for them; only then will he have earned the right to carry a sword.

When Rennewart reflects upon the consequences of his forgetfulness, wondering whether he has hindered his progress towards loyal service in

Willehalm's army, Wolfram rewards the young warrior for his self-reflection. When Rennewart finds his *tinel*, it has been burned in the fires of breaking camp, and made stronger by the heat.[29] Then, on his way back with it, Rennewart encounters the retreating Frenchmen at Petit Punt, and his resolve is now equal to the task of checking their loyalty, thereby performing an important and decisive function for both his character's development and for the Christian army going into battle. He frightens them into rejoining the battle, turning the tide in favour of Willehalm's forces.

It is during the course of this second battle that Rennewart comes into his own, realising his innate nobility and his significant role in God's plan of victory. The height of this realization in the *Willehalm* fragment comes when Rennewart recognizes the sword's superiority over his crude *tinel* as a weapon – and, though he has carried the sword at his side all the while, 'it is in the crisis of the battle that Rennewart reaches the maturity which makes his sword appropriate'.[30] After his *tinel* is shattered by the crushing blow Rennewart delivers to Purrel on the latter's dragon armour, he fights with his fists until he is reminded by Kibelin to draw the sword at his side. This is paralleled almost exactly in *Aliscans*, yet the meaning that has been attached to the scene by Wolfram's careful narration proves more climactic in nature, pointing towards a more refined idea of chivalry.

> Dist Renoart: 'Ceste arme entre souëf[z].
> Bien ait la dame qui la me ceint au lez!
> Se ge cuidasse que costel fussent tel,
> [A Monloon n'en eüst nus remés;]
> Tos les eüsse avec moi aportez'.
>
> (*Alisc.* CLXI, 6979–6982.)[31]

> […]
> Dist Renoart: 'Mout me merveil, par Dé:
> Si petite arme qui a tel poësté!
> [Ja nus frans hom qi teint a bonté
> N'en deuroit estre senz .V. a son costé;
> Se l'une faut, que l'altre ait recovré.]
> Par moi seront paien desbareté'.
>
> (*Alisc.* CLXII, 6983–6993)[32]

Rainouart says,

> 'This weapon is easy to wield. Blessed be the lady who fixed it to my side! If I had known that blades were like this, I would not have left one at Montlaon; I

would have brought them all with me [...] God, how marvellous that such a small weapon can have such might! No good man should be without five at his side. If one fails, the others can be used. I will put the pagans to flight!'[33]

Rainouart's boyish excitement at the discovery of the facility with which the blade may be used is tempered in *Willehalm*. His reaction is more introspective, although still practical:

> er warf ez umbe in der hant,
> er lobt im valze und ekken sîn,
> er sprach 'diu starke stange mîn
> Was mir ein teil ze swaere:
> du bist lîht und doch strîtpaere.'

(Wh 430, 28–431, 2)

> (Rennewart tossed the sword about in his hand, praising its groove and its edges, saying: 'My strong club was a little too heavy, but you are light and battle-worthy all the same.')[34]

Rennewart undoubtedly has respect for this blade beyond its ability to cut his enemy, although in *Aliscans* his enthusiasm is more comical, less refined by the inner chivalry that the later, thirteenth-century audiences would appreciate. Rainouart rushes to the ships to free the prisoners taken in the first battle, among them Bertrand, Guillaume's nephew. Liberated and eager to join the second battle, Bertrand asks Rainouart to capture a horse for him from one of the Saracens. Rainouart obliges by dealing mighty blows to the mounted enemies – but, not yet used to the ease of the blade, each time he strikes he manages to kill both the rider and and the horse. As horse after horse falls, Bertrand looks on impatiently, giving him advice on how to deal blows.

> 'Dex', dist Bertran, 'trop me voiz deleant;
> N'avrai cheval por quoi vois attendant;
> car a ces cops n'avra ja nus garant.'

(Alisc. CVIII, 5702–5704)

> ('God', says Bertrand, 'you're taking too long;
> I'll never get the horse I am waiting for,
> there is no protection against your blows.')[35]

Finally a mount is spared the blow that kills his master and Bertrand is satisfied. Rainouart's development as a knight in *Aliscans* centres on his learning how to use this weapon properly, while the thirteenth-century Rennewart must learn self-control; he must become worthy before his innate ability shines through, allowing him to use the sword without having been taught. This inner chivalry carries a strong spiritual underpinning.

Spirituality and reflection

It was the infusion of a spiritual and ethical code into the elite warrior image that transformed knights into chevaliers, and added a social as well as professional dimension to the role. That chivalry became more closely integrated with spirituality in the twelfth century is evident from the fact that, for the first time in European history, the warrior, his accoutrements and his society were religiously consecrated; they were also motivated and even directed by the Christian Church. It may therefore be asserted that this is the point at which knighthood became chivalry.

This is also the period during which spiritual chivalry in the Arab world began to be more widely practised as an institution, and literature emerged as one of its most important vehicles. It was timely for these diverse cultures in the twelfth century to gain a deeper sense of spirituality in a moral code and a more ethically defined chivalry. Their contact with each other resulted in, among many things, a spiritual and ethically grounded code for chivalric orders, both religious and military, as well as the influence that is apparent in literature.

In almost every romance and *chanson de geste*, a knight may be observed to take a journey from his home, encountering obstacles and difficulty in a quest for knowledge, redemption, love and God.[36] The quest for the Grail in its many manifestations exemplifies such a journey, and Wolfram's *Parzival*, in its quest for inner virtue, is no exception. That Wolfram is interested in the spiritual aspects of chivalry is clear from his reworking of *chansons de geste* material; in this he was partly guided by the times (the German cultural historical perspective, as well as the influences of a wider repertoire of vernacular literature), and also, no doubt, by his own sensibilities and inclinations.

One of the phenomena that made a lasting mark on European chivalry as an institution was the influence of the Church. The Church played a sizeable role in furthering the ideal of the Christian knight, and its influence added to chivalry's status: with it, the notion of 'defender' gained strength, and knighthood became coupled with piety. This latter point seems to have been at its strongest around the time of the First Crusade, starting with the address of Pope Urban II at Clermont in 1095.[37] The literature contemporary with *Willehalm*, and also that of its sources composed before it, extends from the period before the Crusades were called to just after the Third Crusade, led by Richard the Lionheart, Philip II of France and Frederick Barbarossa, Holy Roman Emperor.[38]

As the majority of the *chansons de geste* of the *Cycle de Guillaume* were probably composed before the call of the First Crusade, one can scarcely speak of them as pure Crusade literature. They do have elements that may be seen as consistent with Crusade ideology, however, and this is possibly due to their having been recorded in writing during the time of the First Crusades, or just before.[39] The role of the Church proper in the development of chivalry was more a functional one, assuming the power of the feudal lord in the age of the decline of French royal authority that never fully assumed its moral obligations of the defence of a country and protection of the poor in the early Middle Ages.

Two of the main goals of chivalrous life were 'fame in this world, and salvation in the next',[40] and it was the piety of the eleventh century that began to entwine the two. Likewise, it was the 'interweaving of Christian with heroic and secular motifs [that became] characteristic of the treatment of the crusade in chivalrous narrative and poetry'.[41] Maurice Keen prudently separates the secular from those ecclesiastic influences on chivalry, moral directives from the more recent Church prescripts that sought to give chivalry the purpose of the Crusade.[42] This may be seen in the literature that spans the timeframe of the blossoming of chivalry. The Gautier and Ramón Lull prescripts for chivalry, for instance, written in the form of the *Decalogue* and directives to protect Christianity, attest to the impact of crusading ideals on chivalry as an institution, with a code of practice set out by the Church as it appeared following the First Crusade.[43]

Ideological paradoxes are often overlooked, however, when considering the tremendous impact that the image of the chevalier and his ethos had upon medieval society, and still has upon society today.[44]

This drive to propagate Christianity throughout the world via chivalry, and the image of the spiritually guided knight, was an indication that European chivalry had come of age.

With the Crusades, knighthood and the ideals of chivalry were given a religious basis; this was more concrete than spiritual, with God as the knight's liege-lord, and honour defined by religion.[45] It was only later that crusading ideology became part of aristocratic knightly pursuits in France and her literature, and even later in Germany that true crusading ideology played any definitive role in the chivalry and literature of the courtly audience. When treated by German authors such as Wolfram, those pre-Clermont themes of Christian knighthood take on a deeper, self-reflective angle, presenting contradictions in terms of worldviews and religious views, although without denying the firm faith in the Christian Church that characterized the medieval world order.

The portrayal of the knights in *Willehalm*, both Christian and Saracen, invites the audience to reflect on the ideals identified as crusading; this is owing to the stance of its source *chanson de geste* material. The Crusade ideology itself is not as pronounced in *Willehalm*; but the reactions to it, and the reflection of the contradictory directives of the Church, are questioned. The *chansons de geste* played to the Crusade and Reconquista experiences of the audience, experiences from which the German audience was more removed. The German view was subtly different from that of the *chansons de geste.*

The probing of Christian morality and directives in *Willehalm*, when viewing Wolfram's works from a political standpoint, is perhaps possible, if we consider the environment of the author. Hermann I of Thuringia, Wolfram's patron, was a member of the Hohenstaufen federation to return Frederick II to the throne of the Holy Roman Empire during the dispute for the investiture following the election of Otto of Brunswick in 1209. Hermann, however, also revealed an inclination towards criticism of papal decree and some aspects of the Cluniac reform relating to the power struggle between Church and State.[46] Whether or not Hermann's political inclinations matched those of Wolfram, or whether Wolfram's works reflected the views of his patron, Kurt Reinhardt sees certain evidence of this in that Parzival's 'vocation to the kingship of the Holy Grail reads like a commentary on the political and spiritual implications of the Hohenstaufen claims to the *Sacrum Imperium*'.[47]

Wolfram's depiction of the chivalric view of the Christian moral imperative to convert or kill seems to be based more upon the late twelfth-century courtly code of ethics and the spiritual chivalry that was part of it, than a commentary on his contemporary political environment. It is mentioned by heathen and Christian characters alike, within Willehalm's extended family by marriage to Gyburg, that a better solution than war would be to behave according to the family solidarity propriety would demand, were it not for Tybalt's lust for vengeance and inheritance land. However, Christian Crusade ideology is in play in that any provocation or move towards the acquisition of land by the Saracens must be answered by a consolidated Christian military victory.

Fighting wars in the name of love earned renown, possibly land, and of course honour; fighting wars for revenge protected the honour of an illustrious clan; and fighting to defend Christian lands earned eternal salvation. The war in *Willehalm*, however, is depicted in a more personal and human way by Wolfram, who tells his audience: '*diz engiltet niht wan sterben, und an freuden verderben*.'[48] Willehalm, just like his compatriots, his adversaries and his wife, the Saracen queen of Orange, is bound to a code of chivalry; this code is an important part of his temporal success as well as his spiritual salvation, and it is by nature self-reflecting and introspective. This being so, it would be impossible for Willehalm to look upon unfolding events without asking certain questions: these include justification for loss of life, and how to preserve divine grace without undermining worldly honour.

The Saracen knight in *Willehalm* is subject to the same code of chivalry as his Christian adversary,[49] and Richey saw in this a more inward-looking as opposed to secular reflection of chivalry.

> [That] Wolfram, carrying the self-reliance of knighthood into the domain of thought, could set forth as a sure conviction what others expressed but tentatively [...] Nobility – *werdekeit* – is the touchstone of chivalry, and implies [...] a stronger confidence in the kinship of God and man.[50]

The development in Rennewart's character is expressed in his increased self-control: he learns to check both his temper and his strength, for instance, moderating them in a chivalrous way. In doing this, his innate nobility is then recognized by society. Lofmark draws out the medieval concept of character development with regard to Rennewart when he writes that no evolution of the person is expected, and no essential change necessary. Rather, inherent character qualities are realized by conquering impediments, and the development comes in the 'revelation of true nature', in 'putting the natural qualities into their proper order', in being what God meant one to be.[51] This may certainly be said for Rennewart, whose task it is to realize God's purpose for him.

In becoming a true knight, Rennewart's battles are not for personal glory, as are Rainouart's; instead, they are 'distinctly represented as service to the Christian cause', which 'subordinates him to a cause greater than himself and raises him by giving him a place and purpose in world history and a direct relationship with God (as the tool that executes the divine will) to which Rainouart of *Aliscans* could not aspire'.[52]

Rennewart's nobility is concealed from the main characters, but not from the audience, and this allows them to best witness the transformation taking place. In Orange Rennewart seeks refuge in Gloriette's kitchens, and Wolfram tells the audience the sad story of his enslavement. When his temper is tested, Rennewart cannot control himself. He kills the chef in a violent outburst, but laments bitterly that if Willehalm only knew his lineage, things would be different. He takes comfort under the cloak of Gyburg, his sister and Orange's queen, as his noble heritage dawns on him, and his duty becomes clear. Becoming God's tool is what gives Rennewart's character its value in *Willehalm*, and it is through his realization of his innate nobility, his becoming a knight, and Wolfram's allusions to his investiture, that he is able to fulfil that charge.

An integral part of the chivalry that Rennewart attains, and of the victory that Wolfram depicts in *Willehalm*, is the guidance and protection by the hand of God – which comes with embracing both the Christian religion and chivalry's spirituality. In *Aliscans*, Rainouart is never depicted as anything other than Christian in his inclinations; he swears he is a Christian and he is not bereft of certain medieval Christian values such as charity.[53] It is Louis who refuses to let him be baptized, although Guillaume later permits both the baptism and his marriage to Aélis, his actual conversion to Christianity not being necessary until the end of the story.[54] In all of this, we see a very different perspective on religion from that which appears in *Willehalm* more than a century later. Wolfram has been said to contemplate religious and chivalric values side by side; in doing so, he attributes certain values to the Saracens, which is why he cannot portray Rennewart with the same naïve Christianity with which he is represented in *Aliscans*.[55] Like his attainment of knighthood, the completion of the spiritual complement of chivalry must slowly be achieved by Rennewart, culminating in his anticipated baptism, formally accepting the Christian faith and submitting to the guidance of God.

The refining code of courtly love

If the Church played a key role in the maturity of European chivalry, so too did the ideal of courtly love and the veneration of ladies. The poetry of the troubadours found a well-disposed audience in France among the ruling ranks of chevaliers and their ladies. Troubadours recorded deeds and family lineages, and expanded on the virtues of chivalry; the tradition would later develop into the characteristic genre, romance. The refinement of chivalry through spirituality is evident in the courtly romances that were being composed at this time, with love as the primary agent. In examining the development of both the figure and the term *chevalier* in Old French and Provençal texts to works by Chrétien, Margaret Switten finds that 'the *chevalier* is invited to rise above killing and plundering to embrace an essentially spiritual ideal: maintaining Christianity in the face of the Saracens; attaining *pretz* and *valor* through love of women or of God'.[56] Love became the dominant feature of medieval literature, exemplifying itself through chivalry and service. Love evolved into the most ennobling and refined expression of knightly devotion; this was marked by loyalty and duty to the beloved, and a complex set of self-imposed literary rules which invited inconsistency and conflicting directives, as well as contradictory, often paradoxical morals.

For the warrior knight of *Aliscans*, love was 'a frivolous distraction from his feudal duties', a pleasure that was 'found in a well-groomed social existence; and the gradual refinement of manners brought with it an appreciation of the contribution made by women, an appreciation in fact of women themselves'.[57] But to the knights in *Willehalm*, the woman was responsible socially for raising men to their greatest heights.[58] Love in medieval literature reflected a respect for women and spirituality, and was marked by feudal, chivalric and religious undertones; diverse elements were combined into a custom of duty. This was the embodiment of the *amor cortois*, 'the conception of knightly service as the corollary of love, without which knighthood itself [was] unthinkable'.[59] Again, the ideals inspiring this courtly code must be sought further afield than the Rhenish courts and the troubadours of medieval France.

We now turn our focus to Spain, the staging area for the Muslim conquest of Europe aspired to for centuries after Tours and Poitiers (AD 732) – resulting in a significant conflict spanning Carolingian history and legend – and untamed territory south of the Marches held by the tenacious Aymeri of Narbonne and Guillaume d'Orange in the *Cycle de Guillaume*. We can also see, 300 years later in the eleventh and twelfth centuries, an example of an intercultural European environment in which the richness of the cultures of the Orient combined with the institutions, industriousness, curiosity and Christian values of the Occident. One of the most enduring points of contact, the Umayyad Caliphate, introduced many Arabo–Islamic concepts into Spain; these included centres for learning and some magnificent libraries.[60] The Caliphate of Cordoba fell in 1031, and until about 1086 'the period was one of pleasure and luxury, wine and love, but it was also a period of culture'.[61] The eleventh and twelfth centuries were also a period of 'French involvement, militarily and politically, in Spanish affairs'[62] – and in and out of this cultural centre came and went diplomats, poets, knights, captives, slaves, pilgrims and clergymen. It is not difficult to imagine the relative ease of French and Spanish contact in the twelfth century; one has but to follow the pilgrimage route back from Compostela.

Literature and poetry were among the farthest-reaching and most popular influences of the Orient via Spain. The encouragement of literary pursuits was one of the traditional manifestations of royal power among Arabs; and, consequently, each of the petty kings arising in Spain after the fall of Cordoba boasted court poets. These were trained in the classical Arabic tradition,[63] one of the more prolific of them being Cordoban Ibn Hazm.[64] Court poets precipitated the advent of wandering poets, the troubadours, who employed Arabic metrical forms. In a multilingual and cosmopolitan Spain, troubadours sang songs of love, in keeping with the Arabic ideal; these had a structure resembling *zadjal*[65] and were accompanied by the *'ud*, or lute, the 'instrument par excellence de la musique arabe'.[66] In his article on the transmission of ideas from al-Andalus to Europe, Chejne asserts that 'given the historical setting and circumstances, it is very unlikely that such a popular genre did not penetrate into the popular folklore of Spain and through it into neighbouring European countries'. He also explores the evidence of the oral transmission of Arabic-influenced legends, Arabic versions of courtly love, chivalry and epic, and also oriental proverbs, anecdotes, humour, wisdom and novels;[67] all of these, Chejne contends, would have travelled with the troubadours.[68] If Rychner's studies are taken into account, then the music and composition methods of the *chansons de geste* composers – as he presents them – point to a distinctly southern influence.[69]

In Provence, an atmosphere of permissiveness reigned; the nobility were relaxed, heretical religious movements were widespread and Ovidian literature was popular, with wandering scholars given to composing erotic verse and drinking-songs. These factors combined to bring about an environment that was amenable to travelling troubadours, and this, in turn, is how the 'courtly love' of Baghdad, a 'refined concept of love as an ennobling passion, in whose service a man might exhaust a lifetime's aspirations and, if need be, find death without dishonour',[70] found its way into southern France. Furthermore, that the refined European concept of courtly love and love-service was profoundly influenced by Arabo-Islamic ideas becomes even more convincing when one considers some earlier poems, such as *Floire and Blancheflor*. *Floire and Blancheflor* portrays the Saracens as having honour equal to the Christians, and Helen Cooper remarks of it that:

> love is a feature of both the classical and the Breton material, but the first vernacular European work to ground its whole plot and motivation solely in love, *Floire et Blancheflor*, probably came from a different cultural source, Arabic Spain: the same culture that may have inspired some elements in the Provençal tradition of love-poetry.[71]

Distinguishing 'romance literature' from 'romantic poems', Alison Weir writes that a particular kind of romantic poem, the *lais*, 'sang of love', and also that 'it was the poets of the south, the *troubadours*, who popularised the concept of courtly love, revolutionary in its day'. and inspired by Arab writers.[72] She also makes mention of the manner in which the *lais* were transmitted; composed in *langue d'oc* and sung to the accompaniment of various kinds of musical instruments, they challenged the contemporary image of women, 'according them superiority over men, and [laying] down codes of courtesy, chivalry and gentlemanly conduct'.[73] All of this adds weight, then, to the hypothesis that the ideals of chivalry and the courtly code came from the southern regions of France, and thence from Spain and the Islamic Mediterranean.

The *fin'amors* that was so popular in twelfth-century French literature filtered through to Germany as *hohe Minne*; one of its routes of travel was from Poitiers along the Danube and Rhine, where its sentiments were expressed in the twelfth-century poet, Friedrich von Hausen's work, that the lady was God's wonder, and venerating her was a divine duty.[74] This means of travel may be seen as a kind of traffic between courts on either side of the Rhine, not only in the form of troubadours and *jongleurs*, who were not documented as having made the trip into Germany as often as they were documented having traversed the borders of medieval France, but also kings, princes and other members of the nobility.[75] Of particular note is the legend of Hermann I of Thuringia, who would later become Wolfram's patron, growing up in Paris. A letter exists from his father, Ludwig II, to Louis VII of France, asking permission to send two of his sons to the French court; it describes how one of them, Hermann, was well versed in literature.[76] Bumke writes that the first examples of German courtly poetry were indeed derived from French models, due in no small part to this commerce between French and German courts:

> Den größten Einfluß hatten aber zweifellos die weltlichen Fürsten, die damals bereits auf dem Weg zur Landesherrschaft waren und die ihre Höfe der modernen französischen Adelskultur öffneten.
>
> (The lay-nobility had without doubt the greatest influence; during that era they were building their kingdoms and opened their courts to the modern French courtly culture.)[77]

The *chansons de geste* material found a new audience on the far side of the Rhine. There, epics such as Stricker's *Karl* and two reworkings of the *Rolandslied* were produced, in addition to many adaptations of Arthurian material – and it was this literature, in turn, which began to disseminate the culture of French chivalry: 'for generations the German nobility had sent its offspring to French schools and courts to be educated [because] France had become the home of Chivalry itself and was educating other countries towards that goal'.[78]

The shift from the heroic tone of *Aliscans* to the courtly emphasis on *fin' amors*, with its knightly Christian duty and an emphasis on spirituality, was achieved by Wolfram through changes to characters and subtle plot modifications. A courtly code may be seen in the behaviour and role of women in *Willehalm*; they are softer, while exerting the same subtle and profound influence and serve to remind the knights of what motivates service, bringing the courtly ethic of love, service and reward into the foreground. The battles are depicted as motivated by a duty to liege-lady, as well as revenge and imperial duty. In *Willehalm* it is Gyburg, not the hero, who is the focus of the Saracen attack; it is also she who provides Rennewart's armour and sword, and it is she to whom Rennewart is in service, not Willehalm.

Rennewart is not only in service to Gyburg through the acceptance of knightly accoutrements; love-service also plays a part, this in his relationship with Alyze, King Louis' daughter. In *Aliscans*, Aélis' love for Rainouart blossoms as she watches him wash the dung from his *tinel*, an act symbolising the cleansing of Rainouart's purity. In *Willehalm*, Wolfram allows the relationship to develop more gradually. In childhood, Rennewart was presented to Alyze as a playmate; later, Alyze persuades her father to offer him to Willehalm. Her kiss at his departure, and her sense of guilt at his treatment at Montlaon, symbolize the growing courtly acceptance of Rennewart as a knight. Rennewart now has a duty to Willehalm; he is also in the service of a lady, for love. By convincing her father to give him to Willehalm, Alyze has made it possible for Rennewart to accompany the army and relieve Orange; she has also enlisted Rennewart's service for herself. Even Willehalm recognizes that Rennewart belongs to the princess; this may be seen in the way he asks her permission before speaking to Rennewart, after acquiring him from Loys.[80] If Alyze's departure kiss is accepted as a symbol of his service, then marriage becomes a possibility – as does the possible reconciliation of differences between Terramer and the Christian Narbonnais.

When the army arrives to relieve Orange, Wolfram's description of Rennewart's appearance leaves little doubt as to his intentions for the character. Without uttering a word, Rennewart walks down the great hall of Glorjet to the head of the forces assembled there to eat. All of the relief troops regard him: '*in gienc des rîchsten mannes suon, des houbet krône bî der zît truoc: daz was gar âne strît*.'[81] Wolfram then describes how the perspiration running down Rennewart's dirty skin exposes a shining interior, and also his strength: '*der starke, niht der swache, truoc ougen als ein trache vorm houbte, grôz, lûter, lieht*.'[82] Still not having spoken, the impression given by Rennewart in the palace at Orange is considerable and goes beyond his rough exterior:

> man kôs der muoter êre
> an im, diu sölhe vruht gebar.
> al sîn antlütze gar
> ze wunsche stuont und al die lide.
> sîn clârheit warp der wîbe vride:
> ir necheiniu haz gein im truoc.
> ich sag iu lobs von im genuoc,
> genaehet er baz dem prîse
> und bin ich dannoch sô wîse.

(Wh 271, 6–14)

> (You could detect in him the nobility of the mother who had borne such a child. His whole face and all his limbs were perfection itself, and his handsome appearance earned him the approval of women, so that not one of them was ill-disposed to him. I shall have plenty to say to you in praise of him if he gets closer to renown, and if I am still clever enough for that.)[83]

Already, before the battle and before, indeed, he has even been introduced to the court at Orange, there is a detectable difference in his demeanour and reception from that in Montlaon. He is formidable because his inner nobility is, if not recognized, then certainly intimated. His strength is seen less as brutish than as an indication of his capabilities. His physical beauty is noticed rather than his clumsiness. Most telling of all is his attractiveness to court women, a sign that Rennewart has come of age; his station is now recognized. Now that he can recognize himself as noble, he can become a knight, and he must see that his chivalry serves well and properly, that it is directed by love-service, and by God, and not merely by his own desire for revenge. This will not be an easy lesson for Rennewart; he will be taunted by the chef as well as in the coming battle by knights and warriors. But Wolfram has given the audience a clear indication of his standing, and the possibility of his acceptance into courtly society.

Wolfram compares Rennewart here to the young Parzival, and gives similar reasons for his initial lack of knowledge in terms of courtly behaviour:

> eins dinges mir geloubet:
> *er was des unberoubet,*

sîn blic durh rost gap sölhiu mâl
als dô den jungen Parzivâl
vant mit sîner varwe glanz
der grâve Karnahkarnanz
an venje in dem walde.
jeht Rennewart al balde
als guoter schoene, als guoter kraft,
und der tumpheit geselleschaft.
ir neweder was nâch arde erzogn:
des was ir edelkeit betrogn.

(*Wh* 271, 15–26)

(One thing you can believe, for no one could take this away from him: through the grime he shone forth like the young Parzival when Count Karnahkarnaz came upon him on his knees in the forest, so radiant in his beauty. Right now you are to attribute a similar beauty to Rennewart, as well as the same inexperience. Neither of them had been brought up in accordance with his lineage and so they were robbed of their nobility.)[84]

Wolfram refers to a story with which the audience is already familiar; this establishes both Rennewart's claim to nobility and also that he has an important role to play in *Willehalm*, if he can only gain the proper experience and wisdom. Rennewart comes to stand before Willehalm, offering his services to him, as well as to Gyburg and the Narbonnais princes, with all of the courtliness demanded of his station, and all the knights assembled looking on. It remains for him to take command in battle and turn back the fleeing Frenchmen, the crowning achievement to his chivalry coinciding with his use of the sword and his anticipated baptism into the Christian fold he has helped to defend.

* * *

In *Aliscans*, strength and the defence of the Christian realm are the key attributes of warrior-knights and heroes. In *Willehalm*, chivalry takes on a spiritual dimension, and the emphasis shifts; honour must still be gained in worldly trials, but now – in *Willehalm* – it needs to be achieved without compromising the salvation and promise of redemption granted to Christian knighthood and its spiritual values. This refined sense of the chivalric ideal represents the interplay between justice and right in both medieval Europe and the Arabo-Islamic world as found in the obligation of service, the highest honour aspired to by the knight. This coming of age of chivalry is mirrored in the development of the epic figure of Rennewart, from twelfth-century Aquitaine to thirteenth-century Thuringia. Whereas we see a comical yet formidable giant who fights for the Christians against the Saracen threat in *Aliscans*, in *Willehalm*, Rennewart, almost as if Parzival had been his example, realizes his inner nobility, pledges his love-service to Alyze, reflects on his spiritually guided sense of morality, accepts accoutrements from Gyburg, and learns to use his sword in battle. Rennewart's development exemplifies those keystones of the new European chivalry: investiture, symbol and service; spirituality and self-reflection; and the duty to courtly love service.

Wolfram, 'his language dark and heavy, expressing a dynamic vitality of thought, emotion and imagination that would never submit to the clarity and symmetry of the literary conventions of the age',[85] reveals an attitude towards chivalry influenced by the geographical-historical environment in which he wrote. Even if Wolfram did not have immediate contact with the diverse cultures that influenced the development of chivalry, it is evident that these ideas and concepts were in wide circulation – and it would be naïve to assume that this intuitive and curious author was not aware of them, whether first, second or even third hand.[86] Just as these ideals integrated with literary expression, so too was Rainouart, the Saracen knight of *Aliscans*, transformed in *Willehalm*, mirroring the refinement of European knighthood into chivalry.

Notes

1 *Aliscans* survives in 13 complete manuscripts of varying length, as well as numerous fragments. See Bumke, Joachim. *Wolfram von Eschenbach*, 8th edn. Vol. 36, Sammlung Metzler. Stuttgart: Verlag J. B. Metzler, 2004, pp. 381–3; Ferrante, Joan M. *Guillaume d'Orange: Four Twelfth-Century Epics*, trans. and ed. Joan M. Ferrante, Records of Western Civilization. New York: Columbia University Press, 2001, pp. 9–22; and Régnier, Claude ed. *Aliscans*, 2 vols, Les Classiques français du Moyen Age. Paris: Honoré Champion, 1990, Vol. 1, Introduction, pp. 7–11. *For dating, see* Ferrante, op. cit., p. 10; Régnier, op. cit., vol. 1, Introduction, p. 40.

2 *Des manec getoufter man engalt, ze Alitschanz ûf den plân (Many a Christian paid, on the battlefield of Aliscans).* Wh 10, 16–17. See Wolfram von Eschenbach. *Willehalm*, ed. Werner Schröder, trans. Dieter Kartschoke. Berlin: Walter de Gruyter, 1989; and Wolfram von Eschenbach. *Willehalm*, trans. Marion E. Gibbs and Sidney M. Johnson. London: Penguin, 1984. It is generally accepted that Wolfram's model was the 'M', manuscript of *Aliscans*. The 'M' manuscript,

believed to be the closest extant version to what Wolfram's source would have been, is dated from the fourteenth century and is at St Mark's in Venice: label Venise, Marciana fr. VIII, CIV, 5. See Pérennec, René. *Wolfram von Eschenbach.* Paris: Belin, 2005, pp. 113–14; Régnier, op. cit., p. 8; Gibbs and Johnson, op. cit., pp. 232–3; Holtus, Günter ed. *La versione franco-italiana della 'Bataille d'Aliscans': Codex Marcianus fr. VIII[=252].* Series ed. Kurt Baldinger. Vol. 205, Beihefte zur Zeitschrift für romanische Philologie. Tübingen: Max Niemeyer Verlag, 1985; and Lofmark, Carl. *Rennewart in Wolfram's 'Willehalm' A Study of Wolfram von Eschenbach and his Sources.* Cambridge: Cambridge University Press, 1972, pp. 51–9. There are certain alternatives that must be considered too, such as manuscripts no longer extant, or oral transmission with comparative variation. See Bumke, Joachim. *Wolfram von Eschenbach,* pp. 384–8. See also Pérennec, op. cit., pp. 113–14.

3 Rennewart bears a striking resemblance to some romance figures, such as Gareth in Mallory's *Le Morte d'Arthur,* who has large hands and works in the kitchens. The scene in which Gareth is about to joust with Lancelot (who then pulls out) is reminiscent of the scene in which Guillaume and Rainouart appear as if they are about to joust, but Guillaume tells him he is only coming to help him carry his *tinel* (*Alisc.* LXXVIII). Because this is a later work, it may indicate the popularity of the Rainouart character type. Wolfram's *Willehalm,* however, does not include this incident.

4 Huby-Marly, Marie-Noël. 'Willehalm de Wolfram von Eschenbach et la chanson des Aliscans'. *Études germaniques* 39 (1984): 388–411, p. 403.

5 *Alisc.* LXIV–LXXV.

6 See Lofmark, op. cit., p. 241.

7 Bumke, Joachim. *Studien zum Ritterbegriff im 12. und 13. Jahrhundert.* Heidelberg: Carl Winter, 1964, p. 94. Bumke also writes that 'die deutsche Rittervorstellung der Blütezeit ist nicht denkbar ohne den Impuls aus Frankreich' (p. 95).

8 See Owen, D. D. R. *Noble Lovers.* London: Phaidon Press, 1975, p. 13.

9 Ghali, Wacyf Boutros. *La Tradition chevaleresque des Arabes.* Paris: Plon-Nourrit, 1919, p. 3.

10 Ghali, op. cit., pp 13–14.

11 Ghali, op. cit., pp. 8–9. Ghali also quotes from a letter from El-Malek-el-Nacer (1080–1225), which he proposes establishes that occidental chivalry did not exist as either a concept in itself or an institution until the twelfth century (p. 28).

12 See Chejne, Anwar. 'The Role of al-Andalus in the Movement of Ideas Between Islam and the West'. In *Islam and the Medieval West: Aspects of Intercultural Relations,* ed. Khalil I. Semaan. Albany: State University of New York Press, 1980, pp. 110–33. Some scholars discount the significance of any influences from the Islamic Mediterranean upon the chivalry of France, while others entertain the possibility that it was great. John Jay Parry presents one reason for the former

view in a pert footnote: 'Opposition to the theory of Arabic influence seems to be due largely to the reluctance of the modern school of French scholars to admit that French literature is indebted to any source outside its own country and ancient Rome.' Andreas Capellanus. *The Art of Courtly Love*, trans. John Jay Parry, ed. W.T.H. Jackson, Records of Civilization, Sources and Studies. New York: W.W. Norton, 1969, p. 7, fn 31.

13   Makdisi, George. 'On the Origin and Development of the College in Islam and the West'. In *Islam and the Medieval West: Aspects of Intercultural Relations*, ed. Khalil I. Semaan. Albany: State University of New York Press, 1980, pp. 26–49, p. 42.

14   Ghali, op. cit., p. 35.

15   See Ghali, op. cit., p. 33. Nikita Elisséeff also discusses several influences of Arabic design upon the Franks in the Levant – such as baths, the windmill, the number zero, paper, military tactics and a mobile cavalry, siege engines, innovations to defences and fortifications (e.g. keeps and towers, parapets, walls and *lisses*), as well as innovations to armour that include the display of a coat of arms and the noble recreation of the hunt, which originated in Persia. See Elisséeff, Nikita. 'Les échanges culturels entre le monde musulman et les Croisés à l'époque de Nur ad-Din b. Zanki (m. 1174)'. In *The Meeting of Two Worlds: Cultural Exchange between East and West during the Period of the Crusades*, ed. Vladimir P. Goss. Michigan: Medieval Institute Publications, 1986, pp. 39–52. See also Reinhardt, Kurt F. *Germany: 2000 Years*, Vol. 1. New York: Continuum, 1990, pp. 98, 109.

16   See p. xxiv of the Introduction by Mahmud Shelton of Kashifi Sabzawari, Husayn Wa'iz. *The Royal Book of Spiritual Chivalry (Futuwat Namah Yi Sultani)*, trans. Jay R. Crook, ed. Seyyed Hossein Nasr. Chicago, IL: Great Books of the Islamic World, 2000. That Arabic chivalry existed only as a religious order before the twelfth century (Ghali, op. cit., p. 32) can be seen in the phenomenon of chivalric orders and their organization, which included guilds of artisans and came about in the ninth and tenth centuries. See Nasr, Seyyed Hossein. 'The Rise and Development of Persian Sufism'. In *The Heritage of Sufism, Volume I: Classical Persian Sufism from its Origins to Rumi (700–1300)*, ed. Leonard Lewisohn. Oxford: Oneworld, 1999, pp. 1–18, p. 9.

17   See Mahmud Shelton, in Kashifi Sabzawari, op. cit., p. xxi.

18   See Fahrner, Rudolf. *West-Östliches Rittertum: Das ritterliche Menschenbild in der Dichtung des europäischen Mittelalters und der islamischen Welt*, ed. Stefano Bianca. Graz: Akademische Druck- und Verlagsanstalt, 1994, pp. 83–9, in which examples of poetry as diplomatic relations are given. Ghali also gives examples of embassies and treaties concluded between Arabic caliphs and European kings; see Ghali, op. cit., p. 19.

19   See *Medieval Persian Chivalry and Mysticism* (above) by Milad Milani.

20   See Mahmud Shelton, in Kashifi Sabzawari, op. cit., p. xxiv.

21 Grabar, Oleg. 'Patterns and Ways of Cultural Exchange'. In *The Meeting of Two Worlds: Cultural Exchange between East and West during the Period of the Crusades*, ed. Vladimir P. Goss. Michigan: Medieval Institute Publications, 1986, pp. 441–6, p. 443.

22 Huda mentions Nur ad-Din's successors and adds Zangi to his name: Huda, Qamar-ul. 'The Light Beyond the Shore in the Theology of Proper Sufi Moral Conduct (Adab)'. *Journal of the American Academy of Religion* 72, 2 (2004): 461–84, p. 464. Nikita Elisséeff goes into some detail about the institution of the Abbasid caliphate and the powers and duties of the office of iman as jurist and spiritual counsellor. See Elisséeff, Nikita. *L'Orient musulman au Moyen Age 622–1260*. Paris: Armand Colin, 1977, pp. 150–61.

23 See Mahmud Shelton, in Kashifi Sabzawari, op. cit., p. xxiii. Saladin's nobility in word and deed is illustrated in several charming, possibly fictional stories – one in which his brother is invested by Richard the Lionheart during a battle of the Third Crusade, another in which he sent two new horses to Richard when he learned that the king's horse had died in the midst of battle. Fahrner, op. cit., pp. 18, 88.

24 Fahrner, op. cit., p. 88. Though Fahrner gives no reference to the source of this story, it is referred to in other works, many of them citing Lane-Poole, Stanley. *The Story of Cairo*, 3rd edn. London: J.M. Dent, 1918, p. 193; and Lane-Poole, Stanley. *Saladin and the Fall of Jerusalem*. New York, 1898, p. 354, where Fahrner appears to have found his information, including the exchange of fruit and horses (above); see Lane-Poole, op. cit., *Saladin*, pp. 387ff. See also Newby, P.H. *Saladin in His Time*. London: Faber and Faber, 1983, p. 50; and Hindley, Geoffrey. *Saladin*. London: Constable, 1976, p. 55. However, the stories remain unsubstantiated.

25 Loewen, op. cit., p. 557.

26 See Fahrner, op. cit., pp. 83–9.

27 *Wh*, 295–6.

28 *Wh*, 296, 10–11. That his sword is not used until later in both *Aliscans* and in *Willehalm*, when he can no longer use his *tinel* (because it has been broken), seems to suggest a similarity to those swords in romance that could only be used by certain worthy people, at certain times, or under certain circumstances. See Williams, Andrea M.L. *The Adventures of the Holy Grail: A Study of La Queste del Saint Graal*. Oxford: Peter Lang, 2001, pp. 101–28.

29 There has been speculation on the symbolism in the burning of Rennewart's club, namely Lofmark's comment that 'the strengthening of his club in the fire is comparable to Rennewart's own experience, becoming more deadly and resolute in his purpose through the disgrace he has suffered'. Lofmark, *Rennewart*, op. cit., p. 162. There is also the possibility of religious symbolism here as well, as Rennewart turns towards the Christian God and accepts his role as knight.

30 Lofmark, *Rennewart*, op. cit., p. 163.

31   These lines correspond to *laisse* CXX, 6169–6172 in the 'M' ms. The line in this citation, absent in the 'A' and 'M' editions, is in brackets and corresponds to *laisse* CLXV in the 'S' ms.

32   Lines in brackets from 'M' ms. *laisse* CXXII, 6258–6260.

33   My translation.

34   Gibbs and Johnson, op. cit., p. 210.

35   Ferrante, op. cit., pp. 242–3. Ferrante's translation is from the Oxford/Halle edition of the 'S' manuscript which, while contrasting with the 'A' and 'M' mss. in many aspects, is consistent in this passage; her translation brings out the humour of the *chanson de geste*.

36   See Cooper, Helen. *The English Romance in Time; Transforming Motifs from Geoffrey of Monmouth to the Death of Shakespeare*. Oxford: Oxford University Press, 2004, p. 46. A correlation may be drawn, then, between a spiritual quest for the ideal to the quest motifs in the romance literature of the twelfth and thirteenth centuries.

37   See Keen, Maurice. *Chivalry*. New Haven, CT: Yale University Press, 1984, pp. 44–5; Flori, Jean. 'L'idée de croisade dans quelques chansons de geste du cycle de Guillaume d'Orange'. *Medioevo Romanzo* 21, 2–3 (1997): p. 476, 496–506; and Reinhardt, op. cit., pp. 106–7.

38   The first *chansons de geste* of the *Guillaume* cycle have been placed as early as the late eleventh century, though later findings have designated *Couronnement* as the earliest to have been written down, dating about 1131, and *Aliscans* around 1185. See Ferrante, op. cit., pp. 15–16. Wolfram's *Willehalm* is generally believed to have been composed before 1215; see Richey, Margaret Fitzgerald. *Studies of Wolfram von Eschenbach*. Edinburgh: Oliver and Boyd, 1957, pp. 36–7; and Bertau, Karl. 'Versuch Über Wolfram'. In *Wolfram von Eschenbach: neun Versuche über Subjektivität und Ursprünglichkeit in der Geschichte*, ed. Karl Bertau. Munich: C.H. Beck, 1983, pp. 145–65, pp. 146–8; Bumke, Joachim. *Mäzene im Mittelalter: die Gönner und Auftraggeber der höfischen Literatur in Deutschland 1150–1300*. Munich: C. H. Beck, 1979, p. 168.

39   Flori, Jean. 'La Croix, la crosse et l'épée. La Conversion des infidèles dans la *Chanson de Roland* et les chroniques de croisade'. In *Plaist vos oïr bone cançon vallant? mélanges offerts à François Suard: études recueillies par Dominique Boutet, Marie-Madeleine Castellani, Françoise Ferrand et Aimé Petit*, ed. François Suard. Lille 3: Villeneuve d'Ascq, 1999, pp. 261–72, p. 262. See also Bloch, Marc. *La société féodale*, 2 vols. Paris: Albin Michel, 1939–40, Vol. 1, p. 157.

40   Keen, op. cit., p. 54.

41   Keen, op. cit., p. 55.

42   The power struggle between the German Emperor Henry IV and Pope Gregory VII and the ensuing Cluniac reform, which put an end to the imperial power of

lay investiture and monasteries and granting it solely to Rome, likely forged a rift between secular and ecclesiastic influence over knighthood, as well as contributing to the power struggle between Church and State. See Reinhardt, op. cit., pp. 74–5.

43 See Cooper, op. cit., pp. 42ff., Keen, op. cit., p. 16, and Bloch, op. cit., Vol. 1, p. 57.

44 Switten, Margaret. 'Chevalier in Twelfth-Century French and Occitan Vernacular Literature'. In *The Study of Chivalry: Resources and Approaches*, ed. Howell Chickering and Thomas H. Seiler. Kalamazoo: Medieval Institute Publications, 1988, pp. 403–47, p. 434. '*Chevalier* has as its central etymological meaning a man on horseback, a figure that played a key role in twelfth-century vernacular literature' (p. 403). Likewise, Bumke addresses the etymology of *Knecht* and *Ritter* in German literature and history, and their changing meanings from soldier to service to nobility. See Bumke, *Studien zum Ritterbegriff*, op. cit.

45 See Wentzlaff-Eggebert, Friedrich-Wilhelm. 'Kreuzzugsidee und Mittelalterliches Weltbild'. *Deutsches Vierteljahrschrift für Literaturwissenschaft und Geistesgeschichte* 30 (1956): 71–88, pp. 76–8; and Reinhardt, op. cit., p. 108.

46 See Reinhardt, op. cit., pp. 74f., 92f.; Bumke, *Höfische Kultur*, op. cit., pp. 656f.; also Bumke, *Mäzene im Mittelalter*, op. cit., pp. 163–5.

47 Reinhardt, op. cit., p. 153.

48 *Wh*, 10, 25–26. 'This fighting will settle for nothing less than death and loss of joy.' Gibbs and Johnson, op. cit., p. 22.

49 See: Hathaway, Stephanie. *Saracens and Conversion: Chivalric Ideals in Aliscans and Wolfram's Willehalm*. Oxford: Peter Lang, 2012.

50 Richey, op. cit., p. 115.

51 Lofmark, *Rennewart*, op. cit., pp. 144–5.

52 Lofmark, *Rennewart*, op. cit., pp. 95–6.

53 In an incident in the peasants' bean field, Rainouart's compassion shows itself; he berates the Saracens for stealing and destroying the harvest, saying that it is the livelihood of the farmer and his family. *Alisc.* CLXXI–CLXXIII.

54 Lofmark sees this depiction of Rainouart as an indication of the kind of explicit form that comprised religion in the *chansons de geste*. See Lofmark, *Rennewart*, op. cit., p. 129.

55 Lofmark, *Rennewart*, op. cit., pp. 132–5.

56 Switten, op. cit., p. 434.

57 Owen, op. cit., p. 22.

58 See Jackson, W. T. H. *The Challenge of the Medieval Text: Studies in Genre and Interpretation*, ed. Joan M. Ferrante and Robert W. Hanning. New York: Columbia University Press, 1985, p. 8.

59 Richey, op. cit., p. 117.

60 See Vernet, Juan. *La Cultura Hispanoárabe en Oriente y Occidente*. Barcelona: Ariel, 1978, pp. 15–37. Armand Maurer outlines some Islamic philosophers who

were influential in the development of scholasticism in Europe, noting that the translation of Greek philosophical texts in the Abbasid Caliphate from Persia to Spain was of great importance to European thought, and that 'the Moslems' knowledge of Greek science, mathematics and philosophy, and their original creations in these areas, were far in advance of the Christian West'. See Maurer, Armand A. *Medieval Philosophy*, ed. Etienne Gilson, 2nd edn. Etienne Gilson Series 4. Toronto: Pontifical Institute of Medieval Studies, 1982, p. 94. That Umayyad Spain played a prominent role in the distribution of Arabic translations is evident, as mentioned in Alison Weir's biography of Eleanor of Aquitaine: 'Thanks to the rediscovery of the works of Aristotle, and Greek and Roman writers […] hitherto preserved by Arabs and disseminated through wider contact with Moorish Spain and the Orient, scholars became reacquainted with classical learning.' Weir, Alison. *Eleanor of Aquitaine: by the Wrath of God, Queen of England.* London: Jonathan Cape, 1999, p. 28. See also Reinhardt, op. cit., pp. 109–10.

61 See John Jay Parry's Introduction to Andreas Capellanus, op. cit., p. 7.

62 Ferrante, op. cit., p. 25.

63 See John Jay Parry's Introduction to Andreas Capellanus, op. cit., p. 7.

64 Ibn Hazm, or Abu Muhammad 'Ali ibn Ahmad ibn Sa'id ibn Hazm (eleventh century), was a Muslim philosopher, historian and theologian whose writings inspired courtly love, and who is mentioned in almost every text on Muslim Spain and early medieval courtly poetry. See Parry's Introduction to Andreas Capellanus, op. cit., p. 8; Vernet, op. cit., pp. 332–5; and Dozy, op. cit., pp. 574–80.

65 *Zadjal* was a form of popular poetry in the eleventh and twelfth centuries in Andalusia that evolved into the poetry of the Arabic Jews and of the Berbers. It appears in the first texts of Languedoc. This pursuit was to become the virtuous diversion of knights. Elisséeff also writes that 'l'idéal occidental était alors célibataire, sacerdotal, et hiérarchisé, ce qui aboutit aux ordres de chevalerie et, par réaction, à la poésie courtoise empruntée à la littérature arabe (*adab*)', showing the relationship between chivalry and courtly poetry. Elisséeff, 'Les échanges culturels', op. cit., p. 41. Anwar Chejne also writes of *zadjal*, 'the similarity between this Andalusian poetry and that of Europe is so striking as to form and content, that it cannot be relegated to coincidence'. See Chejne, Anwar. 'The Role of al-Andalus in the Movement of Ideas Between Islam and the West'. In *Islam and the Medieval West: Aspects of Intercultural Relations*, ed. Khalil I. Semaan. Albany: State University of New York Press, 1980, pp. 110–33, p. 121.

66 Elisséeff, 'Les échanges culturels', op. cit., p. 41.

67 See: Elisséeff, 'Les échanges culturels', op. cit., p. 41.

68 In the introduction to his edition of the Occitan poem *Flamenca*, Jean-Charles Huchet writes that 'c'est encore le roman des origines de la lyrique occitane que

la critique a tour à tour cherchées dans d'hypothétiques productions populaires
perdues, dans des emprunts à la lyrique arabe d'Espagne'. Huchet, Jean-Charles ed.
Flamenca: Roman occitan du XIIIe siècle. Paris: Union Générale d'Editions, 1988,
p. 18.

69   See Rychner, op. cit.

70   Owen, op. cit., p. 23.

71   Cooper, op. cit., p. 28.

72   Weir, op. cit., p. 8.

73   Weir, op. cit., p. 9.

74   See Fahrner, op. cit., p. 263.

75   French scholars write of the indebtedness of German vernacular literature to the
     influences of the Romance countries, and specifically the interaction between
     members of the nobility. Gesa Bonath writes: 'l'éclosion d'une littérature profane
     en Allemagne doit beaucoup aux contacts entre l'aristocratie allemande et celle
     de ses voisins romans, qui s'établissent surtout à la suite du mariage de Frédéric
     Barberosse avec Béatrice de Bourgogne'. Bonath, Gesa. 'Reflets des croisades dans
     la littérature allemande'. In *Les Épopées de la croisade.* Stuttgart: Franz Steiner
     Verlag Wiesbaden, 1987, p. 103, pp. 105–118.

76   Bumke provides evidence that Margarethe van Cleve was married to Ludwig III,
     whose brother Heinrich brought with him – *c.* 1180 – Veldecke's unfinished *Eneit*,
     and whose other brothers, Hermann and Friedrich, commissioned its completion,
     showing an active exchange of literature and ideas between French and German
     resources. See Bumke, *Mäzene im Mittelalter*, op. cit., p. 159.

77   Bumke, *Mäzene im Mittelalter*, op. cit., p. 10.

78   Curschmann, Michael. 'The French, the Audience, and the Narrator in Wolfram's
     "Willehalm"'. *Neophilologus* 59, 4 (1975): 548–62, p. 558.

79   See Hathaway, Stephanie. 'Women at Montlaon: The Influential Roles of the
     Female Characters in Court Negotiations in *Aliscans* and Wolfram's *Willehalm*'.
     Neophilologus 93, 1 (2009): 103–21.

80   *'Bien sei venuz' er zuo im sprach mit der jungen künigin urloup. Wh* 192, 14–15.
     ' "Welcome" said [Willehalm] to [Rennewart] with the permission of the princess'
     (my translation).

81   *Wh* 269, 28–30. 'It was the son of the most powerful ruler of the time who had
     come in and there was no disputing this'. Gibbs and Johnson, op. cit., p. 138.

82   *Wh* 270, 25–27. 'The powerful man – no weakling, this – had eyes in his head like
     a dragon, huge, clear and shining'. Gibbs and Johnson, op. cit., p. 139.

83   Gibbs and Johnson, op. cit., p. 139. Though Rennewart's mother is not identified,
     it is clear that Wolfram distinguishes between those characteristics that are the
     result of the influence of women, and those that are from Terramer the warrior.
     Nobility appears to have been a maternal inheritance, honour paternal.

84   Gibbs and Johnson, op. cit., p. 139.

85   Reinhardt, op. cit., p. 153.

86   See: Knapp. Fritz Peter. '*Leien munt nie baz gesprach*: Zur angeblichen lateinischen Buchgelehrsamkeit und zum Islambild Wolframs von Eschenbach.' *Zeitschrift für deutsches Altertum und deutsche Literatur* 138, 2 (2009): 173–84, in which Knapp looks at Wolfram's possible literary influences.

References

Andreas Capellanus. *The Art of Courtly Love*, trans. John Jay Parry, ed. W. T. H. Jackson, Records of Civilization, Sources and Studies. New York: W. W. Norton, 1969.

Bertau, Karl. 'Versuch Über Wolfram'. In *Wolfram von Eschenbach: neun Versuche über Subjektivität und Ursprünglichkeit in der Geschichte*, ed. Karl Bertau. Munich: C. H. Beck, 1983, pp. 145–65.

Bloch, Marc. *La société féodale*, 2 vols. Paris: Albin Michel, 1939–40.

Bonath, Gesa. 'Reflets des croisades dans la littérature allemande'. In *Les Épopées de la croisade*. Stuttgart: Franz Steiner Verlag Wiesbaden, 1987, pp. 105–18.

Bumke, Joachim. *Studien zum Ritterbegriff im 12. und 13. Jahrhundert*. Heidelberg: Carl Winter, 1964.

—*Mäzene im Mittelalter: die Gönner und Auftraggeber der höfischen Literatur in Deutschland 1150-1300*. Munich: C. H. Beck, 1979.

—*Wolfram von Eschenbach*, 8th edn, Vol. 36, Sammlung Metzler. Stuttgart: Verlag J. B. Metzler, 2004.

Chejne, Anwar. 'The Role of al-Andalus in the Movement of Ideas Between Islam and the West'. In *Islam and the Medieval West: Aspects of Intercultural Relations*, ed. Khalil I. Semaan. Albany: State University of New York Press, 1980, pp. 110–33.

Cooper, Helen. *The English Romance in Time; Transforming Motifs from Geoffrey of Monmouth to the Death of Shakespeare*. Oxford: Oxford University Press, 2004.

Curschmann, Michael. 'The French, the Audience, and the Narrator in Wolfram's "Willehalm"'. *Neophilologus* 59, 4 (1975): 548–62.

Elisséeff, Nikita. *L'Orient musulman au Moyen Age 622-1260*. Paris: Armand Colin, 1977, pp. 150–61.

—'Les échanges culturels entre le monde musulman et les Croisés à l'époque de Nur ad-Din b. Zanki (m. 1174)'. In *The Meeting of Two Worlds: Cultural Exchange between East and West during the Period of the Crusades*, ed. Vladimir P. Goss. Michigan: Medieval Institute Publications, 1986, pp. 39–52.

Fahrner, Rudolf. *West-Östliches Rittertum: Das ritterliche Menschenbild in der Dichtung des europäischen Mittelalters und der islamischen Welt*, ed. Stefano Bianca. Graz: Akademische Druck- und Verlagsanstalt, 1994.

Ferrante, Joan M. *Guillaume d'Orange: Four Twelfth-Century Epics*, trans. and ed. Joan M. Ferrante, Records of Western Civilization. New York: Columbia University Press, 2001.

Flori, Jean. 'L'idée de croisade dans quelques chansons de geste du cycle de Guillaume d'Orange'. *Medioevo Romanzo* 21, 2–3 (1997): 496–506.

—'La Croix, la crosse et l'épée. La Conversion des infidèles dans la Chanson de Roland et les chroniques de croisade'. In *Plaist vos oïr bone cançon vallant? mélanges offerts à François Suard: études recueillies par Dominique Boutet, Marie-Madeleine Castellani, Françoise Ferrand et Aimé Petit*, ed. François Suard. Lille 3: Villeneuve d'Ascq, 1999, pp. 261–72.

Ghali, Wacyf Boutros. *La Tradition chevaleresque des Arabes*. Paris: Plon-Nourrit, 1919.

Grabar, Oleg. 'Patterns and Ways of Cultural Exchange'. In *The Meeting of Two Worlds: Cultural Exchange between East and West during the Period of the Crusades*, ed. Vladimir P. Goss. Michigan: Medieval Institute Publications, 1986, pp. 441–6.

Hathaway, Stephanie. *Saracens and Conversion: Chivalric Ideals in Aliscans and Wolfram's Willehalm*. Oxford: Peter Lang, 2012.

Hindley, Geoffrey. *Saladin*. London: Constable, 1976.

Holtus, Günter ed. *La versione franco-italiana della 'Bataille d'Aliscans': Codex Marcianus fr. VIII [=252]*. Series ed. Kurt Baldinger. Vol. 205, Beihefte zur Zeitschrift für romanische Philologie. Tübingen: Max Niemeyer Verlag, 1985.

Huby-Marly, Marie-Noël. 'Willehalm de Wolfram von Eschenbach et la chanson des Aliscans'. *Études germaniques* 39 (1984): 388–411.

Huchet, Jean-Charles ed. *Flamenca*: Roman occitan du XIIIe siècle. Paris: Union Générale d'Editions, 1988.

Huda, Qamar-ul. 'The Light Beyond the Shore in the Theology of Proper Sufi Moral Conduct (Adab)'. *Journal of the American Academy of Religion* 72, 2 (2004): 461–84.

Jackson, W. T. H. *The Challenge of the Medieval Text: Studies in Genre and Interpretation*, ed. Joan M. Ferrante and Robert W. Hanning. New York: Columbia University Press, 1985.

Kashifi Sabzawari, Husayn Wa'iz. *The Royal Book of Spiritual Chivalry (Futuwat Namah Yi Sultani)*, trans. Jay R. Crook, ed. Seyyed Hossein Nasr. Chicago, IL: Great Books of the Islamic World, 2000.

Keen, Maurice. *Chivalry*. New Haven, CT: Yale University Press, 1984.

Knapp. Fritz Peter. '*Leien munt nie baz gesprach*: Zur angeblichen lateinischen Buchgelehrsamkeit und zum Islambild Wolframs von Eschenbach'. *Zeitschrift für deutsches Altertum und deutsche Literatur* 138, 2 (2009): 173–184.

Lane-Poole, Stanley. *Saladin and the Fall of Jerusalem*. New York, 1898.

—*The Story of Cairo*, 3rd edn. London: J. M. Dent, 1918.

Lofmark, Carl. *Rennewart in Wolfram's 'Willehalm' A Study of Wolfram von Eschenbach and his Sources*. Cambridge: Cambridge University Press, 1972.

Makdisi, George. 'On the Origin and Development of the College in Islam and the West'. In *Islam and the Medieval West: Aspects of Intercultural Relations*, ed. Khalil I. Semaan. Albany: State University of New York Press, 1980, pp. 26–49.

Maurer, Armand A. *Medieval Philosophy*, ed. Etienne Gilson, 2nd edn. Series 4. Toronto: Pontifical Institute of Medieval Studies, 1982.

Nasr, Seyyed Hossein. 'The Rise and Development of Persian Sufism'. In *The Heritage of Sufism, Volume I: Classical Persian Sufism from its origins to Rumi (700–1300)*, ed. Leonard Lewisohn. Oxford: Oneworld, 1999, pp. 1–18.

Newby, P. H. *Saladin in His Time*. London: Faber and Faber, 1983.

Owen, D. D. R. *Noble Lovers*. London: Phaidon Press, 1975.

Pérennec, René. *Wolfram von Eschenbach*. Paris: Belin, 2005.

Régnier, Claude ed. *Aliscans*, 2 vols, Les Classiques français du Moyen Age. Paris: Honoré Champion, 1990.

Reinhardt, Kurt F. *Germany: 2000 Years*, Vol. 1. New York: Continuum, 1990.

Richey, Margaret Fitzgerald. *Studies of Wolfram von Eschenbach*. Edinburgh: Oliver and Boyd, 1957.

Switten, Margaret. 'Chevalier in Twelfth-Century French and Occitan Vernacular Literature'. In *The Study of Chivalry: Resources and Approaches*, ed. Howell Chickering and Thomas H. Seiler. Kalamazoo: Medieval Institute Publications, 1988, pp. 403–47.

Vernet, Juan. *La Cultura Hispanoárabe en Oriente y Occidente*. Barcelona: Ariel, 1978.

Weir, Alison. *Eleanor of Aquitaine: By the Wrath of God, Queen of England*. London: Jonathan Cape, 1999.

Wentzlaff-Eggebert, Friedrich-Wilhelm. 'Kreuzzugsidee und Mittelalterliches Weltbild'. *Deutsches Vierteljahrschrift für Literaturwissenschaft und Geistesgeschichte* 30 (1956): 71–88.

Williams, Andrea M. L. *The Adventures of the Holy Grail: A Study of La Queste del Saint Graal*. Oxford: Peter Lang, 2001.

Wolfram, von Eschenbach. *Willehalm*, ed. Werner Schröder, 1st edn. Berlin: Walter de Gruyter, 1978.

—*Willehalm*, trans. Marion E. Gibbs and Sidney M. Johnson. London: Penguin, 1984.

Part 3

Love and Literature

Illustration of an Arab and a European minstrel singing together, from the
Cantigas de Santa Maria, Cantiga CXX, folio 125r. b–I–2.
permission Patrimonio Nacional, Madrid

5

Humour and Sexuality

Twelfth-century Troubadours and Medieval Arabic Poetry

Jerónimo Méndez

Far from a traditional conception of courtly love and the idea of love as a melancholy illness (or *amor hereos)*, defined by Andreas Capellanus in his *De amore* (AD 1186) as a '*passio quaedam innata procedens ex visione et immoderata cogitatione formae alterius sexus*', there were some troubadours who expressed their idea of love in different terms. Guilhem de Peitieu, Bernart Marti, Rimbaut d'Aurenga, Arnaut Daniel and other twelfth-century poets depicted their relationships as well as their sexual desires from an obscene and humorous point of view. They were the first male romance voices on sexuality and women from a cynical and even jocular perspective. Prior to them, indeed, some Arabic medieval poets such as Abu Nuwās (AD 747–815) cultivated the *khamriyyat* poetry and wrote frivolous and licentious lines known as *mujūn* literature, a product of the early Abbasid period,[1] which presents a similar shameless attitude in the face of heteroerotic and even homoerotic love.

The main aim of this chapter is to show briefly how these Arabic poets as well as the troubadours configure together some thematic antecedents of the *fabliaux*, the Italian *novellini* and the Catalan satirical narrations of the fourteenth and fifteenth centuries. Their works involve some of the most famous literary topics on sex and feminine sexuality in the Middle Ages, in addition to representing the anti-courtly sentiment of early medieval literature in the Middle East and Europe as an interesting intercultural chain of literary motifs.

Some examples of *mujūn* and *khamriyyat*: wine and orgies in Arabic poetry

In the ninth and tenth centuries, *mujūn* was highly popular with the ruling elite of the Abbasid caliphate in Baghdad, where true *mujūn* first flourished. Learned and religious people were also fascinated by it, for example, the vizier Ibn 'Abbad (*c.* AD 936–995). Frivolous and humorous descriptions of indecent and obscene manners appear often in combination with scurrilousness and shamelessness in the stanzas of *mujūn* literature.

The definition of *mujūn* given by the *Encyclopedia of Arabic Literature*[2] reads:

> Closely related to *khalāʿa*, the throwing off of societal restraints, *mujūn* refers behaviourally to open and unabashed indulgence in prohibited pleasures, particularly the drinking of wine and, above all, sexual profligacy. *Mujūn* literature describes and celebrates this hedonistic way of life, frequently employing explicit sexual vocabulary, and almost invariably with primarily humorous intent (...) Pre-Islamic poetry sometimes describes sexual adventures (most notably in the *Muʿallaqa* of Imru' al-Qays), but without the graphic and waggish qualities of true *mujūn*; and while pre-Islamic and Umayyad abuse poetry (*hijā'*) is often extremely coarse, and can also provoke laughter, its defamatory intent sets it off clearly from *mujūn's* essential lightheartedness.

In short, *mujūn* is a word that literally means 'shamelesness'.[3] Different *mujūn* poets such as Bashshār, al-Husayn ibn al-Dahhāk, and famous ninth-century poets Abu Tammam, al-Buhturi and Ibn al-Muʿtazz composed homoerotic and heteroerotic love poems. Homoerotic poetry was certainly not unwelcome at the caliphal court, and some caliphs actively encouraged it, like the libertine caliph al-Amin (reigned AD 809–813) who patronized Abu Nuwās and liked *boy-girls* (*ghulamiyat*), slave girls in boys' clothing, tying up their hair and painting artificial moustaches on their faces.

Baghdad poet Ibn al-Hajjāj (*c.* AD 941–1001), whose poetry added to its already graphic sexual description a new element of scatological humour (*sukhf*), is considered by some authors to be the most popular *mujūn* writer of his time. But the best *mujūn*, written with style and sarcasm, may be found in the work of one of the earliest Abbasid poets: Abu Nuwās, often considered to be the greatest of the classical Arabic poets. This author celebrated in exquisite verses the joys of the tavern and of seducing boys (*ephebes*) and occasionally girls, often in the richest descriptions.

The genre known as *khamriyyat* or Bacchus poetry, in which Abu Nuwās was the most famous master, demonstrates the constant praise of wine. This kind of poetry is frequently related to the *mujūn* owing to its occasional obscenity concerning young boys who were responsible for serving the wine at the tavern. In this sense, the Bacchus theme is inseparable from the amorous theme in the poetry of Abu Nuwās. The young and beautiful server of the wine is at the same time the server of other pleasures. The verses of the passions resulting from the consumption of wine and those of infatuation with wine boys are mixed up in two states of drunkenness: the alcoholic one and the erotic one. Besides the wine boys are characters of ambiguous sexuality; they are androgynous. In this sense we may say there is an obvious duality in the poetry of Abu Nuwās: on the one hand, the chastity and femininity of the love of wine (a feminine word in Arabic), and on the other hand, the obscenity and androgyny of the love for the wine boys. This duality entails a poetic and philosophical contrast: it is asceticism opposite to hedonism, reality confronted by idealism, the licentiousness choking the *udhrī* love, the virginal love, the courtly love understood in a traditional way.[4]

Unfortunately, the *mujūn* literature is a little-appreciated genre by Arabists owing to its high dose of jocular obscenity, and, as a result of this, very few of these poems have been translated from Arabic. However, there are some published and translated anthologies of *khamriyyat*, and having a look at several samples from the work of Abu Nuwās demonstrates some repeating literary motifs.

Often in the poetry of this 'modernist' author, scenes of pleasure while drinking wine at the tavern are preceded by lines that show scorn for the bellicose lifestyle of Arabian people and the yearning for the ruins of the *nasib* as an old-fashioned contemptible ideology:[5]

> What do I have to do, tell me, men,
> with swords and battles?
> The only star I have as a guide
> is that one of enjoyment and music.

> (p. 25)

> Forget the ruins, that are next to evil,
> the world where we're living is a fleeting house.
> Honour and drink wine, the drinker exclaims [....]

> (p. 52)

And Abu Nuwās has no problem showing himself as a poor and naughty libertine:

> They brought a woman to me,
> who was considered pretty.
> – You have achieved, sister,
> I'll be the stud she wants,
> if she accepts my faults.

> Does she know yet that I am a pervert,
> a fact that everyone is worried about,
> that my Islam is tepid,
> and that I am rather poor?
>
> (p. 27)

The author also appears like a libertine who enjoys young wine boys in nocturnal and anti-religious orgies, as we can see in the following lines:

> When the night was come,
> I turned passionate
> to the boy who I saw so pretty
> and I had considered an ugly one before
> […]
> I satisfy my desire
> over the back of a solicitous boy
> and I wake up in the morning
> cursing the drunkenness
> though it has been generous.
>
> (p. 30)

> I buy disobedience at good price
> and I exchange faith for orgies.
>
> (p. 58)

Often, the homoerotic figure of the wine boy is called *gazelle* in the Bacchus poetry, and occasionally he is called *little camel* or *roe-deer*. In the poetry of Abu Nuwās, there are several terms related to the meaning of 'gazelle' (*ghazal*) that refer particularly to the wine boys: *shadin* is a baby gazelle, *raisha* is a young gazelle, and *dhabi* or *dhabiyya* means an antelope. All these words are used in order to call the wine boy and they configure together an erotic icon of the beauty canon preferred by the authors of the age. The following passages are erotically significant in this sense, where we can appreciate some poetic and quite refined evidences of this kind of homosexual relations:

> Better the hindquarters
> of a gazelle which, with your desire,
> goes at a trot [or] at a gallop.
>
> (p. 72)

> When sleepiness fell in his like-galena black eyes,
> I went to him – the lover is not patient –

and I kissed eager his shoulder and his chest:
his back worked as a belly, like a carpet on the floor.

(p. 83)

[…] He's walking and bending,
he is like the branch of the willow which is moved by the wind at dusk.
I would give everything for this seductive gazelle.
He wears a suit undone and how many times we've smelled
the fresh rose of his cheeks and mixed the wine
with his fresh and sweet saliva.

(p. 88)

A finely obscene passage that is especially familiar in *mujūn* poetry tells of one night when the poet and his friends arrive at a tavern and the tavern keeper offers them a beautiful young boy to serve them wine until daybreak. So, Abu Nuwās tells us irreverently:

And one by one we were taking him
and it was for us as if we had broken
the fast imposed by the Ramadan month.
We spent all the night dragging the tails
that hang from the dress of perversions,
considered by God as the worst lechers;
modesty aside, I must say.

(p. 207)

On another occasion the drinkers go into a Christian monastery where wine was usually produced. A beautiful young monk – the wine boy in this case – is now called *gazelle* by the poet. Abu Nuwās explains how he penetrates this monk at daybreak, here with licentious, military vocabulary:

When we all woke up,
I went straight to him dragging the clothes,
the battering ram ready for breaking.
And I beat him with my lance,
and he was awoken by the injury.

(p. 215)

In another, related poem, there is another *gazelle* which has:

under the golden embroidered clothes,
white legs, and behind him

> a big dune of virgin snow
> which was ridden without the saddle,
> like horsemen from there to *Merw*.
> Always at the end of a course
> we praise the lists that we've been treating on.

(p. 232)

Here we also find an equestrian and military vocabulary used to describe an erotic scene: a new *gazelle* is 'ridden without the saddle', a metaphor for the sexual act. The mentioned white 'dune' refers to his bottom, according to the beauty canon of the age; and the 'list' – the enclosed field of combat at a tournament – recalls the amorous place, which means the boy with whom the lover has had a good time.

As we can see, homoerotic love appears in Abu Nuwās related to the physical pleasures of the wine orgies, as well as to an ideology that we can identify with the *shuubiyyat* thinking (scorn at the lifestyle of Arabian people). All of this is presented as a provocation that sometimes arrives at the humorous and the obscene. In the obscene, typical of the *mujūn* literature, we can find some equestrian and military metaphors that will be used more frequently in the later erotic poetry and that will coincide with poetic images used by some twelfth-century Provençal troubadours.

Before Abu Nuwās there were other revellers and lechers, for example, the Umayyad caliph al-Walid Ibn Yazid, who received the caliphate on a day when he was having just such a drunken orgy. But Abu Nuwās, as we have seen, wanted to be an *ibahi*, a morally dissolute person until the final consequences, a public libertine without a sense of decency.

Nevertheless, we can say that in Arabic poetry the courtly love and the anti-courtly love sentiments are two sides of the same coin. Alvaro Galmés de Fuentes points out how some Arabic authors demonstrate this concept well:[6] Al-Wasshā, the refined defender of chaste love; Ibn al-Rumī; Jamīl, the representative of the *udhrī* love; Ibn Quzmān; Ibn Jafāja of Alzira, Abū-l-Shalt of Dénia, and al-Gazāl. Of the al-Andalus poets, all of them cultivated, more or less, the satire of the *udhrī* love,[7] the exaltation of *khamr* (wine), or the praise of a dissolute lifestyle based on physical pleasures. They occasionally cultivated cynical misogyny too, as well as the *ibāhī* love in their poetry.

Abū-l-Shalt of Dénia, for example, describes the shameless scene of a trio, in which a servant called Shāf takes part, in an explicit *mujūn* poem:

Shāf, *his master and his lady:*
[…]
the husband over those two
and the wife underneath.
She is supporting the husband
and the husband mounts the servant.[8]

In another example, al-Gazāl expresses cynical misogyny in this way: 'women really are like saddles/and the saddle is yours whilst you don't dismount,'[9] employing an equestrian vocabulary too.

Anti-courtly love of troubadours: the other side of the coin

Bearing in mind the main features of the *mujūn* literature and *khamriyyat* poetry, the words of Abu-Haidar concerning the possible correspondence of a burlesque and obscene element in the troubadours' poetry may be quite interesting:

> Without necessarily 'stirring up' notions of literary influences, it can well be compared in its function to the burlesque element of *foudatz*, more or less manifest in some of the troubadour compositions, and bulking large in the works of the first troubadour known to us, Guillaume IX of Aquitaine.[10]

The truth is that the poetry of Guilhem IX, count of Poitiers and duke of Aquitaine (AD 1071–1126), has been considered by some scholars to be bipolar. He consciously staggers between a prototypical manifestation of courtly love (pure and chaste like the *udhrī* love), and a mode of expression of erotic affairs which may be considered humorous and even obscene. That attests to the greatness of the first troubadour of the Middle Ages, and this duality is clearly detectable several centuries before in Abbasid authors such as Abu Nuwās. His funniest poems were to be recited when men were drinking wine together, or on military expeditions surrounded by their companions (*companho*). One well-known poem by him is *Companho, faray un vers qu'er covinen*,[11] which presents an erotic theme and a cynical mode of expression employing equestrian vocabulary. After the two introductory stanzas, an obscene metaphor fills the composition: two ladies are compared with two good young horses that will be *mounted* by the count with great pleasure. The two ladies/horses are so good that he doesn't know which of them to choose, showing a hypothetical confusion.

In the poem *Farai un vers, pos mi sonelh,*[12] which may be considered a *gap* (a sample of a knight's boastfulness), Guilhem pretended to be mute when he bumped into two other ladies, and so:

> La una-m pres sotz son mantel
> et mes m'en sa cambra, el fornel;
> sapchatz qu'a mi fo bon et bel,
> e-l focs fo bos,
> et eu calfei me volenter
> als gros carbos
> [...]
> 'Sor, del bainh nos apaireillem
> e del sojorn.'
> Ueit jorn ez ancar mais estei
> az aquel torn.
>
> (p. 133)

> (One of them took me under her cloak
> she led me to her room, next to the fireplace;
> know it was good and fine to me
>   and the fire was good,
> and I became warm with pleasure
>   next to the thick charcoals
> [...]
> 'Sister, get ready to take a bath,
>   and for pleasure.'
> Eight days and more yet I stayed
>   in that situation.)

In this poem, Guilhem uses a direct vocabulary: '*las fotei*' (I fucked them); also, he shows his manly vainglory admitting he enjoyed himself with the ladies '*cent e quatre vinz et ueit vetz*' (188 times over eight days) and, as a result of this, he refers to a sexually transmitted disease: '*mal avegz*' (pain I had).

The troubadour Bernart Marti (around the mid-twelfth century) uses a humorous and naughty tone in his poem *Bel m'es lai latz la fontana,*[13] where he talks about a beautiful naked lady under the curtain: '*l'ai despoillada sotz cortin'obrada.*' Arnaut Daniel (*c.* 1180–1195), in his *Pois Raimons e'n Truc Malecs,*[14] uses metaphorical language but his meaning is sufficiently clear:

corns (arse), *cornar* (to blow into the *corns*), *penchenilh* and *penilh* (pubis) in a realistic and mocking description of a sodomite act. On the other hand, Blacatz (*c.* 1194–1236) likes eroticism in his poem *Segner Blacaz, ben mi platz e m'ajensa*, where we find the theme of *jauzir* (to enjoy) with the lady, and in his *En R'aimbautz, ses saben*, the theme of '*jazer sotz cobertor*' (to lie under a bedspread) and the motif of '*tenir nuda*' (hugging the naked lady).

Elias d'Ussel (*c.* 1200) has a *tenso: N'Elyas, conseill vos deman*,[15] where eroticism is present from the first stanza. Aimeric, the other character who participates in the *tenso* (a debate about poetry or love affairs between two troubadours), is considering whether he should respect the oath of not forcing the lady at night, while Elias shows such frankness and cynicism in his answers:

> Car'ieu era ab midonz jazen
> E n'avia faich sagramen
> Faria l'o, so-us assegur,
> Qui que m'en tengues per parjur
> […]
> L'o farai, puois plorarai m'en
> Tro qe'm perdon lo faillimen.

(p. 178)

> (If I were with my lady in bed
> and I had sworn not to do that,
> I would do it, I'm sure,
> though someone considered me a traitor
> […]
> I would do that to her, and then I'd cry
> until she forgave my fault.)

In the thirteenth century, Daude de Pradas (*c.* 1214–1282), in his poem *Amors m'envida e-m somo*,[16] uses an equestrian vocabulary too, and an uninhibited attitude that contrasts with the typical conception of courtly love:

> Amors vol ben que per razo
> eu am midonz per mai valer,
> et am piucella per tener,
> e sobre tot qe-m sia bo
> s'ab toseta de prima sella,
> qand es fresqueta e novella,
> don no-m cal temer que j-am traia,
> m'aizine tant que ab lieis jaia

un ser o dos de mes en mes,
per pagar ad amor lo ces.

(p. 1547)

(Love requires a reason
that I love a lady to venerate her,
and I love a maiden to possess her;
and over all it will be good
if she is a lass first of the saddle,
when she is fresh and young;
thus I mustn't be afraid she will betray me,
so I could sleep with her
one night or two, every month,
in order to pay Love for the pleasure.)

So we can see that all these poets and more, such as Rimbaut d'Aurenga, Marcabru, Bernart d'Auriac, Montan, Cercamon or Alegret, among other thirteenth-century troubadours, in their parodying, obscene and even cynical lines, constitute examples of the '*contre-texte*' of so-called courtly love, as Pierre Bec writes.[17] All of them choose a love expressed in physical terms, the enjoyable exaltation of sexuality, the satire or the misogyny, without idealized motifs, banishing from their poems any trace of the conventions of the *fin'amors* and even ridiculing or inverting it in a similar way in which *mujūn* poets – and Abu Nuwās in his *khamriyyat* – scorned the *udhrī* love and sang of the material pleasures of life.[18]

As Galmés de Fuentes said, this bipolarity of Provençal poetry, especially in the case of Guilhem IX of Aquitaine, has disconcerted the critics.[19] Jeanroy saw in this anti-courtly sentiment the only Arabic influence from al-Andalus.[20] Nelli, on the other hand, believes that the raciest pieces are the older ones, attributed to an explicit youth, and that the more serious ones are later, written in the mature age of the author; so the poet passed from a rude eroticism to another, more idealized one.[21] However, as Galmés de Fuentes and other critics have observed, this proposed order of pieces doesn't appear in any manuscript.

In any case, from a wider and more intercultural perspective, it is interesting to note that specific sexual metaphors related to the equestrian world appear first in the Arabic poetry (from Abu Nuwās) and become the poetic method of the first twelfth-century troubadour and later Provençal poets. Similar images and metaphors may be found in several *fabliaux* such as *C'est de la dame qui aveine demandoit por Morel sa provende avoir*,[22] where the vulva is animalized and it is called 'Morel' like a kind of horse or donkey that constantly demands its *oats*; or *De la damoisele qui n'ot parler de fotre qu'i n'aust mal au cuer*,[23] where the penis of the protagonist is called '*polain*' (colt) in a jocular and so erotic passage. We can find images and metaphors in some late medieval satirical works as *Col·loqui de dames*,[24] a fifteenth-century anticlerical dialogue, preserved in a Catalan manuscript where the *horse* provides a metaphor for the penis and the sexual capacity of priests. These are the same erotic images that appear even in the narrative Italian tradition as well as in the tenth *novella* of the ninth day of the *Decameron*, for example, where a priest, father Gianni, tries to do an *enchantment* to a certain country woman in order to transform her into a mare during a humorous scene that is interrupted by her husband at the moment when the priest tries to put the *coda di cavalla* (a mare's tail) onto the woman in order to finish his naughty and lubricious spell. But all these works and examples are, in fact, other fascinating chapters of medieval literature that should be properly explored from a comparative and intercultural point of view.

Anyway, if we come back to the intercultural relation proposed in the title of this section, we may conclude that it is difficult to speak of a direct Arabic influence, but we can observe among the Arabic poets and the *langue d'oc* troubadours a certain convergence in the themes and treatment of sexuality. There are some inevitable differences too: homoerotic love, for example, is non-existent in the poetry of troubadours and, if homosexual relations do occur, it is in order to make fun of them because of a very different cultural context. What is undeniable is the persistence of a poetic *modus operandi* which takes root in a sort of erotic animalization of the desired object (wine boys in the case of some Arabic authors, women in the case of Provençal poets) and, inverting the social and literary conventions, turns amorous passion into a subversive, even humorous way of writing poetry through the centuries.

Notes

1   There is a very good synthesis in Spanish for helping to understand this period in Vernet, Juan. *Literatura árabe*. Barcelona: Labor, 1972, p. 75.

2   Meisami, Julie Scott and Paul Starkey (eds). *Encyclopedia of Arabic Literature*, Vol. II. London and New York: Routledge, 1998, pp. 546–7. In Allen, Roger and D.S. Richards (eds). *Arabic Literature in the Post-classical Period*. Cambridge:

Cambridge University Press, 2006, p. 350. We can also read about this kind of poetry; and one can also find *mujūn* in famous Arab erotic works like *The Perfumed Garden* and *The Ring of the Dove*.

3   Cachia, Pierre. *Arabic Literature: An Overview*. London: Routledge, 2002, p. 50.

4   This paragraph is a summary of Ferrer, Jaume and Anna Gil (trans.). *Abu-Nuwàs. Khamriyyat: poesia bàquica*. Barcelona: Proa, 2002, pp. 77, 195.

5   All the following passages are translated from Ferrer, Jaume and Anna Gil (trans.). *Abu-Nuwàs. Khamriyyat: poesia bàquica*. Barcelona: Proa, 2002 (a Catalan translated anthology).

6   Galmés de Fuentes, Álvaro. *El amor cortés en la lírica árabe y en la lírica provenzal*. Madrid: Cátedra, 1996, p. 123.

7   A discussion about this kind of scorn or satire can be found in Ashtiany, Julia *et al.* (eds). *The Cambridge History of Arabic Literature. Abbasid Belles Lettres*. Cambridge: Cambridge University Press, 1990, p. 163:

> Humour is evinced, too, in the creative manner in which poets used poetic tradition, either turning a convention upside down in order to poke fun at it while at the same time exploiting it, or manipulating it for their own purposes, for example, in order to provide a contrast with their own experiences. In both cases, poets managed to produce poetry of supreme irony. Two conventions will suffice to illustrate the point: the 'Udhrī tradition, and the motif of weeping over the deserted campsite.

8   From Veglison, Josefina ed. *La poesía árabe clásica*. Madrid: Hiperión, 2002, p. 247 (a Spanish translation).

9   Galmés de Fuentes, op. cit., p. 123.

10   Abu-Haidar, J. A. *Hispano-Arabic Literature and The Early Provençal Lyrics*. Richmond: Curzon Press, 2001, p. 5.

11   Riquer, Martín de ed. *Los trovadores: historia literaria y textos*, Vol. I, p. 128. Barcelona: Ariel, 1983.

12   Riquer, op. cit., Vol. I, p. 133.

13   Riquer, op. cit., Vol. I, p. 248.

14   Nelli, René. *Ecrivains anticonformistes du Moyen-Age occitan. La femme et l'amour*. Paris: Phébus, 1977, p. 79.

15   Nelli, *Ecrivains,* op. cit., p. 178.

16   Riquer, op. cit., Vol. III, p. 1547.

17   Bec, Pierre. *Burlesque et obscénité chez les troubadours: Le contre-texte au Moyen Age*. Paris: Stock, 1984, p. 12. In this work, we can find an interesting difference between eroticism and the obscene of troubadour poetry:

> Nous pensons donc qu'il ne faut pas confondre [....] l'habituelle ambigüité, rhétorique et conceptuelle, de l'érotisme troubadouresque, qui manie volontiers et sciemment l'euphémisme, la polysémie et la périphrase, avec l'obscénité délibérément ludique et affirmé come telle, du contre-texte.

18 The pleasures of life are discussed in Verdon, Jean. *Le Plaisir au Moyen Age*. Paris: Perrin, 1996. We can find out about the sexual act from a clinical and social perspective in the medieval West, the preliminaries of love, and relations with the Church and the religious rejection of pleasure.

19 Galmés, op. cit., p. 128.

20 Jeanroy, Alfred. *La Poésie Lyrique des troubadours*. Genève: Slatkine, 1973, pp. 72–3.

21 Nelli, René. *L'Erotique des troubadours*. Toulouse: Edouard Privat, 1963.

22 Montaiglon, Anatole de and Gaston Raynaud (eds). *Recueil général et complet des fabliaux des XIIIe et XIVe siècles*, Vol. I, p. 319. Paris: Librairie des Bibliophiles, 1872.

23 Montaiglon, op. cit., Vol. V, p. 24.

24 Martín, Llúcia ed. *Col·loqui de dames*. Available from http://www.cervantesvirtual.com/FichaObra.html?Ref=20155 (accessed 23 March 2009).

References

Abu-Haidar, J. A. *Hispano-Arabic Literature and The Early Provençal Lyrics*. Richmond: Curzon Press, 2001.

Allen, Roger and D. S. Richards (eds). *Arabic Literature in the Post-classical Period*. Cambridge: Cambridge University Press, 2006.

Ashtiany, Julia *et al.* (eds). *The Cambridge History of Arabic Literature. Abbasid Belles Lettres*. Cambridge: Cambridge University Press, 1990.

Bec, Pierre. *Burlesque et obscénité chez les troubadours: le contre-texte au Moyen Age*. Paris: Stock, 1984.

Cachia, Pierre. *Arabic Literature: An Overview*. London: Routledge, 2002.

Ferrer, Jaume and Anna Gil (trans.). *Abu-Nuwàs. Khamriyyat: poesia bàquica*. Barcelona: Proa, 2002.

Galmés de Fuentes, Álvaro. *El amor cortés en la lírica árabe y en la lírica provenzal*. Madrid: Cátedra, 1996.

Jeanroy, Alfred. *La Poésie Lyrique des troubadours*. Genève: Slatkine, 1973.

Martín, Llúcia ed. Col·loqui de dames. Available from http://www.cervantesvirtual.com/FichaObra.html?Ref=20155 (accessed 23 March 2009).

Meisami, Julie Scott and Paul Starkey (eds). *Encyclopedia of Arabic Literature*, Vol. II. London and New York: Routledge, 1998.

Montaiglon, Anatole de and Gaston Raynaud (eds). *Recueil général et complet des fabliaux des XIIIe et XIVe siècles*, 6 vols. Paris: librairie des Bibliophiles, 1872.

Nelli, René. *L'Erotique des troubadours*. Toulouse: Edouard Privat, 1963.

—*Ecrivains anticonformistes du Moyen-Age occitan. La femme et l'amour*. Paris: Phébus, 1977.

Riquer, Martín de ed. *Los trovadores: historia literaria y textos*, 3 vols. Barcelona: Ariel, 1983.

Veglison, Josefina ed. *La poesía árabe clásica*. Madrid: Hiperión, 2002.

Verdon, Jean. *Le Plaisir au Moyen Age*. Paris: Perrin, 1996.

Vernet, Juan. *Literatura árabe*. Barcelona: Labor, 1972.

6

Ladies, Lovers and *Lais*

A Comparison of some Byzantine Romances
with the Anglo-Norman *Guigemar*

Andrew Stephenson

A small, under-studied group of medieval Byzantine romances bears a striking resemblance to courtly French literature of the twelfth century. The Eastern Greek and the Western Frankish societies already shared a common literary inheritance from Classical and Late Antiquity when the two cultures met and intermingled during the Crusades of the eleventh and twelfth centuries, and beyond. In this chapter the characteristics of these romances will be surveyed and various theories about dating and sources summarized. The pivotal role of Eleanor of Aquitaine will also be considered and suggestions made for further study to attempt to understand possible relationships between the two groups of tales.

Two passages depicting romantic encounters between a knight and his beloved appear similar and, indeed, the separate tales from which they come share many corresponding elements: an exiled knight; a magical encounter where destiny and love are intertwined; the discovery of a noble but unattainable lady; secret consummation of their passion; trials, separations and adventures; the ultimate reuniting of lover and beloved.

> The lady … immediately granted him her love; then he kissed her. They lie down together and converse, kissing and embracing often. I hope they also do whatever else others do on such occasions.[1]

> With this he … put his arm around her and the two fell. Even the trees … re-echoed their many kisses and embraces. Later, when they had gratified their desires … they kissed tenderly and separated.[2]

An initial reading suggests a common genre, but the first quotation is from a tale from the courtly culture of twelfth-century France; the second is from a little-known and little-understood group of medieval romances.

The first excerpt is from *Guigemar,* one of the *lais* of Marie de France. Guigemar is a young knight who shows no interest in love. When he is out hunting he wounds a hind but is in turn wounded by his own arrow. The hind speaks to him and tells him that he will only be healed by a woman who will suffer for him. He embarks on a magic ship and arrives at an ancient city – the capital of the realm – where he will be healed. There he discovers a guarded grove where the young wife of the lord is kept imprisoned: the wife heals his wound and the couple consummate their love for each other. With the fear of discovery Guigemar departs, but not before the lady ties his shirt in a knot and tells him that he may only fall in love with she who can untie the knot. Guigemar sails away and returns to his court. After another two years imprisoned in the tower, the lady finds the door unlocked one day and sails away in a boat that is waiting. She eventually comes to Guigemar, easily unties the knot in his shirt and they are reunited.

The second tale tells of Velthandros, the second son of a king. Having been persecuted by his father, Velthandros departs from the court, despite the attempts of his elder brother to dissuade him (a parallel may be seen with the lack of family position and inheritance of knights such as in Chrétien de Troye's *Yvain*). Knights from the court follow Velthandros and plead with him that if he leaves he will not attain such privileges as he now has and will live a life of servitude. They attempt to restrain him by force and ten of them are killed. Velthandros comes to a stream that contains a band of fire and eventually discovers a castle built of gold, diamonds and sardonyx from which the stream flows. An inscription informs him that this is indeed Love's Castle and that entering is ill advised; of course he enters. In a magnificent hall is a sapphire statue of a figure whose tears are the source of the stream while its sighs are the source of the fire. An inscription on the statue informs Velthandros that he is suffering from his love for the princess Chrysandza (whom he has not met). Another – male – statue bears an inscription that tells Velthandros that Love has determined the destiny of Velthandros and the princess. Velthandros then comes into the presence of Love himself who has Velthandros judge the fairest of forty beautiful women.

Velthandros continues his journey and meets the prince of a city who is out hunting and who takes him to his palace and accepts him as one of his household. When Velthandros is introduced to the princess Chrysandza he recognizes her as the woman he judged best in the beauty pageant and she recognizes him as the judge. Of course, their love is kept secret but after the passing of two years and two months they become somewhat frustrated. Velthandros is discovered soon after they have been together but by an elaborate ruse the prince is convinced that Velthandros is actually in love with Chrysandza's maid, who is then married to Velthandros in order to allow Velthandros to remain at the court and to continue to see Chrysandza. The clandestine relationship continues for another ten months, after which the lovers finally escape with the maid and three squires. The night of the escape is stormy and in the confusion the lovers are separated and their companions killed. The lovers wander along opposite banks of a river and when they find the bodies of the maid and one of the squires each thinks the other is dead. Eventually, though, they are reunited and come to the coast where they discover a ship sent by Velthandros' father to search for him. They return to his homeland where he discovers that his elder brother is dead; the two lovers marry and Velthandros is declared king.

Despite the similarities to Marie's *lai*, this second story is not from Western Europe but is one of a group of three that are included within a small genre of Byzantine verse romances. This genre comprises – in one assessment – only eleven extant stories, all of which are concerned with romantic love.[3] Of these eleven, six have Western European originals and five are generally regarded as being Greek originals.[4] Two of these five are Greek in content – *The Tale of Achilles* and *The Tale of Troy* – and the remaining three are often claimed to be Greek in origin but with Western elements incorporated.[5] These three are *Velthandros and Chrysandza*, *Kallimachos and Chrysorroi* and *Livistros and Rodamni*. However, examination of both the dating of the composition of the romances and of their content reveals that these claims of a Greek origin cannot be regarded as definitive.

The arguments surrounding the dating of the three romances are complicated and, owing to the Eastern and Western elements and influences, it has been usual to examine them against the background of the major – but not the only – East–West contact of the period: the Crusades. The First Crusade took place from about 1096 to 1099, the Second from about 1147 to 1149 and the Fourth, which resulted in the sack and occupation of Constantinople, from about 1204 to 1206. This contact with the Franks and Latins and their subsequent settlement in Byzantium and the Holy Land led to many cultural influences in both directions.

One of the arguments concerning the dating and origin of the romances is based on language. Constantinople was occupied by the Franks from 1204 until 1261 but Frankish states and culture survived long after this in the East. The form of the Greek language that had been used for administration in the Byzantine world was then influenced by that of the Frankish administrators.

The understandable lack of much appropriate administrative vocabulary in the vernacular Greek of the day resulted in the use of many Western – mainly French and Italian – loan words and concepts. Consequently, the form of Greek used for the romances that were composed during this period reflected these influences.[6]

Based on linguistic evidence, the elements in the romances themselves and the lack of any direct internal or external dating evidence, Gavin Betts suggests that the romances were composed during the fourteenth century.[7] While maintaining that the romances are original Greek compositions, Betts acknowledges the significant Western elements that were incorporated: jousts, magic, the supernatural and especially castles.[8] (The Byzantine emperor Manuel Komnenos, who reigned from 1143 to 1180, had twice been married to Western princesses and is considered to have introduced jousting to the East.[9]) Cyril Mango similarly points out that castles in these romances are not originally Byzantine and that knights, maidens, witches and dragons are clearly medieval and point to the twelfth and the first half of the thirteenth centuries, whereas other tales clearly show a Classical heritage. He notes that names such as Velthandros/Belthandros and Rodophilos are actually the Frankish names Bertrand and Rudolf.[10] Roderick Beaton, however, goes further and considers that the magical castles that feature in all these romances have central structural importance and are clearly connected to the French romances, such as the twelfth-century prose Arthurian romances of Chrétien de Troyes.[11]

Beaton suggests that in the case of *Velthandros* the geography with its echoes of crusaders and the name forms used could indicate composition during the twelfth or thirteenth centuries: internal literary evidence in the romances would not conflict with this but as yet there is no external evidence available to either support or refute such a dating.[12] Hans-Georg Beck, however, considered such Frankish elements as no more than the inclusion of familiar details from the twelfth-century court in Constantinople.[13] Both Beck and J.B. Bury noted the marked influence of Late Antique and exclusively Byzantine motifs in these romances and considered the Western courtly elements as merely superficial additions.[14] More recently, Panagiotis Agapitos has suggested a date of composition between the thirteenth and fifteenth centuries.[15] These suggested dates ranging from the twelfth to the fifteenth centuries demonstrate the lack of agreement among scholars and the difficulties of ascribing sources to the romances.

The number of romances comprising the genre is surprisingly small, as is the number of surviving manuscripts. *Velthandros* and *Kallimachos* each survive in only one manuscript, both dating back to the early sixteenth century and *Livistros* survives in five mss. from the same period that, however, vary so much among themselves that it is not possible to establish a clear relationship between them.[16]

This variation in the manuscripts that do exist and the nature of some of the language used leads Betts to suggest that there may have been a tradition of recitation but he does not consider this to support a true oral tradition.[17] Elizabeth Jeffreys is more positive, however. She notes that there is no clear evidence of any one dialect in the romances that could help establish the area in which they originated.[18] She compares this to the research on Homer and the mixture of dialects and retention of archaic forms in an oral tradition if they suited the purpose of the author or oral poet and the metre of the poem.[19] Jeffreys suggests that the romances that survive are indeed the result of combining oral works with written methods.[20]

For one of the three romances – *Kallimachos and Chrysorroi* – there does appear to be some external evidence of authorship and date. Based on a separate epigram, the author is possibly Andronikos Komnenos and this suggests a composition date of 1310 to 1340. This is accepted with reasonable certainty by Jeffreys[21] and Mango,[22] but is dismissed by Betts as being mistaken.[23] An external reference also means that *Livistros and Rodamni* must have been written prior to 1418.[24]

Against this discussion of the dating of the romances it is useful to consider their structure and the various elements and motifs. These have an influence on dating and also on ideas about origins and sources as well as contact and transmission between Byzantium and Western Europe.

For a reader familiar with French courtly literature of the twelfth century and later, the first impression upon reading the Byzantine romances is one of recognition. The romances are secular tales about courtly love and are particularly reminiscent of the *lais* of Marie de France, written around 1160 to 1199.[25] Her *lais* reflect the Byzantine romances in that they are in verse, are written in the vernacular language and are relatively short, unlike the longer prose romances of Chrétien de Troyes. The structural elements of the two groups are also very similar:

- A royal prince leaves his home for adventure.
- In a magical location he discovers a noble lady with whom he falls in love.
- There is a series of trials or adventures and the love is consummated secretly.

- A reversal of fortune or the discovery of the lovers leads to a separation.
- The separation seems to become permanent, with at least one of the lovers often assumed to be dead.
- The estranged lovers meet again, recognize each other and are married and welcomed back by the family of the prince.

These elements have been discerned in both the *lais*[26] and the romances.[27] Beaton has tabulated the structure of *Velthandros and Chrysandza* and considers the resulting symmetrical model to be consciously intended by the author.[28] However, what is of central importance for the present discussion is that a detailed examination reveals that not just these same structural elements but also their symmetrical arrangement are seen to be clearly evident in *Guigemar* (Figures 6.1 and 6.2).

Figure 6.1 *Velthandros and Chrysandza*: table of narrative structure

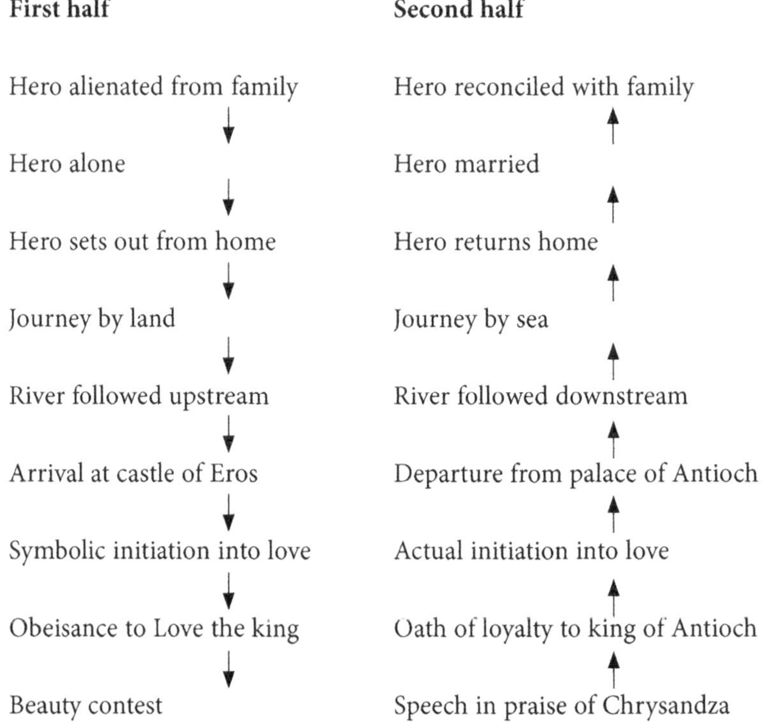

Source: From R. Beaton, *The Medieval Greek Romance* (London, 1996; 2nd edn), 123.

Figure 6.2 *Guigemar*: table of narrative structure

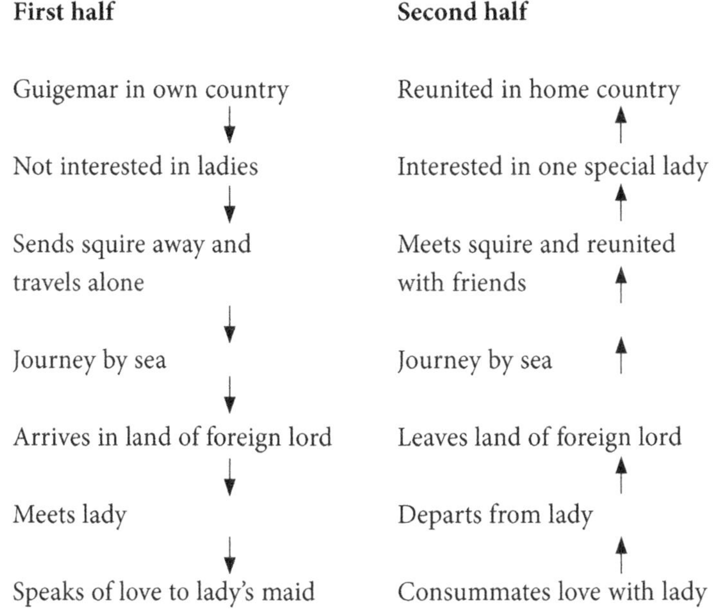

The *lai* is 886 lines long, if it is accepted that the *Prologue* was intended to stand separately.[29] In the mathematically central episode, the maid realizes that her lady is in love with Guigemar; the maid then observes to Guigemar that he, too, is obviously in love with her lady. With the maid thus acting as intermediary, their love can now be realized (lines 431–55).

Moving away from this pivotal point in both directions, the mirroring of the elements of the *lai* is revealed. In the first half, Guigemar becomes obsessed with love for the lady whom he has just met; in the second half, he consummates his love with her. Prior to meeting the lady, Guigemar arrives in the land of a foreign lord; afterwards, he departs from this foreign land. The journeys both to and from this foreign land are by sea. Prior to his outward sea voyage, Guigemar is hunting with his companions and his squire; following the return voyage, Guigemar is reunited with his squire and then with his friends. Early in the *lai* we are told that Guigemar has no interest in love and ladies; by the end he only has eyes for one special lady. And of course the *lai* commences and finishes with Guigemar in his native land.

The shared elements and motifs cause as much confusion of opinion about the origins of all the tales as does the dating. While the acceptance of a particular date of composition affects ideas about contact and transmission between East and West, the acceptance of a particular stance on the textual influences affects the dates that can satisfactorily be attributed.[30]

The underlying assumption for many scholars of the past century and a half has been that much Byzantine literature was of inferior quality and its development had stagnated; thus the fresh influence from the West provided much-needed inspiration and reinvigoration and gave rise to this group of romances in a more popular, vernacular idiom.[31] As previously discussed, Betts maintains that the Byzantine romances are Eastern originals but do have Western elements; he is also surprisingly confident that there are no Western sources that remain to be discovered.[32] However, Betts also states that the romances are in fact the result of a Western genre adapted so successfully in the East that the origins are no longer visible.[33] This circular reasoning serves to obscure rather than support his discussion. Beaton suggests that the presence of French speakers in the twelfth century may well have influenced the development of the Greek vernacular literature.[34] Similarly, Jeffreys sees many Western influences, such as courtly love and descriptions of Western dress, but notes that there is also a tradition of romance literature in Greek and so there is some continuity from this as well.[35] Some of the romances include tournaments[36] and Velthandros becomes a liegeman to the prince of Antioch:[37] these are Frankish elements.

Central to the romances is the idea of courtly love. Like Jeffreys, Mango sees this as a Western influence: he considers that the attitude displayed towards love, premarital sex (and extra-marital, as in the two romances being considered here) and the lovers being naked together are not Greek elements but show the Byzantines being influenced by the attitudes of the West (but in his opinion lacking, however, the quality of the French literature that he sees them as imitating).[38] Betts, on the other hand, sees the open inclusion of sexual consummation as based on Greek literary tradition and, in order to retain it, all mention of Christianity has been excluded from the romances. Further, he considers that it was because secular romantic love was common to both Greek and French literature that the two could meld so well.[39] Romantic love in Greek literature had its origins in the Greek novel that developed in the Hellenistic world.[40] Elements included escape from the ordinariness of daily life to a world of excitement and adventure, travel to exotic locations and the triumph of romantic love over adversity.[41] The Greek novel continued under the Roman occupation as well as under Christianity and enjoyed a revival in the twelfth century.[42] However, the escapism in Greek works was traditionally to a remote time, whereas the contemporary, chivalric nature of the fantasy world in these tales is characteristic of Western romances.[43]

Influences of the East upon the West are also readily discernible. Prior to the arrival of the crusaders, the Medieval West had little if any knowledge of the magnificence of Byzantium and the riches of Constantinople.[44] Indeed, it was this richness that led to the sacking of Constantinople during the Fourth Crusade in 1204.[45] Beaton suggests that the shared elements of ambience and the matter of the Eastern and Western romances are due to the consequent influence of the East upon the West.[46] To further complicate the relationships, there is evidence in both literatures of common borrowings from Classical literature, especially from Ovid and his description and analysis of the development of love.[47]

As well as the possibility of such general influences between East and West through the agency of the Crusades, there is, of course, one figure who is specifically and importantly linked to the Crusades as well as to the flowering of courtly literature in France: Eleanor of Aquitaine. Her grandfather was William IX (1071–1127), Duke of Aquitaine, the earliest troubadour whose songs have survived[48] and who was also a Crusader: he arrived in Constantinople and Antioch in 1101.[49] Travelling on the Second Crusade with her first husband, Louis VII of France, Eleanor arrived in Constantinople in October 1147.[50] After several weeks experiencing the exotic environment of the imperial capital, Eleanor and Louis departed for Jerusalem. In March 1148 they arrived in Antioch where Eleanor's uncle, Raymond of Poitiers, was prince.[51] Raymond knew the troubadour culture of Aquitaine and his oriental court resembled it in many regards.[52] While staying with her uncle, Eleanor would have experienced the mixing of familiar aspects from her own culture with many more unfamiliar and exotic elements. Antioch had been occupied during the First Crusade in 1098 and was by now home to a mixture of Franks and Saracens, Christians and Muslims. At the same time that this rich oriental atmosphere would have been new to Eleanor, it would have also seemed reminiscent of the blending of cultures in Bordeaux where there were Jews, Negroes and Moors.[53]

While in Antioch Eleanor spent little time with her husband and instead associated with her uncle Raymond so much that contemporary accounts suggested a sexual relationship between them.[54] After their eventual return to France, the marriage between Louis and Eleanor was annulled in 1152 and shortly afterwards Eleanor married Henry, Duke of Normandy, the son of Count Geoffrey of Anjou and soon to be King Henry II of England.[55] This marriage thus brought England and large areas of France together under the control of Eleanor and her husband. The establishment of courtly culture, the growth of troubadour poetry and the development of courtly romances are all closely related to Eleanor's influence and the spread of Angevin rule,[56] as well as to the broadening cultural effect of the Crusades.[57]

One of the most important centres for the development of the French romances was the court of Marie de Champagne, the daughter of Eleanor and Louis. It was here that the romances of Chrétien de Troyes were written in the late twelfth century. But Marie de France – the author of the *lais* here compared to the Byzantine romances – is also generally understood to have been connected to Henry and Eleanor. While there is some debate about her identity, she is usually considered to be Mary, Abbess of Shaftesbury, the daughter of Geoffrey Plantagenet, Count of Anjou, and therefore sister to Henry II.[58] She was writing from approximately 1160 to 1215[59] and was present at the court of Eleanor and Henry.[60]

Marie's sources are usually considered to be Celtic and, more immediately, Breton.[61] However, Arabic, Greek and other oriental elements have also been discerned.[62] The theory of Breton sources has been discounted by some as merely a fashion evident in the literature of the period[63] and it has also been suggested that the origins of the *lais* are actually Latin but transmitted via Celts.[64] In *Guigemar*, for example, the major motifs are only slightly related to Celtic ones.[65] A further interpretation is that the elements and motifs in Marie's *lais* are not proof of origin so much as evidence of Marie's familiarity with contemporary styles, traditional themes and the vernacular literature of the day.[66]

It remains to consider the possibilities for understanding further the relationship, if any, between the group of three Byzantine romances and the *lais*. It can be seen that there are theories about influences and transmission from East to West and West to East, as well as a sharing of common sources from Antiquity. The theories about dating become circular: any assumed date affects the discussion about sources in the same way that assuming a particular source or influence affects the subsequent discussion about dating. The only agreement seems to be that, with the current state of knowledge, ideas about influences, transmission and dating are inconclusive.[67] One possible way forward is a close analysis of the themes, motifs and structure of the three Byzantine romances and a comparison with the French literature. This comparison would, in the first instance, be with the *lais*, since they bear the most immediately recognizable relationship to the Greek tales in scope, content and format: both genres are relatively short and in verse form. To date, the three Byzantine romances have mainly been studied in the context of the linguistic development from the artificially maintained administrative language of Attic Greek to the vernacular of the Middle Ages and ultimately to Modern Greek.[68] Further investigation may well help unravel the complexities of the relationships and illuminate this obscure but fascinating genre of romantic literature.

Notes

1   Marie de France. 'Guigemar', ed. and trans. R. Hanning and J. Ferrante. In *The lais of Marie De France*. Grand Rapids: Baker, 1995, p. 45.

2   'Velthandros and Chrysandza'. Trans. G. Betts. In *Three Medieval Greek Romances*. New York: Garland, 1995, p. 21.

3   Betts, ix; for an alternative and equally valid categorization see P. A. Agapitos. 'Genre, Structure and Poetics in the Byzantine Vernacular Romances of Love', *Symbolae Osloenses* 79 (2004): pp. 7–101, at pp. 12–17.

4   C. Mango. *Byzantium: The Empire of the New Rome*. London, 1994, pp. 251–2; Betts, p. xxi.

5   R. Beaton. *The Medieval Greek Romance*, 2nd edn. London: Routledge, 1996, p. 101; Agapitos, 'Genre', p. 17; Betts, p. xxii.

6   Betts, p. xx.

7   Betts, pp. ix, xxi.

8   Betts, pp. xix, xxii.

9   Beaton, p. 19.

10 Mango, p. 252.

11 Beaton, pp. 159–62.

12 Beaton, p. 220.

13 Agapitos, 'Genre', p. 11.

14 Cited in P. A. Agapitos. *Narrative Structure in the Byzantine Vernacular Romances: A Textual and Literary Study of 'Kallimachos', 'Belthandros' and 'Libistros'*. Munich: Institut für Byzantinistik und Neugriechische Philologie der Universität, 1991, p. 8.

15 Agapitos, 'Genre', p. 9.

16 Agapitos, *Narrative Structure*, pp. 23–36; Betts, p. xxix; Beaton, pp. 104–6. The manuscript of *Velthandros* is in Paris, that of *Kallimachos* is in Leiden and those of *Livistros* are in the Vatican, Leiden, Naples, Paris and the Escorial in Spain.

17 Betts, pp. xxix–xxx.

18 E. Jeffreys. 'The Later Greek Verse Romances'. In E. Jeffreys, M. Jeffreys and A. Moffatt (eds). *Byzantine Papers: Proceedings of the First Australian Byzantine Studies Conference*. Canberra: Humanities Research Centre, Australian National University, 1981, pp. 116–27, p. 119.

19 Jeffreys, p. 120.

20 Jeffreys, p. 123.

21 Jeffreys, p. 117.

22 Mango, p. 251.

23 Betts, p. xxxvi n6.

24 Jeffreys, p. 117.

25 Hanning, p. 8.

26 Hanning, pp. 1–27 *passim*.

27 Beaton, pp. 109, 121–5.

28 Beaton, pp. 127, 249 n38.

29 Hanning, p. 55.

30 See Beaton, pp. 18–21, for intricate arguments about the dating of the texts and East–West or West–East influences varying from text to text.

31 Agapitos, *Narrative Structure*, pp. 5–6.

32 Betts, p. xxii.

33 Betts, p. xxviii.

34 Beaton, p. 20.

35 Jeffreys, p. 116.

36 Jeffreys, p. 116.

37 'Velthandros and Chrysandza', p. 19; see also Mango, p. 252.

38 Mango, pp. 252–3; see also Beaton, p. 109.

39 Betts, p. xxvi.

40 Betts, p. xvii.

41 Betts, p. xviii.

42 Betts, p. xix.

43 Betts, pp. xxiii, xxx.

44 E. J. Mickel. *Marie De France*. New York: Twayne, 1974, p. 25.

45 S. Runciman. *A History of the Crusades*, 3 vols. London: Penguin, 1965, Vol. 3, pp. 123–4.

46 Beaton, p. 19.

47 Jeffreys, p. 117; Mickel, p. 27.

48 F. Heer. *The Medieval World: Europe 1100–1350*. London: Weidenfeld, 1993, p. 124.

49 Runciman, Vol. 2, pp. 27–30; A. Weir. *Eleanor of Aquitaine: By the Wrath of God, Queen of England*. London: Pimlico, 2000, pp. 10–11.

50 Weir, p. 59.

51 Weir, p. 66; Runciman, Vol. 2, p. 278.

52 Weir, p. 66.

53 Heer, p. 127.

54 Runciman, Vol. 2, p. 279; Weir, pp. 66–9. Heer, p. 127, even suggests that this relationship fits into the tradition of courtly love and Eleanor's role as patron.

55   Heer, p. 128; Weir, pp. 94–5.

56   Heer, p. 130.

57   Mickel, p. 24.

58   Mickel, p. 21; Hanning, pp. 5–7.

59   Hanning, p. 1.

60   Hanning, p. 7.

61   C.A. Marechal ed. *In Quest of Marie De France, a Twelfth-Century Poet.* Lewiston:
     Edwin Mellen, 1992, p. 15.

62   Marechal, p. 9.

63   Mickel, p. 51.

64   Mickel, pp. 52, 98.

65   Mickel, pp. 59, 74–5.

66   Mickel, pp. 22–3.

67   Beaton, pp. 20–1; Betts, p. xxviii; Jeffreys, p. 118.

68   Agapitos, 'Genre', p. 9; Betts, p. x; Jeffreys, p. 118.

References

Agapitos, P. A. *Narrative Structure in the Byzantine Vernacular Romances: A Textual
     and Literary Study of 'Kallimachos', 'Belthandros' and 'Libistros'.* Munich: Institut für
     Byzantinistik und Neugriechische Philologie der Universität, 1991.

—'Genre, Structure and Poetics in the Byzantine Vernacular Romances of Love',
     Symbolae Osloenses 79 (2004): 7–101.

Beaton, R. *The Medieval Greek Romance*, 2nd edn. London: Routledge, 1996.

Heer, F. *The Medieval World: Europe 1100–1350.* London: Weidenfeld, 1993.

Jeffreys, E. 'The Later Greek Verse Romances'. In E. Jeffreys, M. Jeffreys and A. Moffatt
     (eds) *Byzantine Papers: Proceedings of the First Australian Byzantine Studies
     Conference.* Canberra: Humanities Research Centre, Australian National University,
     1981, pp. 116–127.

Mango, C. *Byzantium: The Empire of the New Rome.* London: Phoenix, 1994.

Marechal, C. A. ed. *In Quest of Marie De France, a Twelfth-Century Poet.* Lewiston:
     Edwin Mellen, 1992.

Marie de France. 'Guigemar' ed. and trans. R. Hanning and J. Ferrante. In *The lais of
     Marie De France.* Grand Rapids: Baker, 1995.

Mickel, E. J. *Marie De France.* New York: Twayne, 1974.

Runciman, S. *A History of the Crusades*, 3 vols. London: Penguin, 1965.

'Velthandros and Chrysandza'. Trans. G. Betts. In *Three Medieval Greek Romances.* New
     York: Garland, 1995.

Weir, A. *Eleanor of Aquitaine: By the Wrath of God, Queen of England.* London:
     Pimlico, 2000.

7

Performance and Reception of Greek Tragedy in the Early Medieval Mediterranean

Amelia R. Brown

When the first production of Aeschylus' *Oresteia* ended in 458 BC, the audience at the City Dionysia in Athens must have realized that they had seen a masterpiece from one of their greatest dramatists. Yet no Athenian could have imagined that plays based on the *Agamemnon*, the *Libation Bearers* and the *Eumenides* would still be performed more than 2,000 years later, on other continents and in other languages.[1] Indeed, the performance history of the *Oresteia* offers unique insights into the history of tragedy itself: how a dramatic art invented in Athens spread east and west throughout the Ancient Mediterranean, spawned multiple performance traditions and written texts, and endured economic and religious pressure. But in the millennium from the first performance of Aeschylus to the sixth-century end of Greek tragic drama as he would have recognized it, tragedy was by no means a fossilized or frozen institution. Though modern scholarship generally focuses on Greek tragedy in fifth-century BC Athens, Early Medieval audiences across the third- to sixth-century Mediterranean did demonstrably view tragic performances.[2] Literary, artistic and archaeological evidence demonstrates continued familiarity with tragic plots and characters, and a careful examination of the manuscript tradition of the plays of the *Oresteia* contributes some new evidence for performance of these venerable plays in Late Antiquity.

While tragedy originated in Athens, even during Aeschylus' own lifetime productions of his plays were performed outside of that city. He himself made two trips to Sicily, where he put on at least one of his plays; after he passed away there in 456 BC, the Athenians voted to grant a chorus to anyone wishing to re-perform his works.[3] By the end of the century, both Aristophanes and Euripides could expect that audiences would recognize references to the *Oresteia* in their own plays, and agree with the shade of Aeschylus in the *Frogs* that his works had outlived him.[4] While some saw the plays of Aeschylus revived in the city or demes of Athens, others had access to written texts circulating among the literate public. Many other Greek cities then incorporated theatre into their existing festivals of Dionysus or founded new competitions in the fourth century BC, and the works of Aeschylus spread throughout the Greek-speaking Mediterranean along with those of his contemporaries and successors.[5]

By the early fourth century BC, Aeschylus, Sophocles and Euripides were already enshrined as the greatest Greek tragic poets; widespread re-performance, adaptation and school textbook use ensued in the Hellenistic period and under the Roman Empire. Although Euripides was the most popular, revivals of the other two poets are also documented by inscriptions and vase paintings.[6] In 386 BC, the performance of one 'Classical' fifth-century tragedy put on by an actor was instituted at the City Dionysia, and later that of one 'Old' comedy.[7] By the 330s BC, the theatrical reforms of Lycurgus included the erection of statues of these three great tragic poets, and codification of the texts of their plays.[8] The fact that he felt it necessary to legislate official versions shows that different versions of the plays were in circulation, probably due to widespread re-performance and the inevitable alterations of actors and directors.

In Hellenistic Alexandria, scholars at Ptolemy's Library acquired Lycurgus' texts of the three great tragedians, and produced complete editions of their plays for schools and interested patrons of drama.[9] For Aeschylus, these texts were eventually whittled down to include only the seven plays surviving to our day, and above all the widespread 'Byzantine Triad' of *Prometheus Bound, Seven Against Thebes* and *Persians*. However, papyrus scripts from Roman Egypt reflect a continuing performance tradition too, a tradition also revealed by the diversity of our extant manuscripts.[10]

Indeed, even as the *Oresteia* was being studied in schools, the rules of tragic performance were changing, expanding to include other forms and genres with tragic elements. Already by the second half of the fifth century BC, Aeschylus' tetralogy format of three tragedies and a satyr play had been largely replaced by separate stand-alone plays, and the whole *Oresteia* was rarely if ever performed; by Roman times, and probably earlier, individual plays were also regularly emended, the choruses often eliminated, and one actor's part highlighted.[11] The costumes of tragedy became more and more elaborate: ornately embroidered, padded robes, large masks with high crests (the *onkos*) and thick-soled platform boots (*kothornoi*).[12] These changes inevitably made the performance of tragedy more stately and stylized, and drew more attention to the actors, who by the fourth century BC had risen in importance to become some of the most wealthy and important men in Athens and elsewhere.[13] Their political rise was matched by that of the high, narrow stage above the orchestra, and they increasingly performed in front of painted or carved panel scenery on a multi-level stage building, assisted by stage machinery, hidden passages and fake blood.[14]

The popularity of tragic (and comic) drama also led to greater professionalism and specialization in theatrical professions during the Hellenistic age. Poet-directors and professional actors assembled troupes and staged re-performances of the classic works at a growing number of competitions and festivals, in Greece and throughout the Mediterranean. From inscriptions at Delphi, we learn that the usual troupe included three actors, one flute player and a *didaskalos* (director-poet).[15] The chorus is often patently still in existence, and necessary for productions, yet it seems to have been less and less involved in the action of new tragedies.[16] Chorus members, along with costumiers and other drama professionals, may have travelled around with troupes, but they seem more often to have been locals, attached to a particular city's theatre. In the third century BC, the growing numbers of people involved in the theatre organized themselves into the *Technitai Dionysou* (Artists of Dionysos), a network of dramatists' guilds centred around Athens, the Peloponnese (Nemean-Isthmian), the coast of Asia Minor (Ionia-Hellespont) and the Ptolemaic realm (Egypt and Cyprus). Members of these guilds travelled far and wide outside of their home areas, and negotiated with cities and festivals for a range of benefits and honours.[17]

In the wake of the Hellenising of the East, a Western power began its own expansion: Rome. By the end of the third century BC, Rome's military had conquered the Hellenized centres of southern Italy, and a cultural conquest in reverse, which included Greek dramatic traditions, was moving north. Latin translations and adaptations of Greek tragedies began to be produced in Rome in the late third century BC by multilingual poets of southern Italian origin like Livius Andronicus and Quintus Ennius. Drawing on various forms of Italian drama as well as the Classical and contemporary Greek drama, these poets, along with Greek expatriates, assembled groups of actors, performed on temporary free-standing wooden stages, founded their own festivals, and formed a *Collegium* in Rome as a counterpart to the Artists of Dionysos.[18] Latin actors were never as well respected as their Greek counterparts, however, and Roman theatre from its beginnings had associations with the lower classes, associations which eventually produced problems for Greek drama with the Christian fathers.

While Euripides was the most popular Classical tragedian at Rome, as he was in the East, Aeschylus enjoyed some revivals too. Around 200 BC, the poet Ennius produced a *Eumenides* probably based on Aeschylus' play, and Pacuvius and Accius also wrote now-lost plays based on the story of Orestes. Beyond direct adaptations, however, Latin dramatists also modified older works, often eliminating the chorus: as Shakespeare would later, the Latin poets drew on the Classics and their own contemporaries for new stagings of old stories. As drama gained popularity in Italy, other towns in the West built permanent theatres and created *Ludi Scaenici* (Dramatic Games). In these towns, as in Rome, and increasingly in the East, drama was as much a political as a religious event, being staged by local officials to garner public support in elections.[19] These differences notwithstanding, by the second century BC Greek actors were performing Greek drama in Rome, while Latin actors toured not only Italy, but the heartlands of theatre in the East, and at the heels of conquering Roman armies in Gaul, Spain and North Africa.[20]

The expansion of Hellenistic and then Roman drama brought other entertainment to theatres too, however: gladiatorial combat, animal fights, pantomimes, mimes and spectacles of many other kinds. At the dedication of the Theatre of Pompey in 55 BC, the first stone theatre in Rome itself, performances of tragedy (including Accius' *Clytemnestra*) had to compete for attention with 'athletic contests, music, gladiators, races, and the hunting of wild beasts', according to Cassius Dio.[21] At the end of the Republic, theatrical performances were staged increasingly in the service of politicians; when the emperors became theatre patrons, their interests were not often beneficial for actors, especially of Greek tragedy.[22]

Seneca's tragedies are extremely important, as they are our only surviving examples of Roman tragedy. The debate about whether they were intended for performance, and inspired in part by the *Agamemnon* of Aeschylus, continues.[23] However, without a doubt he wrote performable plays using a five-act form featuring dialogue and a chorus, derived from Hellenistic tragedy.[24] Though his *Agamemnon* does not have the same form as Aeschylus' play, and many of the speeches could stand alone, it is still a tragic play concerned with the same characters and themes as Aeschylus' play.[25] At the very least the existence of this play reflects the continuing relevance of the story, and its expression through dramatic presentation in a Rome where Nero was also composing an *Oresteia*.[26]

Productions of Greek tragedy continued: an ecumenical Dramatists' Guild was organized throughout the Roman Empire, while drama remained an important part of festivals and civic life in the East.[27] The Classics increasingly dominated these festivals; the last performance of new plays at Athens' City Dionysia seems to have taken place in the first century, although the festival long continued solely with revivals.[28] A continuum of performance emerged during the early Empire, ranging from full-scale productions of the Classics in Greek or Latin, down through private shows in small odeons and dinner theatre, to the recitation of parts of plays in competitions or as part of training in rhetoric.[29] Select plays of the Classical dramatists remained among the core texts of the Greek school curriculum, which many Romans also studied.

New forms of drama – mime, pantomime and performance of excerpts – often co-opted Classical tragedies' stories and elements.[30] The mime was a non-masked show presented by a troupe of male and female actors, which likely resembled vaudeville in its selection of excerpts of plays, animal shows, music and farce.[31] Many mimes incorporated elements of Classical tragedies, but eschewed the masks, boots and stylized gestures of traditional performances.

Pantomime did away with actors and dialogue entirely, presenting the story by means of a solo dancer and accompanying musician and chorus.[32] Many Roman literary sources treat pantomime as the most typical form of 'tragedy' being performed in their day, and rhetoricians like the young St Augustine presented speeches or scenes from tragedy in competitions, as did singers and lyre players.[33] By the time Constantine took the throne, performances of whole Classical Greek tragedies were probably largely a thing of the past, yet the theatres were still full of performances of all types, some of them incorporating elements of the *Oresteia*.

What were tragic performances like in Late Antiquity, and how long do they continue? Tragedy certainly did not end with Christianity; it just became harder to distinguish the reality behind the rhetoric. Several generations of churchmen railed against the theatre, from Tertullian to John Chrysostom, as well as against war, adultery, lawyers and many other sins that still beset us today.[34] The very consistency of these speeches, and the lack of evidence of outright suppression of drama in the fourth century, suggests that we must look outside the early church for evidence of the Late Antique theatre. Theatrical performances of any kind (as we have learned again in modern times) require a performance space, funding, actors and an audience. If we can identify the existence of these features in Late Antiquity, then tragedy must have continued.

It is both very tempting and very difficult to tie the performance of tragedy to the use or abandonment of theatres in Late Antiquity. It is intrinsically difficult to estimate when unroofed theatres went out of use, as they were exposed to the elements from the time of their construction. Remodelling for theatrical reasons, though, surely signifies continued use, while remodelling into houses, stables or churches indicates that performances had ceased. The Theatre of Dionysos in Athens, for instance, received a new stage under Hadrian or the

Antonines, and Phaedros' *bema* (stage) in the fourth century.[35] This *bema* was modified again in the fifth century, to allow for the performance of water spectacles in the flooded orchestra. The theatre at Isthmia, by contrast, was built over and pillaged for building material at about the same time.[36]

The upkeep of theatres and the production of plays required money and social will, too, and perhaps the most compelling evidence for continuing dramatic production comes in the details of financing of spectacles and competitions. Historical and archaeological evidence, especially from Aphrodisias and Antioch, reveals a rich tapestry of festivals: their growth and early support by private foundations and public offices, and, in the fourth and fifth centuries, their wholesale adoption by imperial officials, and decline outside their purview.[37] Some sources of funding were more fragile than others: in the third century foundations tied to loans supposedly suffered from inflation, while those tied to land remained solvent.[38]

Yet in the fifth century, imperial patronage increasingly replaced private support, at the same time as the surviving festivals themselves were being converted into extensions of imperial cult. By the sixth century, the picture is very different: legislation tries to ensure the availability of actors, and imperial funds and officials are responsible for almost all dramatic spectacles; it seems that it was difficult for actors to make a living, and to keep them in their profession. They are increasingly paid out of public money, and seem to belong to specific cities. [39] At some point they also became part of the Blue and Green circus factions, perhaps to ensure competition.[40] Procopius blames Justinian for seizing the funds from cities which used to support theatrical performances; however he also makes his own awareness of Aeschylean tragedy clear, not least in his portrayal of the Empress Theodora as a contemporary Clytemnestra.[41] The implications are clear: productions could only continue after this point in Constantinople and those cities where imperial funds and officials were reliably present. As this list decreased sharply in the sixth century, we must assume a corresponding end to tragic dramatic productions outside the imperial centres; the theatre of Byzantium which survived was of players and singers performing at court, in the Hippodrome or on the road, not in built theatres or as part of public dramatic competitions.[42]

However, so long as the theatres, money, actors and audiences lasted, it is worth asking how Late Antique tragic productions were staged. Did Aeschylus and his successors have any existence outside the classroom and beyond the manuscript? I have gathered a few tantalising pieces of evidence to suggest that tragedy was still a recognized form of drama in Late Antiquity, including even the works of Aeschylus, if in radically different forms and environments from Classical Athens.

First, consider consular diptychs, ivory plaques carved to commemorate the shows given by newly elected consuls, which regularly depict tragic actors alongside mimes, jugglers, acrobats, hunters and charioteers.[43] A diptych of Anastasius from 517 depicts two scenes from mime, alongside three tragic actors, and a hunt set in the theatre.[44] Although these sets of images were standardized, it would not have made sense to include depictions of tragic (or comic) actors if they had ceased to have any meaning for the patrons and recipients of the plaques. In addition, although popular artistic depictions of actors had largely become fossilized by this point, actors on these plaques wear new and individual costumes and masks.[45]

Then there are literary sources which seem to refer to real plays going on in the theatres. While many authors refer to mimes, pantomimes and the like, there are enough references to tragic actors and tragic themes to suggest that this type of production continued. In the third century, Tertullian specifically criticized first the mime, then the tragic actor's *cothurni* and masks, and then the pantomime.[46] Growing up in late fourth-century Carthage, St Augustine described not only his love of theatre and specifically watching tragic plays, but also the respect given to the wealthy citizens who put on the shows, both pantomime and tragedy.[47] That Augustine may even have been familiar with the *Oresteia* is suggested by a fifth-century epic poem by his fellow-Carthaginian Blossius Aemilius Dracontius: the *Tragoedia Orestis*.[48]

Finally, there is the fragmentary but suggestive evidence of the Aeschylean texts themselves.[49] Acting companies may have passed on their material orally, but they must have started with some written text in the case of the Classics, and occasionally refreshed or adapted their repertoire. We know that this was a problem for Aeschylus specifically from very early on, but we have no idea how late it continued. What we do know, however, is that the texts of Aeschylus as we have them show clear evidence of oral transmission, and, in one case perhaps, performance emendation. Such things could have happened already in the fifth century BC, but given the relative rigour (and education) of Lycurgus and the Alexandrian scholars, and the tenth-century date of our earliest manuscripts, I would argue that it is more likely that these changes happened in Roman or Late Antique times.

First of all, R. D. Dawe has pointed out that out of the numerous errors that beset our texts of Aeschylus, the transposition of verses, and especially choral verses, is most likely due to oral transmission.[50] Although they are written in manuscripts as undivided prose, choral verses are always exchanged with ones that they are metrically identical with, and often the sense is damaged to the extent that it is obvious to a reader who understands the content. This type of error would be most likely among people memorising the text who knew the rhythym but did not completely understand what was being said, i.e. actors. Students would also be memorising the plays, but I can hardly imagine the errors of students creeping into the textual transmission, while it is more understandable that a much-performed text would suffer.

There is further evidence for the most commonly memorized (or performed) lines in the *Christos Paschon* (*Christus Patiens*), a Byzantine *cento* drawn from the tragedians, and often ascribed to Gregory Nazianzus.[51] The author of this *cento* drew on two plays of Aeschylus, *Prometheus Bound*, which almost everyone studied in school, and *Agamemnon*, which was part of the seven selected plays of Aeschylus, but not a school text. In this context, it is interesting that the seven lines selected from *Prometheus* come from throughout the entire play, whereas although more than twice as many lines from *Agamemnon* are used, they come from only three passages.

Twelve of these lines are drawn from Clytemnestra's second monologue (587–613), when she has just heard that Agamemnon has returned from Troy, and delivers a speech laced with double meanings, concluding with the ominous line on how bronze cannot be dyed. Three lines come from the subsequent choral ode (681–781), which deals with issues central to the theme of the play: prosperity as never childless, and pride going before a fall; four come from the lament of the chorus for Agamemnon (1448–1550). The inclusion of the last is understandable for its lamentation, with which much of the *Christus Paschon* is concerned, but to me, at least, the first two selections encompass some of the most tragic and ironic parts of the play, and perhaps indicate that the author was familiar with productions or at least editions that highlighted these parts. That such productions existed is strongly suggested by extensive evidence for the performance of tragic monologue set to music, and by papyrus play scripts found in Egypt.[52]

One third-century papyrus from Oxyrhynchus is a text, probably a script, of Euripides' mostly lost *Cresphontes*.[53] The papyrus contains three columns of writing, two of which are intelligible as belonging to parts of the play which were the most tragic, and which, in the original play, should have been separated by much more text than the papyrus allows; the lines are labelled with letters, probably to indicate which actor should take each part.[54] The first scene is of the ironic type where a son is questioning his mother about events of his childhood while concealing his identity from her. The second scene is of the mother preparing to murder her own son, in the mistaken belief that he has killed her son.

With the added help of a passage from Plutarch, it is reasonable to suppose that this is an abridged performance version containing episodes chosen for their tragic irony, pathos, and dramatic tension. Plutarch wrote in *The Eating of Flesh* 2.998.5E:

> Consider also Merope in the play raising her axe against her son himself because she believes him to be that son's murderer and saying, 'This blow I give you is more costly yet –' what a stir she rouses in the theatre as she brings them to their feet in terror lest she wound the youth before the old man can stop her!

The author of the papyrus picked out the most dramatic episodes to perform, with at least two actors, in a small town in third-century Egypt; perhaps this was happening all over the Roman world.

If this selection happened to Euripides, did it not also happen to Aeschylus? I believe that we have modern evidence of a performance abridgement in the two lacunae found in the texts of the *Eumenides* contained in the 'Triclinian' manuscripts (FGTrE), which represent one manuscript tradition, different from the tenth-century M tradition.[55] These lacunae each correspond to a distinct section of text, which can be removed without the sense of the play suffering. The first lacuna (582–644) belongs to the defence of Orestes during his trial at the end of the play; it can be removed with the result that Orestes no longer speaks for himself, but Apollo merely offers the famous defence on his behalf that the child comes only from the father. This is an emendation which does not hurt the sense in the slightest, but makes a shorter, tighter scene. It retains the essential argument of the original, with only the loss of Orestes' redundant self-defence.

The same goes for the second lacuna (778–807), which contains the first of two identical speeches by the Furies, and a soothing reply by Athena, which is almost entirely repeated in the next section. This, again, could be an emendation for dramatic reasons, or merely a scribal error of repetition in the M tradition.[56] I, at least, find this a more persuasive argument than a scribe skipping several pages, or that pages with just this text fell out. There was, it seems, an intermediate stage between whole tragedy and mere recitation or dramatic monologue. When was this emendation made, and the selections mentioned above? The most likely historical period for dramatic emendation and selection of this sort is the Later Roman Empire: after the codification of the manuscripts by the Alexandrian scholars, but before the end of tragic performance.

When, then, was the actual end of tragic performances? There is still no certain date for the end of tragic performance in Constantinople, although it seems to have ended in the rest of the Later Roman Empire in the sixth century. In conclusion, there is one last piece of evidence which may perhaps reflect the continuation of the theatrical tradition in the Byzantine Empire. Besides occasional references to theatre attendance in Constantinople, there is the case of Roswitha of Gandersheim. Alone among Westerners for several hundred years before and afterwards, in the mid-tenth century she seems to have written plays for performance, clearly modelled on those of Terence. It is not, perhaps, a coincidence that she was a contemporary of Theophano, a Byzantine princess from Constantinople married to Otto II, and that she resided in the same abbey as Theophano's daughter.[57]

Notes

1 A recent survey counts 22 performances of plays based on the *Oresteia* in 2003 alone, in eight different countries: Wrigley, Amanda. '*Agamemnons* on the APGRD Database'. In Fiona Macintosh *et al.* (eds), Agamemnon *in Performance 458 BC to AD 2004*. Oxford: Oxford University Press, 2005, pp. 359–435.

2 A recent brief overview of the 'reception of the *Agamemnon* in Greek' in Antiquity notes the great variety of evidence, lauds the new willingness of scholars to include 'low' forms of performance in studies of tragedy, and focuses on the *Hypothesis, scholia* and *Life* of Aeschylus as well as vase painting and the portrayal of Cassandra in *P. Oxy.* 2746 and Philostratus. *Imagines* 2.10: Easterling, Patricia E. '*Agamemnon* for the Ancients'. In Fiona Macintosh *et al.* (eds), Agamemnon *in Performance 458 BC to AD 2004*. Oxford: Oxford University Press, 2005, pp. 23–36. For the traditional (negative) appraisal of the possibility of performance of Aeschylus' dramas after the Hellenistic period. see Rosenmeyer, Thomas G. *The Art of Aeschylus*. Berkeley: University of California Press, 1982, p. 14.

3 Ancient biographical source material on Aeschylus and modern commentary: Page, Denys ed. *Aeschyli Septem Quae Supersunt Tragoedias*. Oxford: Clarendon Press, 1972, pp. 331–4; Radt, Stefan ed. *Tragicorum Graecorum Fragmenta (TrGF) Vol. 3: Aeschylus*. Goettingen: Vandenhoeck & Ruprecht, 1985, pp. 29–108; Wartelle, André. *Histoire du texte d'Éschyle dans l'antiquité*. Paris: Les Belles lettres, 1971, pp. 19–38; Rosenmeyer, *The Art of Aeschylus*, op. cit., pp. 369–76.

4   Aristophanes. *Frogs* 850; Easterling, '*Agamemnon* for the Ancients', op. cit.

5   Easterling, Patricia E. 'From Repertoire to Canon'. In Patricia E. Easterling ed., *The Cambridge Companion to Greek Tragedy*. Cambridge: Cambridge University Press, 1997, pp. 211–227, p. 213.

6   Xanthakis-Karamanos, Georgia. *Studies in Fourth-Century Tragedy*. Athens: Athenian Academy, 1980, p. 23.

7   Easterling, 'From Repertoire to Canon', op. cit., p. 213 n9.

8   Plutarch. *Lycurgus* 841.

9   Easterling, 'From Repertoire to Canon', op. cit., pp. 224–5.

10 Dawe, Roger D. *The Collation and Investigation of Manuscripts of Aeschylus*. Cambridge: Cambridge University Press, 1964, p. 156.

11 Dio Chrysostom. *Oration* 19.5; Easterling, 'From Repertoire to Canon', op. cit., p. 215.

12 Lucian. *On the Dance* 27; Kokolakis, Minos. 'Lucian and the Tragic Performances in his Time'. *Platon* 12 (1960): 67–109.

13 Easterling, 'From Repertoire to Canon', op. cit., p. 217.

14 Special effects: Bieber, Margarete. *The History of the Greek and Roman Theatre*, 2nd edn. Princeton, NJ: Princeton University Press, 1961, pp. 74–9; Beacham, Richard C. *The Roman Theatre and its Audience*. London: Routledge, 1991. Fake blood: Sutton, Dana F. *Seneca on the Stage*. Leiden: Brill, 1986, Appendix I, pp. 63–7.

15 Sifakis, Gregory M. *Studies in the History of Hellenistic Drama*. London: Athlone Press, 1967, p. 73.

16 Sifakis, *Studies in the History of Hellenistic Drama*, op. cit., p. 120.

17 Sifakis, *Studies in the History of Hellenistic Drama*, op. cit., p. 99. On actors see also Ghiron-Bistagne, Paulette. *Recherches sur les acteurs dans la Grèce antique*. Paris: Les Belles lettres, 1976.

18 Beacham, op. cit., pp. 18ff.

19 Beacham, op. cit., p. 16.

20 Beacham, op. cit., pp. 47, 63.

21 Cassius Dio. 39.38.1. For *Clytemnestra* see: Cicero. *Letters to his Family* 7.1.2; Hall, Edith. 'Aeschylus' Clytemnestra versus her Senecan Tradition'. In Fiona Macintosh *et al.* (eds), Agamemnon *in Performance 458 BC to AD 2004*. Oxford: Oxford University Press, 2005, pp. 53–76.

22 Coffey, Michael. 'Notes on the History of Augustan and Early Imperial Tragedy'. In John H. Betts *et al.* (eds), *Studies in Honour of T.B.L. Webster Vol. 1*. Bristol: Bristol Classical Press, 1986, pp. 46–52.

23 Aeschylus' play is judged not to be a major influence by Tarrant, Richard J. ed. *Seneca: Agamemnon*. Cambridge: Cambridge, University Press, 1976, pp. 7ff.; and Hall, 'Aeschylus' Clytemnestra versus her Senecan Tradition', op. cit. Hall

also supports the nineteenth-century view that Seneca did not intend his plays for performance as such, though she recognizes the broad range of tragic 'performance' existing in his era. However, details which support the possibility of actual dramatic production are explored at length by Sutton, *Seneca on the Stage*, op. cit., who summarizes the performance-recitation debate on p. 1 n2.

24 Tarrant, Richard J. 'Senecan Drama and its Antecedents'. *HSCP* 82 (1978): 213–63.

25 Seneca's themes include 'self-perpetuation of crime' and the 'danger of high position', as noted by Tarrant, *Seneca: Agamemnon*, op. cit., p. 2.

26 Philostratus. *Life of Apollonius of Tyana* 4.39.

27 Mitchell, Stephen. 'Festivals, Games, and Civic Life in Roman Asia Minor'. *JRS* 80 (1990): 183–93, pp. 184–5.

28 Pickard-Cambridge, Arthur W. *The Dramatic Festivals of Athens*, 2nd edn, ed. John Gould and David M. Lewis. Oxford: Clarendon Press, 1968, p. 82.

29 On dinner theatre see Jones, Christopher P. 'Dinner Theater'. In William J. Slater, ed., *Dining in a Classical Context*. Ann Arbor: University of Michigan Press, 1991, pp. 185–198. On theatre in education see Bonner, Stanley F. *Education in Ancient Rome*. London: Methuen, 1977, pp. 250ff.

30 Gentili, Bruno. *Theatrical Performances in the Ancient World: Hellenistic and Early Roman Theatre*, 2nd edn. Amsterdam: Gieben, 1979.

31 Wiemken, Helmut. *Der griechische Mimus*. Bremen: Schünemann, 1972; Beacham, op. cit., p. 128.

32 Webb, Ruth. *Demons and Dancers: Performance in Late Antiquity*. Cambridge, MA: Harvard University Press, 2008.

33 Augustine. *On Christian Doctrine* 2.3.4, 2.25.38.

34 Tertullian. *On Spectacles*; John Chrysostom. *On Vainglory and the Upbringing of Children* 77; Leyerle, Blake. *Theatrical Shows and Ascetic Lives: John Chrysostom's Attack on Spiritual Marriage*. Berkeley: University of California Press, 2001.

35 Frantz, Alison. 'The Date of the Phaidros Bema in the Theater of Dionysos'. In *Studies in Athenian Architecture, Sculpture, and Topography. Hesperia Suppl.* 20. Princeton, NJ: American School of Classical Studies at Athens, 1982, pp. 34–9; Sironen, Erkki. 'Life and Administration of Late Roman Attica in the Light of Public Inscriptions'. In Paavo Castrén ed., *Post-Herulian Athens*. Helsinki: Finnish Institute at Athens, 1994, no. 27, pp. 15–62.

36 Gebhard, Elizabeth R. *The Theater at Isthmia*. Chicago, IL: University of Chicago Press, 1973, p. 134; Gregory, Timothy E. 'The Sanctuary of Poseidon and the Broader Isthmus at the End of Antiquity'. Forthcoming.

37 Liebeschuetz, J. H. and Wolf, G. *Antioch: City and Imperial Administration in the Later Roman Empire*. Oxford: Clarendon Press, 1972; Roueché, Charlotte. *Performers and Partisans at Aphrodisias in the Roman and Late Roman Periods*.

London: Society for the Promotion of Roman Studies, 1993; Mitchell, op. cit., pp. 183–93; Jory, John. 'The Masks on the Propylon of the Sebasteion at Aphrodisias'. In Patricia E. Easterling and Edith Hall (eds), *Greek and Roman Actors: Aspects of an Ancient Profession*. Cambridge: Cambridge University Press, 2002, pp. 238–53.

38   Roueché, op. cit., p. 8.

39   Liebeschuetz, op. cit., pp. 141–4.

40   Roueché, op. cit., p. 45.

41   Procopius. *History of the Wars* 1.24.33–7, *Secret History* 26; Ure, Percy N. *Justinian and his Age*. Harmondsworth: Penguin, 1951, pp. 202–3; Hall, 'Aeschylus' Clytemnestra versus her Senecan Tradition', op. cit., p. 56; Webb, Ruth. 'Female Entertainers in Late Antiquity'. In Patricia E. Easterling and Edith Hall (eds), *Greek and Roman Actors: Aspects of an Ancient Profession*. Cambridge: Cambridge University Press, 2002, pp. 282–303.

42   The definition of Byzantine drama in and outside the Orthodox liturgy continues to evolve, and much is still shadowy, due in large measure to the classicising of our textual sources: White, Andrew W. *The Artifice of Eternity: A Study of Liturgical and Theatrical Practices in Byzantium*. Ph.D. Diss., University of Maryland, 2006; Puchner, Walter. 'Acting in the Byzantine Theatre: Evidence and Problems'. In Patricia E. Easterling, and Edith Hall (eds), *Greek and Roman Actors: Aspects of an Ancient Profession*. Cambridge: Cambridge University Press, 2002, pp. 304–24.

43   Natanson, Joseph. *Early Christian Ivories*. London: Alec Tiranti, 1953, nos 44, 46; Bieber, op. cit., pp. 250–3.

44   Natanson, op. cit., no. 46.

45   Green, J. Richard. *Theatre in Ancient Greek Society*. London: Routledge, 1994, p. 168.

46   Tertullian. *On Spectacles* 23.

47   Augustine, *Confessions* 1.10, 3.2.

48   Wartelle, op. cit., p. 360; Bright, David F. *The Miniature Epic in Vandal Africa*. Norman: University of Oklahoma Press, 1987.

49   On the textual tradition of Aeschylus see: Mund-Dopchie, Monique. *La survie d'Eschyle à la Renaissance: éditions, traductions, commentaires et imitations*. Louvain: Peeters, 1984; and West, Martin L. *Studies in Aeschylus*. Stuttgart: Teubner, 1990, pp. 319–54.

50   Dawe, op. cit., pp. 161–4.

51   Sticca, Sandro. 'The Christos Paschon and the Byzantine Theatre'. In Clifford Davidson *et al.* (eds), *Studies in Medieval Drama in Honor of William L. Smoldon on his 82nd Birthday*. Kalamazoo: Western Michigan University, 1974, pp. 13–44; Wartelle, op. cit., pp. 359–360; Puchner, op. cit., pp. 317–18.

52   For Imperial Roman papyrus tragic play scripts, and tragic dramatic poetry lines with musical notation which may well form parts of tragic plays, see: Eitrem,

Samson *et al. Fragments of Unknown Greek Tragic Texts with Musical Notation (P. Osl. inv. no. 1413).* Oslo: Brøgger, 1955; Coles, Revel A. *et al.* (eds), *The Oxyrhynchus Papyri, Part 36.* London: Egypt Exploration Society, 1970, pp. 7–11, no. 2746; Johnson, William A. 'Musical Evenings in the Early Empire: New Evidence from a Greek Papyrus with Musical Notation'. *JHS* 120 (2000): 57–85; Hall, Edith. 'The Singing Actors of Antiquity'. In Patricia E. Easterling and Edith Hall (eds), *Greek and Roman Actors: Aspects of an Ancient Profession.* Cambridge: Cambridge University Press, 2002, pp. 3–38; Gammacurta, Tatiana. *Papyrologica scaenica: I copioni teatrali nella tradizione papiracea.* Alessandria: Edizioni dell'Orso, 2006, pp. 270–3.

53   Turner, Eric G. *et al.* (eds), *The Oxyrhynchus Papyri, Part 27.* London: Egypt Exploration Society, 1962, pp. 73–81, no. 2458; Gammacurta, op. cit., pp. 95–110, no. 10, with intervening bibliography.

54   Turner, Eric G. 'Dramatic Representations in Graeco-Roman Egypt: How Long Do They Continue?' *Antiquité Classique* 32 (1963): 120–128, p. 122.

55   Fraenkel, Eduard ed. *Aeschylus' Agamemnon.* Oxford: Clarendon Press, 1950, p. 7.

56   It is worth noting that Tony Taccone, director of a modern production of the *Oresteia* at the Berkeley Repretory Theater in 2001, selected the scenes he would most like to cut as the first long speech of Clytemnestra, and parts of the trial and aftermath.

57   Tunison, Joseph S. *Dramatic Traditions of the Dark Ages.* Chicago, IL: The University of Chicago Press, 1907; St John, Christopher. *The Plays of Roswitha.* New York: Cooper Square Publishers, 1966.

References

Beacham, Richard C. *The Roman Theatre and its Audience.* London: Routledge, 1991.

Bieber, Margarete. *The History of the Greek and Roman Theatre*, 2nd edn. Princeton, NJ: Princeton University Press, 1961.

Bonner, Stanley F. *Education in Ancient Rome.* London: Methuen, 1977.

Bright, David F. *The Miniature Epic in Vandal Africa.* Norman: University of Oklahoma Press, 1987.

Coffey, Michael. 'Notes on the History of Augustan and Early Imperial Tragedy'. In John H. Betts *et al.* (eds), *Studies in Honour of T.B.L. Webster Vol. 1.* Bristol: Bristol Classical Press, 1986, pp. 46–52.

Coles, Revel A. *et al.* (eds), *The Oxyrhynchus Papyri, Part 36.* London: Egypt Exploration Society, 1970.

Dawe, Roger D. *The Collation and Investigation of Manuscripts of Aeschylus.* Cambridge: Cambridge University Press, 1964.

Easterling, Patricia E. 'From Repertoire to Canon'. In Patricia E. Easterling ed., *The Cambridge Companion to Greek Tragedy*. Cambridge: Cambridge University Press, 1997, pp. 211–27.

—'*Agamemnon* for the Ancients'. In Fiona Macintosh *et al.* (eds), Agamemnon *in Performance 458 BC to AD 2004*. Oxford: Oxford University Press, 2005, pp. 23–36.

Eitrem, Samson *et al. Fragments of Unknown Greek Tragic Texts with Musical Notation (P. Osl. inv. no. 1413)*. Oslo: Brøgger, 1955.

Fraenkel, Eduard ed., *Aeschylus' Agamemnon*. Oxford: Clarendon Press, 1950.

Frantz, Alison. 'The Date of the Phaidros Bema in the Theater of Dionysos'. In *Studies in Athenian Architecture, Sculpture, and Topography. Hesperia Suppl.* 20. Princeton, NJ: American School of Classical Studies at Athens, 1982, pp. 34–9.

Gammacurta, Tatiana. *Papyrologica scaenica: I copioni teatrali nella tradizione papiracea*. Alessandria: Edizioni dell'Orso, 2006.

Gebhard, Elizabeth R. *The Theater at Isthmia*. Chicago, IL: University of Chicago Press, 1973.

Gentili, Bruno. *Theatrical Performances in the Ancient World: Hellenistic and Early Roman Theatre*, 2nd edn. Amsterdam: Gieben, 1979.

Ghiron-Bistagne, Paulette. *Recherches sur les acteurs dans la Grèce antique*. Paris: Les Belles lettres, 1976.

Green, J. Richard. *Theatre in Ancient Greek Society*. London: Routledge, 1994.

Gregory, Timothy E. 'The Sanctuary of Poseidon and the Broader Isthmus at the End of Antiquity'. (Forthcoming).

Hall, Edith. 'The Singing Actors of Antiquity'. In Patricia E. Easterling and Edith Hall (eds), *Greek and Roman Actors: Aspects of an Ancient Profession*. Cambridge: Cambridge University Press, 2002, pp. 3–38.

—'Aeschylus' Clytemnestra versus her Senecan Tradition'. In Fiona Macintosh *et al.* (eds), Agamemnon *in Performance 458 BC to AD 2004*. Oxford: Oxford University Press, 2005, pp. 53–76.

Johnson, William A. 'Musical Evenings in the Early Empire: New Evidence from a Greek Papyrus with Musical Notation'. *JHS* 120 (2000): 57–85.

Jones, Christopher P. 'Dinner Theater'. In William J. Slater ed., *Dining in a Classical Context*. Ann Arbor: University of Michigan Press, 1991, pp. 185–98.

Jory, John. 'The Masks on the Propylon of the Sebasteion at Aphrodisias'. In Patricia E. Easterling and Edith Hall (eds), *Greek and Roman Actors: Aspects of an Ancient Profession*. Cambridge: Cambridge University Press, 2002, pp. 238–53.

Kokolakis, Minos. 'Lucian and the Tragic Performances in his Time'. *Platon* 12 (1960): 67–109.

Leyerle, Blake. *Theatrical Shows and Ascetic Lives: John Chrysostom's Attack on Spiritual Marriage*. Berkeley: University of California Press, 2001.

Liebeschuetz, J. H. and Wolf, G. *Antioch: City and Imperial Administration in the Later Roman Empire*. Oxford: Clarendon Press, 1972.

Mitchell, Stephen. 'Festivals, Games, and Civic Life in Roman Asia Minor'. *JRS* 80 (1990): 183–93.

Mund-Dopchie, Monique. *La survie d'Eschyle à la Renaissance: éditions, traductions, commentaires et imitations*. Louvain: Peeters, 1984.

Natanson, Joseph. *Early Christian Ivories*. London: Alec Tiranti, 1953.

Page, Denys ed., *Aeschyli Septem Quae Supersunt Tragoedias*. Oxford: Clarendon Press, 1972.

Pickard-Cambridge, Arthur W. *The Dramatic Festivals of Athens*, 2nd edn. John Gould and David M. Lewis (eds). Oxford: Clarendon Press, 1968.

Puchner, Walter. 'Acting in the Byzantine Theatre: Evidence and Problems'. In Patricia E. Easterling and Edith Hall (eds), *Greek and Roman Actors: Aspects of an Ancient Profession*. Cambridge: Cambridge University Press, 2002, pp. 304–24.

Radt, Stefan ed. *Tragicorum Graecorum Fragmenta (TrGF) Vol. 3: Aeschylus*. Goettingen: Vandenhoeck & Ruprecht, 1985.

Rosenmeyer, Thomas G. *The Art of Aeschylus*. Berkeley: University of California Press, 1982.

Roueché, Charlotte. *Performers and Partisans at Aphrodisias in the Roman and Late Roman Periods*. London: Society for the Promotion of Roman Studies, 1993.

Sifakis, Gregory M. *Studies in the History of Hellenistic Drama*. London: Athlone Press, 1967.

Sironen, Erkki. 'Life and Administration of Late Roman Attica in the Light of Public Inscriptions'. In Paavo Castrén ed., *Post-Herulian Athens*. Helsinki: Finnish Institute at Athens, 1994, pp. 15–62.

Sticca, Sandro. 'The Christos Paschon and the Byzantine Theatre'. In Clifford Davidson *et al.* (eds), *Studies in Medieval Drama in Honor of William L. Smoldon on his 82nd Birthday*. Kalamazoo: Western Michigan University, 1974.

St John, Christopher. *The Plays of Roswitha*. New York: Cooper Square Publishers, 1966.

Sutton, Dana F. *Seneca on the Stage*. Leiden: Brill, 1986.

Tarrant, Richard J. ed. *Seneca: Agamemnon*. Cambridge: Cambridge University Press, 1976.

—'Senecan Drama and its Antecedents'. *HSCP* 82 (1978): 213–263.

Tunison, Joseph S. *Dramatic Traditions of the Dark Ages*. Chicago, IL: The University of Chicago Press, 1907.

Turner, Eric G. 'Dramatic Representations in Graeco-Roman Egypt: How Long Do They Continue?' *Antiquité Classique* 32 (1963): 120–8.

Turner, Eric G. *et al.* (eds) *The Oxyrhynchus Papyri, Part 27*. London: Egypt Exploration Society, 1962

Ure, Percy N. *Justinian and his Age*. Harmondsworth: Penguin, 1951.

Wartelle, André. *Histoire du texte d'Éschyle dans l'antiquité*. Paris: Les Belles lettres, 1971.

Webb, Ruth. 'Female Entertainers in Late Antiquity'. In Patricia E. Easterling and Edith Hall (eds), *Greek and Roman Actors: Aspects of an Ancient Profession*. Cambridge: Cambridge University Press, 2002, pp. 282–303.

—*Demons and Dancers: Performance in Late Antiquity*. Cambridge, MA: Harvard University Press, 2008.

West, Martin L. *Studies in Aeschylus*. Stuttgart: Teubner, 1990.

White, Andrew W. *The Artifice of Eternity: A Study of Liturgical and Theatrical Practices in Byzantium*. Ph.D. Diss., University of Maryland, 2006.

Wiemken, Helmut. *Der griechische Mimus*. Bremen: Schünemann, 1972.

Wrigley, Amanda. '*Agamemnons* on the APGRD Database'. In Fiona Macintosh *et al.* (eds), Agamemnon *in Performance 458 BC to AD 2004*. Oxford: Oxford University Press, 2005, pp. 359–435.

Xanthakis-Karamanos, Georgia. *Studies in Fourth-Century Tragedy*. Athens: Athenian Academy, 1980.

Part 4

Material Culture

Woodcut of Constantinople by Michael Wolgemut (1434–1519) from *Nuremberg Chronicle*, 1491

8

The Urban Language of Early Constantinople

The Changing Roles of the Arts and Architecture in the Formation of the New Capital and the New Consciousness

Gordana Fontana-Giusti

The complexity and elusiveness of the history of art and architecture in Late Antiquity and the early Middle Ages have been acknowledged most notably through the work and legacy of Alois Riegl.[1] More recently, this subject was addressed in the book by Hans Peter L'Orange,[2] who studied the relationship between the arts and the broader values of the period. Equally, a more profound and multifaceted approach is required within architecture, its theory and its historiography, building upon the exemplary work of Krautheimer and Ćurčić.[3] This chapter will focus on the status of architecture, related arts and the change of consciousness in the fourth century AD in the context of the new capital – Constantinople, the imperial seat for over a millennium, that survived destruction and social upheavals, Crusades and assaults, resulting in the emergence and disappearance of many works of art and architecture.

Focusing on early Constantinople (*c.* AD 324–*c.*337) and the status of the arts and architecture at the time, this analysis observes the city that had managed to regenerate and redefine itself several times. This chapter investigates the way in which this was possible and made achievable by incorporating arts and the knowledge of antiquity into the running of the everyday life of the Empire. The new capital city contributed in this way contributed to the formation of a new mind-set in the early Middle Ages.

In the Preface to his collected seminal works on Constantinople, contemporary historian, and probably the most prolific scholar on Constantinople, Cyril Mango (b. 1928) states that the Byzantine capital and its history were never clearly delineated.[4] In constructing the city's history, scholarship had to draw from stories, chronicles, the lives of the saints and theological treatises of the period, while being indebted to the European connoisseurs and travellers who had observed, taken notes and sketched in the course of their journeys. Mango discusses the fragility and scarcity of documents and adds that most of the time we are only imagining this ancient capital.[5] In his works Mango was filling this lacuna as he made the city his focus in the same way in which Krautheimer and Ćurčić have contributed to the architectural history of Byzantium.

The making of Constantine's *Polis*

The city was part of the imperial project of building the new capital – the New Rome – by reconstructing the small ancient town of Byzantium, chosen by Constantine following the military victory over his rivals in AD 312. This victory

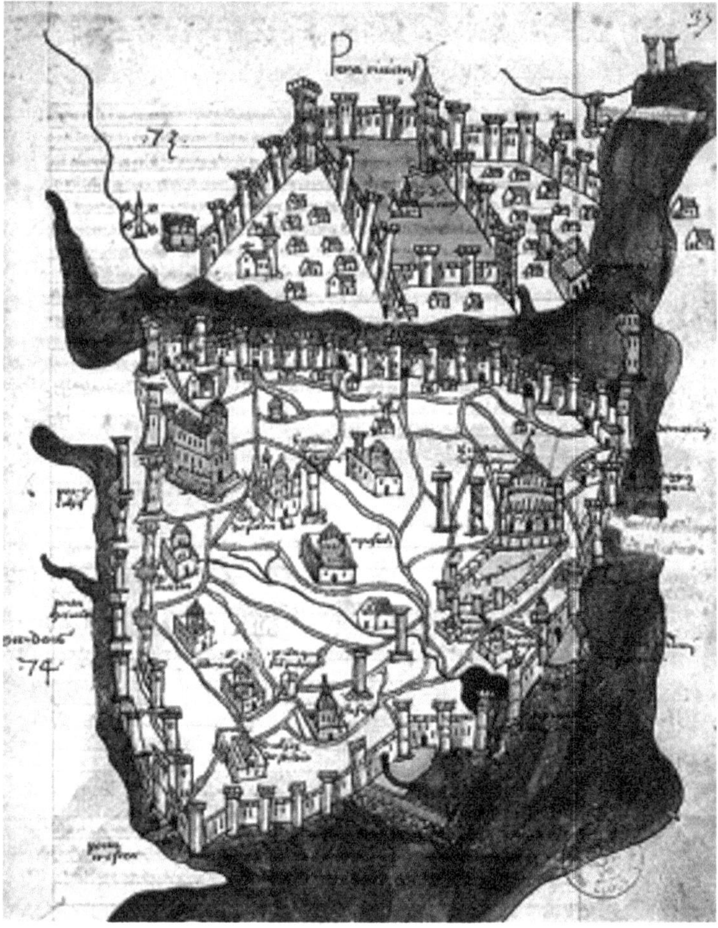

Fig. 1. The oldest map of Constantinople from the fifteenth century by Florentine Christoforo Buondelmonte

in the battle at Milvian Bridge has been linked to Constantine's legendary vision of the cross as the sign under which he was to succeed.[6] The vision was followed by the Emperor's Edict of Milan in AD 313 authorising the licence for Christians to worship freely.[7]

According to William C. Morey, Constantine 'was a man of wider views than Diocletian, and had even a greater genius for organization. The work which Diocletian began, Constantine completed.'[8] Morey argues that it was Constantine who had decisively shaped the Roman imperial project by giving it the final form in which it had exercised its great influence upon modern governments. In other words, through the variety of institutional engagements on different levels, spanning military victories to urban design, Constantine had shaped the legacy of the Roman Empire. It was not so much the early imperialism of Augustus, Morey argues, as the later imperialism of Constantine that had an impact on the subsequent empires of medieval and early modern Europe. The role of Constantine was therefore one of statesman, political reformer and originator of the new Roman capital city.

Historical documents record that on 8th November 324 the city limits were established on the edge of the Bosporus.[9] The emperor had apparently overseen the city's official dedication in a series of ceremonies in the new urban core.[10] According to the available documents, the process of rebuilding the 'New Rome' was completed on 11th May 330, five and a half years after the initiation in a burst of building activity.[11] Little is known about this 'instant city' and a great deal remains speculation. The physical evidence is fragmentary, as the remains and ruins that were left at the end of the fifteenth century were gradually absorbed into the fabric of the modern metropolis. We know that monuments and streets with numerous palaces were built during these five-and-a-half years, as advanced Roman building technology had been fully applied. The techniques of creating large-span viaducts and aqueducts were in place, as was the science of building roads, fortresses, palaces and bridges.[12]

Constantinople was a complex, multi-dimensional city; initiated by the pagan ritual, it was placed under the protection of the tutelary Fortune even though the city was to embrace Christianity.[13] In this respect there are competing streams of interpretation based upon the claims of different historiographers. Some argue that the city was supposed to be Christian in its dedication, while others have related it unequivocally to Rome's pagan tradition. A re-examination of historical documents leads to the conclusion that while religious concerns were indeed the underlining component in determining the plan of the city, the city of Constantine was never meant to be exclusively for

Christians.[14] In other words, religious concerns, while important, were not the only defining element of urban design. The main objective was to create a capital for all inhabitants that would celebrate the imperial rule and provide stability for the Empire spreading east.

The role of the new capital

During the second decade of the fourth century new structures and ostentatious public spaces were superimposed by Constantine's architects upon the existing city of Byzantium – a medium-sized local urban community with some building work undertaken by the Emperor Severus. These included the Severan wall that delineated the protected core of the city. Constantine had a new wall built and laid out the city on a larger scale, adorning it with novel monumental buildings. The building of the 'New Rome' is described in one of the chronicles:

> He renewed the original walls of the city of Byzas and made many additions to them which he joined to the ancient walls and he called the city Constantinople. He also completed the Hippodrome which he decorated with bronze statues and other embellishment, and made in it a *loge* for the emperor to watch (the games from) in imitation of the one in Rome. He built a big palace near the said Hippodrome and connected it with the loge of the Hippodrome by an ascending staircase called *cochlias*. He also constructed a big and very beautiful forum and set up in a centre of it a tall column of purple Theban stone worthy of admiration. At the top of this column he set up a big statue of himself with rays on his head, which bronze statue he had brought from Phrygia. The same Emperor Constantine removed from Rome the so-called Palladium and placed it in the forum that he had built underneath the column (bearing) his statue: this is stated by some inhabitants of Byzantium who have heard it by way of tradition. He had also offered a bloodless sacrifice and confessed the name Anthousa on the Tyche of the city he had renewed.[15]

The urban design thus involved the symbolic reconnection with Rome by means of the Palladium, the enhancement of the city plan, the building of grand imperial buildings and the redesign of public spaces in the new capital. The public squares were in most cases completed with the placement of statuary.

The creation of a New Rome this way poses some significant questions that we will now address. On a general level, what did the formation of the new capital achieve? What kinds of investments in the arts and practices had the creation of this city incorporated? What were the architectural methods used

Fig. 2. Constantine, statuary fragments, Musei Capitolini, Rome

in the making of the institutions such as the Christian Church and the Empire within the city space? What was the role of the statuary in this respect and within a wider epistemological context? What were the effects of this approach upon the city space and the new urban psyche?

The imperial investment in the arts and architecture of the new capital

The making of the new capital meant a sweeping break from the traditions of the old empire. The city of Rome was packed with memories of paganism and relics from the republic. Constantine desired to radically renew the empire and to give it a novel and well-positioned centre.[16] The new capital was considered better placed for defending Roman territory, as the site of the old Greek colony in the

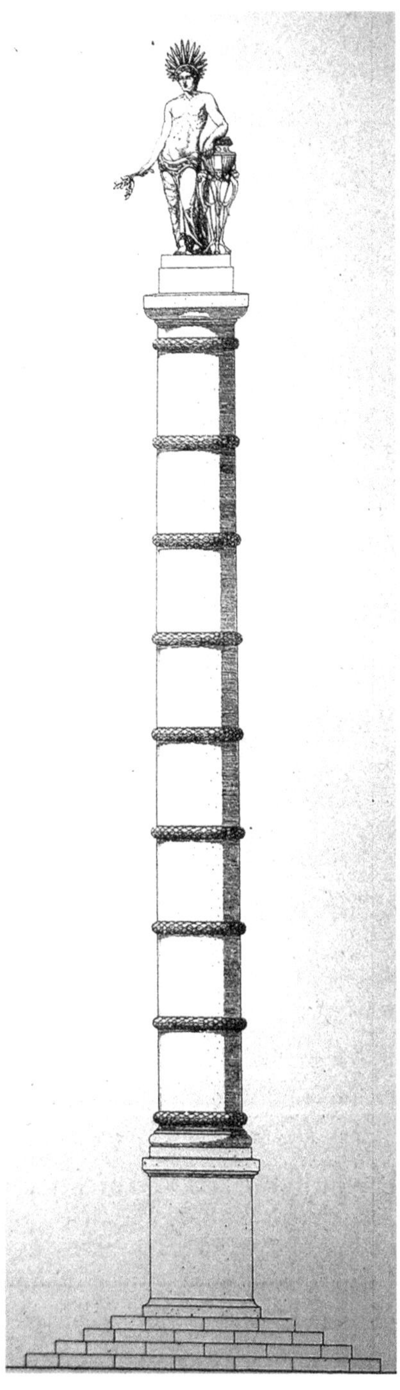

Fig. 3. Constantine's Column as designed

Fig. 4. Constantine's column today

confines of Europe and Asia. This site was regarded favourably for commerce as its port had deep water facilities. Above all, the city was planned for the establishment of a system of government that was considered superior. The formal character of this system was drawing from its Graeco-Roman tradition but also from the experiences of the nearby, long-standing Oriental empires.

It has been understood that the natural function of the old city of Byzantium was to be a gatekeeper to the Black Sea and to tax any related trade. However, the customary assertions about the city's special geographical position and its advantages need to be put under scrutiny.[17] Apart from the exaggerated claims about the conveniences of its location, a number of drawbacks were suffered by the city, such as exposure to attacks from the hinterland, and a lack of sufficient sources of drinking-water. More alarmingly, the new capital did not immediately attract a significant population.

Still, despite these initial difficulties, the city had managed to prosper due to enormous effort and significant imperial investment. The nature of this investment was diverse, including people's skills and knowledge about the arts, the latest building technology and the direct supply of treasures such as the ancient statuary. The transfer of knowledge also included the concentrated sum total of learning and practice of the Liberal Arts and architecture as developed in Late Antiquity.[18]

The learning of the liberal arts centred on the *egknklios paideia*, 'the customary, general education'.[19] The more specialized knowledge of architecture was based on the actual practice and related commentaries.[20] Indeed, the position of architecture and its discourse is not clear, as it was not the art but *techne*.[21] There are few ancient records on architecture in general, and the only remaining text is the one by Vitruvius.[22] Although we do not have direct evidence that would link this treatise to the making of Constantinople, it is probable that Vitruvius' book (or another one of a similar kind) was available and in use. *De architectura* was a useful manual for the dissemination of Roman architecture throughout the Empire. Vitruvius, a Roman architect and engineer (*c.* 80 BC–*c.* 15 BC) had introduced a number of Greek architectural concepts such as order, arrangement, eurhythmy, symmetry, propriety and economy, and had compiled ancient mathematical knowledge such as that of Philo of Byzantium of the second century BC. Philo's work incorporated *Isagoge* – an introduction to mathematics, *Mochlica* – on general mechanics, and *Limenopoeica* – on harbour building. It is likely that other commentaries on specific temples were still circulated in the fourth century separate from Vitruvius'. These sources of knowledge would be involved in and directly relevant for the building of Constantinople.[23]

The investment was equally significant in respect of the imported technology coming directly from the old capital. The young and ambitious builders, architects and artisans were taking advantage of alluring salaries and exemptions from the taxes legislated by the Emperor if they were to join the building effort in Constantinople.[24] The exemplary Roman structures at the time that could have served as models would include the Basilica of Maxentius and Constantine, completed in 312. This was the largest edifice to be constructed, combining the features from Roman baths such as those of Diocletian.

In addition to this investment, treasures, such as the large amount of statuary that was shipped over from Rome and elsewhere, were the most direct and instant contribution to the making of the new capital. The lavish statuary marked imperial power and equipped the city with numerous significations. The central and changing role of the statuary will be addressed later on.

The configuration of the city space, its streets and its architecture

Constantinople made use of the existing city plan of Byzantium whose main features were left in place. The Emperor's intentions were to extend the city utilising the functioning elements. Constantine's architects had therefore retained the two main squares of the Graeco-Roman, largely Severan city: the Strategion (nearby modern Sirkeci station) and the Tetrastoon (to the south of

Fig. 5. Basilica of Maxentius and Constantine, early fourth century, Rome

Hagia Sophia) that were linked by the north-south street. The architects of the new capital also decided to extend the east to west colonnaded street, believed to be built by Severus, thus making it the main artery that came to be known as Mese. Constantine's own Forum, where the famous Porphyry Column stood, was sited just outside the ancient city walls on the axis to the Mese.[25]

Constantine's architects traced the outline of the new city over the old one, even if the former remained largely unbuilt and uninhabited. This meant that the principal street was projected to run straight from the Milion to the Capitol along a distance of 1850m. At the Capitol the Mese branched: one segment of it extended into the northwest past Constantine's mausoleum in the Church of the Holy Apostles, the other southwest to the Golden Gate of the Constantine walls. The only transversal north to south street that can be traced with a degree of certainty ran from the Golden Horn.[26]

The Mese was thus the first artery that was subsequently followed by a series of colonnaded streets in the manner of Greek *stoae* that generously adorned the city space. The city's monumental development was exemplified further in *emboloi* – small roads with colonnades and shops that led up to a central street. These, together with *Tetrastoon*, a columned porch around the courtyard, the Basilica, the Baths of Zeuxippos and the Hippodrome, were the main features in the Constantinian plan. The streets from the old plan were either completed or rebuilt, thus providing the new city centre with the relevant imperial institutions.

The old Tetrastoon was redesigned and dedicated to Constantine's mother Augusta Helena, and named Augusteion. The silver statue of Augusta was placed in the square.[27] The Augusteion's scale was grand: estimates range between 1,750 and 3,500 square metres. This large *chora* – like public space in the heart of the city was thus best suited for ceremonial public functions.[28] As such, the Augusteion remained the place of attraction, natural convergence and gathering.

As mentioned above, the city did not suddenly break from its pagan past; two temples (dedicated to Rhea/Kybele and to Tyche/Fortuna) were also erected by Constantine and his architects in this area.[29]

The liturgy, its spatial arrangement and the early churches

The Basilica of early Constantinople was inherited from the Severan period. It was initially designed as a rectangular peristyle court accommodating a public library, the university and the court of law. For Constantine, the change in liturgy was inevitable, due to the newly established authority of the Church whereby a

Fig. 8. The Serpent Column is an ancient bronze column at the Hippodrome of Constantinople, Istanbul. It was originally 8 m high and was part of an ancient Greek sacrificial tripod from Delphi, relocated by Constantine in 324

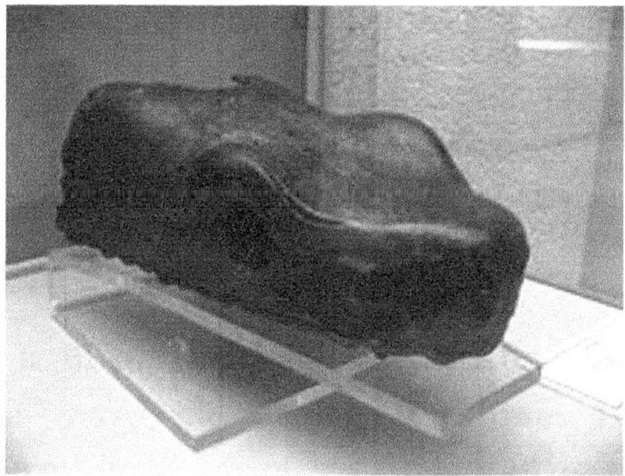

Fig. 8a One of the heads of the Serpent Column is today in the Istanbul Archaeological Museum. The serpent heads remained intact until the end of the 17th century

Fig. 9. Hippodrome of Constantinople as it is today. The Obelisk of Theodosius is in front and the one of Constantine at the back

permanent and unchangeable liturgy was required. Historians have argued that it was because Constantine viewed himself as God's vicar on earth that consequently God became seen as the Emperor of Heaven. Hence the liturgy became a ceremony performed before the Lord or before his representative, the Bishop. Krautheimer and Ćurčić describe it:

> the bishop, clad in garments of high magistrate, entered the church in solemn procession, preceded by the insignia of his official rank, candles and book. Flanked by his presbyters, he was seated on a throne, the *sella curulis* of a Roman official.[30]

It is important to remember that the basilica was the structure best suited for the new liturgy because it contained a big covered meeting hall of the tribunal. Here the magistrate and his assessors would sit on a podium next to a shrine that sheltered the effigy of the Emperor. Originally Roman justice was dispensed only in the presence of the Emperor (or his substitute, the effigy). By an extended analogy the priest did the same, and the arrangement became the *mise-en-scène* for Christian liturgy with the podium becoming an altar space.[31]

However, hardly anything remains of Constantine's church buildings in the new capital. In addition to the Severan basilica, the first Hagia Sophia and Hagia Irene were built, but were replaced in the sixth and the eighth centuries respectively. Hagia Irene reputedly stands on the site of a pre-Christian temple and is believed to be the first church in the capital built by Constantine's architects. Hagia Sophia, built next to the Emperor's palace, was later famously replaced by Justinian. The first Hagia Sophia was a large basilica with double aisle and galleries. It was short and wide, and had an atrium and perhaps a propylaeum. The edifice probably resembled the Basilica of the Holy Sepulchre in Jerusalem and was built with the expertise and technology similar to that applied to the Basilica of Maxentius and Constantine in Rome.

There are no traces of the fourth-century Church of the Holy Apostles, replaced in 536 by Justinian's church. According to Eusebius, the Church of the Holy Apostles rose in the centre of a wide courtyard, surrounded by meeting halls, baths and pools. It was designed on the basis of the cross. The ceiling was gilded and coffered, covering all four arms, while the walls were wrapped with marble. According to this source, a drum, well lit through bronze grilled windows, rose over the crossing, and was apparently surmounted by a conical roof. Below this drum stood the sarcophagus of Constantine, apparently flanked by piers inscribed to the Twelve Apostles. The sarcophagus stood within an enclosure where the liturgy was held at the altar. Thus the building was the mausoleum of the Emperor and a martyrium dedicated to the Apostles.[32] Over the years the central position of Constantine's sarcophagus became inappropriate, as the relics of the apostles were brought there in 356 to 357. The Emperor's remains were later removed into a separate, adjoining mausoleum of a traditional plan, circular and domed. Apostoleion, as it became known, was a martyrium, as were the Basilica at the Holy Sepulchre in Jerusalem, the Holy Nativity at Bethlehem and the tomb of St Peter.[33] In its plan the Church of the Holy Apostles was innovative. The martyrium, rather than being hidden underground or appended to the nave and aisles of a basilica as at Bethlehem, became the very core of the structure. Krautheimer and Ćurčić argue that a new type of martyrium has thus emerged, a self-sufficient structure centred on the focus of worship.

This kind of legacy by Constantine corresponds to his general goal for the adoration he was aiming to establish for both the Church and the Empire.

Subsequently, during the later fourth and early fifth centuries, we find many churches that have copied this arrangement, including the plan with its connotations of the True Cross, the dedication to the Apostles and the centrality of martyrdom.[34]

The impact of Constantine's Holy Apostles and other buildings is impossible to determine, as nothing of the palaces, colonnaded streets or public buildings attributed to Constantine has survived.

Modelling the Church, the Empire and the mores of the imperial life

Constantine believed that one of the imperfections of the old empire was the fact that the emperor was not sufficiently esteemed and cherished. For this reason, and in addition to his large-scale building project, he adopted the insignia of adoration on his personal clothing such as the diadem and the elaborate rich robes of the Asiatic monarchs.

This is not a minor point, since the roles of ornament and splendour that were deployed in the framing and representation of imperial power need to be acknowledged. Constantine and the supporters of his ideology of the new Christian state did not consider the robes to be simply luxuries of clothing as did wealthy Romans. In establishing the practices and ceremonies for the new religion, they embraced a different attitude drawn mainly from the Old and the New Testaments. Constantine's priests and courtiers understood the question of robes within the philosophy of the Scriptures. As in ancient Israel, the primacy of clothing had a metaphysical significance associated with the Hebrew concept of *chabod,* which means splendour, glory and honour, but also importance. Biblical tradition attributed the institution of priesthood to Aaron who was the one who wore the 'glorious garment' (*beged chabod*) (*Sirach 45.9*).[35] This association between robe and priesthood, between clothing and service to God, is embedded in the biblical tradition as God Himself 'clothed with honour and Majesty,/who coverest thyself with light as with a garment' (Psalm 104.12).[36]

Closely connected with God's garments is His dwelling place, His habitation – the Ark of the Tabernacle that Moses founded with Aaron's priesthood. Robes and homes come together for a priest, and the Ark was built at the same time as the priestly robes were made (*Exodus* 39). Furthermore, Solomon's legendary construction of the Temple represented the crowning achievement of this outlook: the House of God was associated with His *chabod,* with his glory.[37]

There are scholarly works on the parallels between the project of Constantine's and Solomon's construction of the Temple,[38] in particular in relation to Constantine's undertakings in Jerusalem.[39] Krautheimer and Ćurčić remind us that, layman though he was, and baptized probably only on his deathbed, Constantine considered himself not to be Solomon but 'the thirteenth Apostle, Christ's vicar on earth – an aspect of the Divinity incarnate, the Invincible Sun, the Sear of Justice'.[40] Constantine believed that he had been divinely appointed to lead Christ's Church to victory and to preside in person at Church Councils that he had convened in Nicea in 325. He pressed for the settling of dogmatic controversies, and used the machinery of government to implement decisions of the Councils. Constantine employed the unlimited means of the imperial power to raise the standing of the Church. By the time of his death in 337 this well-constructed interpenetration of ecclesiastical and imperial power had been achieved.[41]

The historical significance of the First Nicean Council was in being the earliest to attain consensus in the Church through an assembly representing all of Christendom.[42] In pursuing his project, Constantine had included the adoption of the Old Testament while reorganising the court on a thoroughly Eastern model. His oriental-style court consisted of officials who surrounded the Emperor and were raised to the rank of nobility.[43] The establishment of the rank of nobles with their privileges and duties was of strategic importance to the longevity of the Eastern Roman Empire.

The legacy of employing the nobility for the benefit of the state was subsequently adopted by many courts in Europe. The chief officer of the court was the grand chamberlain who was in charge of the imperial palace. The chancellor had a duty of supervision of the court officials. He also had to receive foreign ambassadors (an institution that had been invented under the Byzantine Empire).[44] The quaestor drew up and issued the imperial edicts while the treasurer-general had to control the public revenues. The master of the privy purse had to manage the Emperor's private estate and the two commanders of the bodyguard.

While the concept of responsibility that comes with high rank (*noblesse oblige*) had already existed during the time of Homer, the *topos* had here reinstated itself within the Christian tradition.[45] In the Gospel of Luke, Jesus endorses the concept by saying, 'From everyone to whom much has been given, much will be required; and from the one to whom much has been entrusted, even more will be demanded' (Luke 12.48). Constantine may have been inspired by the Gospels and he may have felt that it was his duty to put into practice the suggestion from Luke and other evangelists.

The city and its mythic legacy

The Trojan Homero/Virgilian connection is not accidental either. The correlation is likely because the new capital was peculiarly situated in the proximity of the ancient city of Troy, saturated with the myths of Aeneas and the narratives of the Graeco-Roman past.[46]

In this context, the gesture of bringing back to Asia Minor the legendary Palladium – a wooden statue (*xoanon*) of Athena Pallas, allegedly stolen by Odysseus and Diomedes from the citadel of Troy and taken to the future city of Rome by Aeneas – is a striking parallel. It opens up a space for the hypothesis that Constantine was not simply going east, but *returning* to the East. The idea of home-coming is the stronger narrative compared to the idea of relocation. Following this logic, Constantine can be seen as the emperor who brought the people of Rome back to their legendary roots in Asia Minor.

The fact that he chose to place the mythic Palladium under his own celebrated Porphyry Column in his forum suggests the importance this myth had for Constantine personally. The actuality that it was subsequently ravaged, probably by crusaders in 1204, suggests that the struggle for legitimacy over this mythic ancestry had continued for centuries after the presumed Palladium's return by Constantine.

Constantinople was therefore a uniquely complex and multifaceted urban and imperial entity. It drew from the myths, arts, knowledge and technology of the ancient Greeks and Romans, incorporating the principles of their achievements within what was projected to be the heart of the Christian Empire. In doing so, the city embodied the old traditions in a novel way believed to be suitable for the new capital.

Constantinople never gave up on its symbolic and religious traditions either, as the saga of the wooden *xoanon* and numerous other statues testify. The religious buildings of all denominations, be it the temples to Kybele, Fortuna, Hagia Sophia or the Hagia Irene, were part of a large imperial building campaign involving both pagans and Christians. In this respect Constantine's city crucially established Christianity not as a conquering force but as one religion, albeit dominant, among many.[47]

The temples and the churches were both positioned in the city centre although detached from the Augusteion and from each other. This arrangement was meant to provide for a variety of religious buildings and sacred spaces, as well as for their safe detachment from the flux of urban life and from each other. The precarious balance was struck by the careful disposition of the series of discrete temples, monuments and their surrounding precincts.[48]

Fig. 7. Nike and a Warrior with Palladium, Louvre, Paris

Constantinople therefore provided a ground and created the space within which the Emperor's vision about religious freedom could come to life following the 313 Edict of Milan that was the official guarantee and the inspiration for these developments. Without the actual conditions provided on the site of Constantinople, the legislation might not have gained its lasting credibility.

The accommodation of different ethnicities and religious cultures was an important part of Constantine's plan. Decisively, the common formal features for all were found in the architectural language of Late Antiquity. All spaces of the capital were determined by using this language that included rich marble towering columns, arches, complex brickwork structures, and a variety of vaults and domes – all prime features of Roman imperial architecture. Typically this language included another central element in the creation of public spaces: the statuary.

This style of building did not remain intact for long. New concerns emerged as both social and private life gradually moved inward. The fact that churches such as Hagia Irene and Hagia Sophia were later rebuilt in a different manner suggests that their ancient form was no longer considered adequate. Above all

Fig. 6. Kybele Rhea from Nicaea (Bithynia), Istanbul Archaeological Museum

this applied to interiors that were increasingly used for meditation and prayer. As such they required a certain design and appearance that could correspond to the heavenly landscape of Christianity – a particular quality that architects of the Justinian era strived to capture.

The statuary, its role, prestige and subsequent demise

From its beginnings in the fourth century the city of Constantinople contained a great number of ancient statuary previously not seen in other medieval cities. This has been referred to by a number of sources from Zosimus onwards. Recently the statuary of Constantinople was studied and addressed by Sarah Bassett.[49] Bassett claims that the creation of the collection of effigies was consciously planned and conceived by the Emperor and his advisers. She argues the point with inspirational eloquence; the attention to statuary was significant at the time of Constantine, and Bassett's claim remains a strong possibility.

However, Bassett fails to present final, conclusive evidence about the statuary being brought into the city on the Bosporus as part of this preconceived plan.

The acquired effigies of Constantinople have included the pre-fourth-century antiquities that were transported from the cities and sanctuaries of the Roman Empire to the newly founded capital. Believed to be organized in a series of related groupings spread throughout the city's public spaces, the sculptures of antiquity were apparently brought in, in an attempt to create a 'civic identity' for the new city. As such, they were showing the city's history, the achievements of its founder and the magnificence of the Roman Empire.

In doing so, these instantly produced public spaces aimed at showing off their prestige and to explain their unique urban pre-eminence. In this process the displacement and repositioning of the statuary, I would argue, demonstrate, confirm and follow the logic of the returned Palladium placed under Constantine's column.

Fig. 10. Group of statues now based in the Archaeological Museum in Istanbul, II century AD, Appollo kitharoidos is presented centrally with the instrument, the muses are around him

Fig. 11. Appollo kitharoidos

Memory and the role of statuary and *loci* in rhetoric

The role of statuary within the city needs to be reviewed further. In doing so I shall refer to two separate theoretical sources and point out their relevance for an enhanced understanding of the role of statuary in urban space. One

Fig. 12. Appollo kitharoidos detail

approach is relevant for our comprehension with regard to statues and memory; the other is instrumental to the overall insight into the emergence of statuary in early antiquity and its role for the so-called bicameral mind.

There is little dilemma about the fact that statuary has been highly important in Antiquity. Effigies were often part of buildings, while they were equally indispensable as free-standing compositional items that articulated the quality of public spaces in ancient cities. The development of architecture and of sculpture is closely and inextricably linked, sometimes symbiotic and at other times a contest. The statuary was traditionally made for deities such as patrons of the city/polis, or for illustrious men – the practice was more associated with the Roman period. The effigy would be placed in the core of the city in order to address the sacred precinct important either for worshipping the divine or for paying respect to the ancestors and city founders. The statuary of *lupa* with Romulus and Remus adorned ancient Rome at every corner, as did the statues of Constantine and his mother Helena in Constantinople. The public spaces with dedicated sculptures were the places of gathering and worship, especially during the days of the calendar when communities came together and evoked the ancestral past. The mechanism of how this phenomenon actually functioned with regard to memory could be best described by reference to the work of

Frances Yates.[50] By looking at her text that explored the relevant ancient sources, it is possible to extrapolate Yates' ideas beyond the places of the house, as she had it, and to extend them into the urban context.

In Antiquity, Yates argues, memory was understood as the guardian of all knowledge. It was seen as the treasure house of inventions and its overall keeper, a function even more significant prior to the invention of the institution of the library.[51] The art of memory centred on the description of the artificial memory outlining its bi-partite spatial structure containing places or backgrounds (*locis*) upon which the images (*imaginibus*) are set and memorized. Yates argues that the character of the images and that of the backgrounds must differ and be distinguishable and clearly visible. A well-outlined, distinct and balanced composition is crucial for maintaining its content within memory.[52]

Following this line of reasoning about images placed upon the background of houses, it could be extrapolated that the statuary may have played an analogous role as memorable images in the city, where the public squares acted as backgrounds.[53] In this context, especially memorable would be those statues that are conspicuous and that adhere long in our minds such as objects of exceptional history, size, distinction, beauty, or even exceptional ugliness. The statuaries collected for the New Rome would have fulfilled these requirements, because they were as a rule distinct for their splendour, provenance and high value. This would suggest that by means of their presence the statues were able to trigger memories related to the history of the Graeco-Roman world from whose regions they originated. Such was the role of the Serpent Column brought from Delphi.

Furthermore, we need to consider not only the Palladium and the ancient statuary, but equally so the Christian relics. The documented travels by Constantine's mother Helena into the Holy Land and subsequent donations of the relics she brought back, including parts of the wooden cross of Christ and the relics of the Apostles, are of relevance here. The ancient statues and Christian relics housed within the Constantinopolitan churches were essential for the new capital, as they provided the sites in the city space where memory could be exercised. The nature of this mechanism of 'con-memoration' was linked to the state of mind that was shaped in rituals, speeches and acts of dedication, rather than in creating archives.

The Emperor's urban project had therefore included and most probably planned for the functioning of memory with the main roles being given to the effigy, to the relics housed in churches and to the overall configuration of the city space, the latter derived as the sum of layers of the newly positioned urban elements superimposed upon the Severan grid.

Even if only intuitively, Constantine and his architects knew that the old Rome could not be right for the new state of mind, as it was saturated with its own significant places and its distinctive configuration embedded in the people's psyche. Constantine's *grand projet* on the Bosporus included a careful rewriting of history and laying down conditions for the future. For the spatial inscriptions of this project the Emperor required a less inundated urban context.

The role of statuary in the urban setting of the New Rome was therefore essential from the outset. On the level of cultural history it provides a significant marker in the process of the development of human consciousness. This role of effigy has not often been considered within wider philosophical and epistemological context as it has usually been appreciated for its aesthetic and representational values. In order to highlight the epistemological role further I shall refer to the works of scholars who have maintained a profound interest and theoretical focus in this respect.

The emergence of the new consciousness

The statuary was revered because it was believed that effigy had certain properties for the human psyche of which the named art of memory could be just a trace. In that sense, where does the statuary of the new imperial capital stand in this process?

We shall briefly look at the selected texts that refer to both: the history of the human mind and the history of sculpture. The relevant texts include a book by the American psychologist Julian Jaynes, who worked within this field in the1970s, and of the contemporary theorist Iain McGilchrist. Jaynes defined the emergence of consciousness in his highly speculative book about early Mesopotamian statuary and the bicameral mind.[54] Thirty years later McGilchrist elaborated on the divided brain and the making of the Western World in his seminal book comprising decades of his research.[55]

Jaynes argues that the ancients did not always possess the power of intro-spective thinking; instead, they probably heard hallucinatory voices coming from the effigies, which they interpreted as those of their gods, king or chief. This interpretation points towards the origins of statuary as auditory, i.e. the effigies were not only looked at but listened to. In the course of the development of Western culture, the auditory aspect has gradually been lost as the reliance on vision overwhelmingly took over. He argues the American psychologist argues that the change from the mode of thinking (which he called the bicameral mind) to consciousness (interpreted as the self-identification of interior mental states) occurred over a period of centuries about 3,000 years ago and was due to the development of metaphorical language and the emergence of writing.

Jaynes relates this phenomenon to the Mycenaean Greeks and uses Homer's *Iliad* as an example where the main characters act in response to the voices they hear (usually from their gods). Jaynes argues that the process of transformation of the human mind that followed took centuries. This implies that a large part of Antiquity was dominated by this underlying conversion of human consciousness. Mesopotamian, Egyptian, Greek and Roman statuary would therefore be implicated in this process.

According to Jaynes, voices and the bicameral mind were gradually ceasing to function so that in Late Antiquity the voices coming from statues gradually unfolded, transformed and flattened into another category: writing. Due to the invention and the practice of writing, the role of the auditory voice became replaced by the visual sign. From then onwards human consciousness that was previously tuned to speech and hearing became more adjusted to writing, signs and images. Consequently, the art of rhetoric that was concurrent to speeches, symposia and auditory functions was modified for the visual usage. Within this economy of transformation, the role of statuary was pivotal as it embodied (or was believed to embody) both the fading voices and the visual properties that were gradually gaining in prevalence. This phenomenon may explain why antiquity paid so much attention to the statuary and applied such skills into their making.

Ancient statuary was therefore not just representing the status of and giving legitimacy to the city. The effigy was profoundly important for the minds and understanding of the citizens. The statues were addressing people's knowledge of the world and of themselves (*gnothi seauton*).[56] In that sense the striving towards naturalism and liveliness that is evident in the progress and maturity of the ancient statuary were most probably attempts to reach out to the voices that were already vanishing during Late Antiquity.

This explanation may be instrumental in understanding why the subsequent early Christian direction towards the abstraction in sculpture and arts in general could be interpreted not as inferior or lacking in liveliness, but rather as a mark of the newly found self-confidence coming from within. The new faith in its confidence did not need to reach out to the voices of the effigy as it was finding pronouncements from within oneself, from within the subject. In doing so, as it has been noted, early Christianity established and affirmed the category of the subject.

This strategically important turn inward that would mark the lives of individuals within Western culture for centuries was part of the formation of the consciousness that is based on self-identification with interior mental processes. The evidence from both Homeric epic and early drama testifies that this was not always the case. The metamorphosis that occurred is consistent with the emerging rhetorical categories of Late Antiquity concerned with the interpretation of the statuary – the notion of *ekphrasis* being central. Through *ekphrasis*, the writers disclosed the details of the emotions and intellectual experience in observation and contemplation of the individual or groups of statuary.

Historians Cyril Mango and Sarah Bassett have argued that as a result of *ekphrasis* the individual passages in early medieval texts are often 'long on interpretation and short on documentation'.[57] While this is an understandable claim, this condition is not to be seen as a drawback or a pitiful lack of evidence as these authors seem to imply. Rather, it could be understood as positive evidence about the state of consciousness at the time.[58] This state of consciousness was less concerned with the physical materiality of the statuary (proportions, colour, quality of the stone, etc.) and more with the effects it was having upon the mind of the observer. The experience that evokes perceptions, thoughts and feelings in relation to past events was what the effigies were meant to trigger and convey.

In doing so the statues mattered because they were able to make a link to both the perceptive and associative knowledge that formed the ancient human psyche. We have lost the access to that level of perceptive knowledge whose traces the ancient statues still embodied as the essential link to the knowledge of the past. This connection was the reason why Constantine embarked upon the great project of the removal of effigies not simply to adorn the new capital. It was probably still possible and meaningful at the time to try to reach out towards the statues' hidden voices. Today we have lost the ability to recognize these traces that Jaynes struggled to rejuvenate and recall.

The minds of the ancients sensed, understood and operated within this delicate condition; because it mattered to them profoundly, the weighty statues were repeatedly shipped around the Mediterranean. From Egypt to Greece, around the Roman World and back, many of the sculptures ended up in the New Rome not to simply adorn the new capital, but to stand as pointers of the experiences and of the knowledge related to the Mediterranean historical and mythic past. The search for these effects of the statuary most probably achieved its climax here in the city on the Bosporus in the fourth century.

The context of the gradual demise of sculpture is marked by the rise and institutionalization of writing, contributing to the emerging category of literature. When the religion based on scripture became finally officially established by Constantine, there was very little left for statuary to do, in an active sense.

Its downfall as the epistemological category was inevitable in a context where letters and literature steadily took over the tasks of memory and rhetoric, and, consequently, the practices of education, arts and crucially, religion.[59]

By the fifth and sixth centuries, the statuary in Constantinople became futile – an ornament of the past – clunky, impractical and useless. At the same time, large churches with impressive interiors were built and the Imperial Library and the Scriptorium flourished. Constructed during the reign of Constantine's heir to the throne Constantius II (AD 337–361), the library was believed to have housed approximately 100,000 volumes of ancient texts.[60] This explains why the practice of collecting statues, having continued to exist for some time after Constantine, ceased soon after. In the sixth century, during the reign of Justinian, the practice of reusing transported effigies had disappeared. The practice of writing chronicles took over. The nature of public life also changed. Importantly, it became more dependent upon reading, libraries and interior spaces such as palaces and monasteries where the learned congregated to read and interpret texts. The urban spaces of Constantinople turned inward as the statue gave way to the book and public squares gave way to salons, while temple precincts were replaced by richly vaulted and complexly domed church spaces.

This condition often raised the question about the so-called 'closing of the mind' that has traditionally been referred to by historians in relation to Late Antiquity. This belief is gradually losing its former authority in light of recent historical work, as the 'closing of the public life' need not necessarily be interpreted as the 'closing of the mind'.[61]

Today, Constantinopolitan scholarship on arts and architecture is again lively because of the need to address the missing part that art history and its powerful medium Renaissance Studies has traditionally tended to undermine: the wider cultural and epistemological character of Byzantine arts and architecture exemplified in its pivotal role in providing the continuity and transformation of ancient experiences and knowledge. Significantly, this transmission has occurred in the libraries, churches, monasteries and scriptoria of Constantinople, where scholars who lived in this adorned city reinterpreted the events of classical antiquity and wrote about their own experiences. While this process is a wider phenomenon not restricted to the capital, it is important to recognize both the underlining continuity and the transformation of the ancient knowledge that was secured via the arts and architecture of Constantinople.[62]

The city and its artefacts have acted both as storage and props for the human psyche, its memory and its overall workings. In this sense the urban project of making the new capital was truly grand and multifaceted. Unfortunately, Constantinople's unrivalled medieval influence and supremacy was in part the reason why it was subjected to destruction. The ancient capital presented the most attractive and rich target for both the crusaders in 1204 and the Ottomans in 1453. Many small artefacts looted, often modelled on ancient statuary, are today on display in various museums across Europe.

With regard to the general question about the intercultural transmission in Late Antiquity and the Middle Ages, it is up to every generation of scholars to discover how deep they are prepared to dig into the subject. As always, this is decided in relation to the present and current views of the future. As one twentieth-century architectural historian has noticed, every analysis seeks only to measure the effects it sets in motion in order to change itself according to the intervening transformations.[63] The certainties that history presents could be read as expressions of repressions. 'True history' is not that which presents itself with indisputable 'proofs' but that which recognizes its own limits and its arbitrariness. The examples of fragments, failed works and unrealized attempts raise issues traditionally suppressed by the completeness of works that have attained seminal status. Errors, demises and erasures often speak more clearly about the difficulties of particular utopias than the grandest of celebrated monuments.

Notes

1   The source that is referred to is the seminal work by Riegl, Alois. *Historical Grammar of the Visual Arts*, trans. Jacqueline Jung. New York: Zone Books, 2004; in addition, Curtius, Ernest Robert. *European Literature and the Latin Middle Ages*. Princeton, NJ: Princeton University Press, 1991, still presents a good and reliable twentieth-century synthesis of the work undertaken by previous generations of scholars. Further sources: Brown, Peter. *The Body and Society, Men, Women and Sexual Renunciation in Early Christianity*. New York: Columbia University Press, 1988; Jacques Le Goff's work on the body in the Middle Ages. In Le Goff, Jacques. 'Head or Heart? The Political Use of Body Metaphors in the Middle Ages', trans. Patricia Ranum. *Fragments for a History of the Human Body*, Part Three. New York: Zone Books, 1989, pp. 13–26; Foucault, Michel. *The History of Sexuality*, Vol. 2, *The Use of Pleasure*, trans. Robert Hurley. London: Penguin Books, 1987, *The History of Sexuality*, Vol. 3, *The Care of the Self*, trans. Robert Hurley. London: Penguin Books, 1990.

2   L'Orange, Hans Peter. *Art Forms and Civic Life in the Late Roman Empire*. Princeton, NJ: Princeton University Press, 1971.

3   Krautheimer, Richard and Ćurčić, Slobodan. *Early Christian and Byzantine Architecture*. London: Penguin Books, 1986.

4   Mango states that we can recall and imagine the Istanbul of the 1780s in Melling's and Choiseul-Gouffier's albums and we can possibly do the same with respect to Istanbul of Suleyman the Magnificent as captured by Melchior Lorich (Lorck) in the second half of the sixteenth century. Mango, Cyril. *Studies on Constantinople*. Aldershot: Ashgate Publishing, 1993. Preface.

5   In this context Mango mentions the work of Gilbert Dagron. See Dagron. *Naissance d'une capital*. Paris: Bibliothèque byzantine, Études 7, 1974.

6   Before the battle at Milvian Bridge near Rome, Constantine had a legendary vision of the cross revealed to him: 'this is the sign under which you will win.' This scene, known as 'in hoc signo vinces', has been depicted in the *Stanze di Raffaello*, 1520, in the Vatican, by Giulio Romano, who was an assistant to Rafael at the time. It also exists as statuary by Bernini (1670) currently also at the Vatican.

7   The Edict of Milan states:

> When I, Constantine Augustus, as well as I, Licinius Augustus, fortunately met near Mediolanurn (Milan), and were considering everything that pertained to the public welfare and security, we thought, among other things which we saw would be for the good of many, those regulations pertaining to the reverence of the Divinity ought certainly to be made first, so that we might grant to the Christians and others full authority to observe that religion which each preferred; whence any Divinity whatsoever in the seat of the heavens may be propitious and kindly disposed to us and all who are placed under our rule. And thus by this wholesome counsel and most upright provision we thought to arrange that no one whatsoever should be denied the opportunity to give his heart to the observance of the Christian religion, of that religion which he should think best for himself, so that the Supreme Deity, to whose worship we freely yield our hearts may show in all things His usual favour and benevolence. Therefore, your Worship should know that it has pleased us to remove all conditions whatsoever, which were in the rescripts formerly given to you officially, concerning the Christians and now any one of these who wishes to observe Christian religion may do so freely and openly, without molestation.

From Lactantius, *De Mort. Pers.*, ch. 48. opera, ed. 0.F. Fritzsche, II, p. 288 sq. (Bibl Patr. Ecc. Lat. XI). Department of History: *Translations and Reprints from the Original Sources of European History*, Vol. 4, pp. 1, 28–30.

8   Morey, William C. *Outlines of Roman History*. New York, Cincinnati, OH, and Chicago, IL: American Book Company, 1901. Morey based his arguments on reading Eutropius, an Ancient Roman pagan historian of the latter half of the fourth century. Eutropius held the office of secretary (*magister memoriae*) at

Constantinople, accompanied the Emperor Julian (361–363) on his expedition against the Persians (363), and was alive during the reign of Valens (364–378), to whom he dedicates his *Breviarium historiae Romanae*.

9　Chron. Paschale I, 527–530. Mango, Cyril. *The Art of Byzantine Empire 312–1453 Sources and Documents*. Toronto: University of Toronto Press and Medieval Academy of America, 1986, p. 7.

10　For more historical references on Constantinople see: Ostrogorski, Georgije. *History of the Byzantine State*. New Brunswick, NJ: Rutger University Press, 1986; Mango, Cyril. *Le développement urbain de Constantinople (Ive–VIIe siecles)*, 2nd edn. Études de topographie Byzantine, I–II, Paris, 1990; Mango, Cyril. *Studies on Constantinople*. Aldershot: Ashgate Publishing, 1993; Mango, Cyril. 'The Triumphal Way of Constantinople and the Golden Gate'. *Dumbarton Oaks Papers* 54 (2000): 173–188; Mango, Cyril and Dagron, Gilbert (eds). *Constantinople and its Hinterland*. Aldershot: Ashgate Publishing, 1995. The recent book by Bassett, Sarah. *The Urban Image of Late Antique Constantinople*. Cambridge: Cambridge University Press, 2004, was inspirational and instructive.

11　Zosimus. See Mango, *Studies on Constantinople*, op. cit., p. 119.

12　For instance, large-scale aqueducts of a kind built in Segovia (second century AD), Spain and Nimes France (first century AD).

13　Mango, *The Art of Byzantine Empire*, op. cit., and Mango, Cyril. *Byzantium: The Empire of New Rome*. New York: Charles Scrivener's, 1980, p. 7. n24.

14　For historical sources on Constantinople, see Gilles, Pierre. *De Bosphoro Thracio libri tres De topographia Constantinopoleos*. Lyon, 1561; Leiden, 1632 and 1635; and Gilles, Pierre. *De topographia Constantinopoleos et de illius antiquitatibus libri quatuor*. Lyon, 1561; Leiden, 1661. The latter is Gilles' major work and there are subsequent eighteenth-century Venetian editions with enriched illustration.

15　Chron. Paschale I, 527–530. See in Mango, *The Art of Byzantine Empire*, op. cit., p. 7.

16　The notion of the 'centre' is important for Christians. It has a strong theological relevance as the centre emanates over the whole and holy (note the same origin of the two terms). I am grateful to my student Lindy Weston who has constantly pointed this out in his own work.

17　See Mango, 'The Development of Constantinople as an Urban Centre', in *Studies on Constantinople*, op. cit., pp. 117–36.

18　Curtius, *European Literature*, op. cit., p. 36. The history of European educational institutions could be traced back to the sophist Hippias of Elis, a contemporary of Socrates. He was regarded as the founder of the pedagogical system, whereby a core study was related to various fields of general knowledge (in Greek).

19　Seneca's *Epistle 88* was the *locus classicus* about the arts and education. Seneca discussed the 'artes liberales' and the 'studia liberalia' – both parts of the *egknklios paideia*. These arts were called 'liberal' because they were worthy of free men. Their purpose was not the achievement of material wealth. Painting, sculpture and other manual arts (*artes mechanicae*) were excluded, while music, being a mathematical subject, had a secured place in the circle of the liberal arts. It could be argued that, by the end of Antiquity, the liberal arts had become the sole authority on learning. Their number had been fixed at seven, and they were arranged in a sequence, which was kept throughout the Middle Ages: grammar, rhetoric, dialectic (the *trivium*), arithmetic, geometry, music, astronomy (*quadrivium*), Curtius, p. 37.

20   Two dominant theories on the subject of the *artes* are: the patristic (of the early Church Fathers), and the secular-scholastic. In Constantinople they have existed in parallel. They are not always easily separable, but they differ in their origin. Philo (20 BC–AD 50), a Jewish scholar from Alexandria, had already added Greek learning and philosophy to his Jewish interpretation of the Holy Scriptures, which he did by transforming the Hellenic sages into pupils of Moses. The Christian apologists of the second century, particularly Justin, took over the same idea and handed it down to the theologians of the Alexandrian school. Thus Clement of Alexandria (Titus Flavius Clemens, *c.* 150 BC–*c.* AD 215) drew the conclusion that Greek learning was established by God and that Christians needed it in order to understand the Scriptures. The Latin fathers were divided on the subject. Ambrose of Milan (333–397) knew Greek philosophy but opposed it.

21   As argued by Riegl in *Late Roman Art Industry,* op. cit. – the fourth and fifth century AD are the least covered periods in the history of arts and architecture.

22   Vitruvius. *The Ten Books On Architecture*, trans. Morris Hicky Morgan. London: Dover Publications, 1960. Vitruvius was possibly *praefectus fabrum* officer in charge of artisans.

23   Vitruvius refers to Pytheos among others, a celebrated architect of the temple of Minerva in Priene in Asia Minor, not too distant from Constantinople. In his *Commentaries* Pytheos asserts that architects need to be accomplished in all sciences and arts even if they cannot reach perfection in each of them (Book 1, 12–17). Due to the influence of Vitruvius' treatise and its later dissemination these ideas have subsequently spread into most European languages and architectural theories. See Vitruvius, *The Ten Books On Architecture*, op. cit.

24   Mango, *The Art of Byzantine Empire*, op. cit.

25   Mango, *Studies on Constantinople*, op. cit., p. 123.

26   op. cit., p. 123.

27   St Helena, as she is known, has been credited for being the first pilgrim to Jerusalem. Upon her return she brought back the parts of the cross on which Christ was martyred, according to legends.

28   *Chora* is a (womblike) receptacle that can hold all and receive all. The concept has been discussed by Plato in *Timaeus* (49–53) in *The Collected Dialogues*, edited by

E. Hamilton and Huntington Cairns. Bollingen Series. Princeton, NJ: Princeton University Press, 1989, and Derrida in 'Point de Folie – Maintenant l' architecture'. *AA Files*, No. 12. London: Architectural Association, 1986.

29 Zosimus, 'The Building of Constantinople', II, 30–31, in Pollitt. *The Art of Rome 753 BC–337 AD*, 212–213. Cambridge: Cambridge University Press, 1983.

30 Krautheimer and Ćurčić, op. cit., p. 40.

31 Ibid., p. 42.

32 Eusebius, *The Life of the Blessed Emperor Constantine*, IV, 15, translation, revised by Ernest Cushing Richardson, http://www.fordham.edu/halsall/basis/vita-constantine.asp.

33 Krautheimer and Ćurčić, op. cit., p. 69.

34 The copies of this arrangement are found at Milan, Ravenna, Ephesus, Antioch, at Gaza and Sichem. The Apostoleion has also made an indirect impact on the formation of basilicas with cross-transepts. The types of plan differ in the East and West; in the East the four arms radiate from the central core, while in the West two lateral arms appear from the longitudinal nave. Krautheimer and Ćurčić, op. cit. p. 70.

35 Perniola, Mario. 'Between Clothing and Nudity'. In *Fragments for the History of Human Body*, New York: Zone Books, 1989, p. 237.

36 The character of the priestly robe can be represented only by reference to the transcendent, which is essentially 'clothed'; in all its relations with human beings it always veils, covers or clothes its power, because one cannot bear the direct sight of God. God said to Moses, 'you cannot see my face: for man shall not see me and live' (*Exodus* 33.20). Perniola, op. cit., p. 238.

37 Perniola, op. cit., p. 238.

38 For example, when discussing the appropriateness of celebrating the *Encaenia*, Michael A. Fraser writes:

> September 13 was a particularly appropriate day for the Encaenia. Not simply because it coincided with the anniversary of Constantine's victory over Licinius and his honouring of the heavenly sign but because that day was also one of a wider theological significance. The Martyrium basilica (built by Constantine) is described by Eusebius as the New Jerusalem, predicted by the prophets of old, namely Ezekiel. The implication, in accrediting Constantine with the building of a New Jerusalem, is that a new Solomon has also arisen. Less than fifty years later the pilgrim Egeria will write that the date of the Encaenia was also the day on which Solomon dedicated the temple. The feast of Solomon's dedication commenced on the 10th day of Tishri, the day of atonement, and ended with the feast of Tabernacles. The feast of the Encaenia occurs in this very same season. According to a software application which calculates the Jewish feasts for any given year, in 335 AD the 10th day of Tishri fell on Saturday 13th September. 'Constantine and the Encaenia'. *Studia Patristica*, 39, ed. Livingston.

39   This project needs to be differentiated from the myth about the 'Donation of Constantine', a forged Roman imperial decree by which the Emperor Constantine supposedly transferred authority over Rome and the western part of the Roman Empire to the Pope. The Western Church has maintained this forgery as truth for centuries, not exposing it fully even after the proof by Lorenzo Valla in the fifteenth century. This account of forgery does not necessarily contradict the account about Constantine bringing the columns to Rome. Constantine apparently brought a set of columns to Rome and gave them to the original St Peter's Basilica. *The Donation of Constantine*, a painting from Raphael's studio, shows these columns in their original location. According to tradition, these columns came from the 'Temple of Solomon', built in the tenth century BC. The columns, now considered to have been made in the second century AD, became known as 'Solomonic'. Constantine is indeed recorded as having brought them from Greece. If these columns really were from one of the temples in Jerusalem, the spiral pattern may have represented the oak tree which was the first Ark of the Covenant, mentioned in Joshua 24:26. The columns have twist-fluting sections.

40   Krautheimer and Ćurčić, op. cit. p. 39.

41   Ibid. p. 39.

42   'Council of Nicaea' in *Encyclopædia Britannica*. Its achievements included the agreements about the relationship of Jesus to God the Father, the construction of the Nicene Creed, settling the calculation of the date of Easter, and the spread and implementation of the early canon. *Encyclopaedia Britannica*, 1911. http://www.1911encyclopedia.org/Council of Nicaea (retrieved 14 March 2010).

43   This assertion is supported by Riegl, Alois. *Spätrömische Kunstindustrie – Late Roman Art Industry,* trans. Rolf Winkes. Rome: Bretschneider, 1985; and in Riegl, Alois. *Historical Grammar of Visual Arts*, op. cit., pp. 69–70.

44   On the emergence of diplomacy in Constantinople, see Graziano, Vittorio. *Ambasciate d'Italia in Turchia*. Catania: Mediterraneum, 1994, pp. 8–42.

45   Homer, *Iliad,* book XII. Sarpedon delivers a well-known *noblesse oblige* speech before attacking the Argive ramparts.

46   *Aeneid,* by Virgil, an epic poem about Æneas of Troy; it is composed in the traditional Homeric metre of hexameters. Written during the last ten years of the poet's life (29–19 BC), it celebrates Roman moral values in the role of its Trojan hero Æneas, who was destined to found a new city in Italy – Rome.

47   Other examples of non-Christian edifices include Constantine building the Triumphal Arch in Rome dedicated to pagan gods, etc.

48   According to historical evidence and its subsequent interpretation, the population of the Byzantine Empire consisted of diverse peoples. Towards the end of the second century AD the various nations under Roman rule tended to assert their individuality. Mango argues that in the time of Justinian, approximately 560,

over 70 languages were spoken inside the capital and throughout the Empire. However, it would have sufficed to know only two languages, namely Greek and Latin, to be able to travel throughout the entire country. The boundaries of the respective languages were often not sharply drawn. It may be argued however that the linguistic boundary ran through the Balkan peninsula along an east–west line; while south of the Mediterranean it divided Libya from Tripolitania. The Balkan lands had a mixed population, but the western half of the Empire was mainly Latin speaking and the eastern half was mainly Greek speaking. These two were the languages of administration and culture, and almost all educated people in the East spoke Greek, just as all educated people in the West spoke Latin. Constantinople and its surroundings were therefore administered in Greek, as we observe in the city and on its monuments. Mango. *Byzantium: The Empire of New Rome*. New York: Charles Scrivener's, 1980, p. 13.

49   Bassett, op. cit., p. 1.

50   Francis Yates explains the subject by referring to the three main antique sources: *Ad Herennium* by an anonymous writer (sometimes attributed to Cicero); *Ad Herennium Libri IV. De ratione dicendi*. The Loeb Classical Library, ed. T. E. Page, with the English translation by Harry Caplan. Cambridge MA, and London: William Heinemann and Harvard University Press, 1954. The second source is Cicero, Marco Tullius. *De oratore,* trans. W. Sutton and H. Rackham, *Readings in Classical Rhetoric*, ed. Thomas W. Benson and Michael H. Prosser. Davis, CA: Hermagoras Press, 1988. The third source is Quintillian, Marcus Fabius. *Institutio Oratoria,* trans. H.E. Butler. Loeb Classical Library. Cambridge, MA: Harvard University Press, 1920; *Ad Herennium* is the key text as the other two assume that the reader is already familiar with the artificial memory. Yates, Frances A. *The Art of Memory*. Chicago, IL: Chicago University Press, 1966, p. 1.

51   *Ad Herennium*, 207. The text distinguishes two kinds of memory, one natural, and the other the product of art. The natural memory is that memory which is embedded in our minds, born simultaneously with thought. The artificial memory is that memory which is strengthened by a kind of training and system of discipline … It is neither more nor less true in this instance than in the other.

52   *Ad Herennium,* 209.

53   *Ad Herennium* dates from the second decade of the first century BC. Addressed to Gaius Herennius, it takes on the subject of Hellenistic rhetorical teachings. It divides the art of rhetoric into four parts: (1) Invention (*inventio*); (2) Disposition (*dispositio*); (3) Delivery (*elocutio*); (4) Memory (*memoria*), and (5) Style (*pronuntiatio*).

54   Julian Jaynes (1920–97) was an American psychologist, best known for his book *The Origin of Consciousness in the Breakdown of the Bicameral Mind*. London: Allen Lane, 1976. He discussed the emergence of consciousness by addressing the

stage prior to it, which he called the period of the bicameral mind. In his book Jaynes demonstrates the characteristics common to civilizations around the globe, 165. I am indebted to my former supervisor Mark Cousins for introducing the work of Julian Jaynes to me.

55   McGilchrist, Iain. *The Master and Emissary – The Dividing Brain and the Making of the Western World*. New Haven, CT, and London: Yale University Press, 2009. I am grateful to Professor John Onians for this reference.

56   Delphic oracle, the aphorism 'know thyself' was inscribed in the pronaos of the Temple of Apollo at Delphi – according to Pausanias (10.24.1).

57   Bassett writes:

> Consider, for example, the description of the orator Demosthenes (cat. no. 53). In the florid language admired by the age, Christodoros identifies and describes his subject with only passing reference to physical appearance. Instead, the author concentrates on re-creating the orator's mental state by alluding to past historical events. This technique allows Christodoros to infer a state of mind from which the orator's thoughts are duly extrapolated. Far more interpretive than factual, this verse is conceived less as a documentation and more as mutual and emotional evocation of a moment. Indeed, the real subject of Christodoros's poetry is not so much observed physical reality as the ephemera of thought and feeling.

Fifth-century description of one of the major thermal foundations in Constantinople, an *ekphrasis* on the statuary in the Baths of Zeuxippos by Christodoros describes 81 statues or statue groups. Bassett, op. cit., p. 9.

58   Christodoros, a Christian poet in the time of Anastasius I (491–518), was influenced by Nonnos of Panopolis (Cameron, 475). Between 491 and 518 he wrote a poem 'On the Pupils of the Great Proclus', an epic on the Isaurian expedition (497–498) of Emperor Anastasius, poems on the history and antiquities of Constantinople and other places, an exposition on statues in the thermae of Zeuxippos in Constantinople, and epigrams. See Cameron, Alan. 'Wandering Poets. A Literary Movement in Byzantine Egypt'. *Historia* 14 (1965): 470–509; and Stupperich, R. 'Das Statuenprogramm in den Zeuxippos-Thermen'. *Istambuler Mitteilungen* 32 (1982): 210–35; *The Coptic Encyclopedia*, ed. Aziz Sourial Atiya. New York: Macmillan, 1989.

59   One of the theoretical difficulties that emerged was the new equalising power of letters. For the Greeks, spirituality and rationality, *muthos* (*mythos*) and *logos*, could coexist without conflict in separate domains. But the idea that *muthoi* could be frozen in a written form and interpreted to make statements of 'truth' (*logoi*) was foreign to the Greeks. As both Freeman and McGilchrist admit, there was resistance to such formations in early Christianity as well, and Christians as much as pagans suffered under Theodosius' decree and imposition of strict rules

coming from Ambrose of Milan. They stand in sharp contrast to the practices
of Constantine. See Freeman, Charles. *The Closing of the Western Mind: The
Rise of Faith and the Fall of Reason*. London: William Heinemann, 2002, 137;
McGilchrist, op. cit., pp. 294–5.

60   Most Ancient Greek texts were written on papyrus that would have deteriorated
in time and had to be transferred to parchment. The project of transcription had
been initiated by Constantine, who organized a group of calligraphers to rewrite
the texts (such as the Holy Scripture) on parchment.

61   See the review by Beard, Mary. Charles Freeman's *The Closing of the Western Mind.
Independent*, 14 September 2002.

62   The other important Mediterranean city in this respect is Alexandria, well known
for its scholars and its library.

63   Tafuri, Manfredo. *The Sphere and the Labyrinth. Avant-Gardes and Architecture
from Piranesi to the 1970s*, trans. Pellegrino d'Acierno and Robert Connolly.
Cambridge, MA, and London: MIT Press, 1987. Paraphrasing from the first
chapter entitled 'The Historical Project'.

Image Credits

Fig. 1. Image in Public domain

Fig. 2. Photo permission Jean-Christoph Benoist

Fig. 3. Gurlitt, 1912, image in public domain, in USA Photo permission Marsyas

Fig. 4. Photo permission Sandstein

Fig. 5. Photo permission MM

Fig. 6. Photo permission Quartier Latin 1968

Fig. 7. Photo permission Jastrow

Figs. 8 and 8a. Photos permission Gryffindor

Fig. 9. Photo by Fontana-Giusti

Figs. 10, 11 and 12. Photos permission Giovanni Dall'Orto

References

Ad Herennium Libri IV. De ratione dicendi. The Loeb Classical Library, ed. T.E. Page,
with the English trans. Harry Caplan. Cambridge, MA, and London: William
Heinemann and Harvard University Press, 1954.

Alberti, Leon Battista. *On the Art of Building in Ten Books*, 1452, ed. and trans.
J. Rykwert, N. Leach and R. Tavernor. Cambridge, MA, and London: MIT Press,
1988.

Bassett, Sarah. *The Urban Image of Late Antique Constantinople*. Cambridge: Cambridge University Press, 2004.

Beard, Mary. Review of Charles Freeman's *The Closing of the Western Mind* (2002). *Independent*, 14 September 2002.

Blanchet, Adrien. *Recherches sur les aqueducs et cloaques de Galle romaine*. Paris, 1908.

Brown, Peter. *The Body and Society, Men, Women and Sexual Renunciation in Early Christianity*. New York: Columbia University Press, 1988.

—*Augustine of Hippo*. Berkeley: University of California Press. 2000.

Cameron, Alan. 'Wandering Poets. A Literary Movement in Byzantine Egypt'. *Historia* 14 (1965): 470–509.

Cicero, Marco Tullius. *De oratore,* trans. W. Sutton and H. Rackham. In Thomas W. Benson, Michael H. Prosser (eds), *Readings in Classical Rhetoric*. Davis, CA: Hermagoras Press, 1988.

The Coptic Encyclopaedia by Aziz S. Atiya. New York: Macmillan, 1989.

Curtius, Ernst Robert. *European Literature and the Latin Middle Ages*, trans. from German by W. R. Trask. New York: Pantheon Books, 1953.

Dagron, Gilbert. *Naissance d'une capital*. Paris: Bibliothèque byzantine, Études 7, 1974.

Derrida, Jacques. 'Point de folie – Maintenant l' architecture', *AA Files,* No 12. London: Architectural Association, 1986, 65–75.

Du Fresne Du Cange, Charles. *Historia byzantina duplici commentario illustrate*. Paris, 1680.

Evans, James Alan S. *The Age of Justinian: The Circumstances of Imperial Power*. London: Routledge, 1996.

Fraser, Michael A. 'Constantine and the Encaenia'. In Elizabeth A. Livingstone ed., *Studia Patristica* 39. Leuven: Peeters, 1997, pp. 25–28.

Freeman, Charles. *The Closing of the Western Mind: The Rise of Faith and the Fall of Reason*. London: William Heinemann, 2002.

Gilles, Pierre. *De Bosphoro Thracio libri tres De topographia Constantinopoleos*. Lyon, 1561; Leiden, 1632, 1635.

—*De topographia Constantinopoleos et de illius antiquitatibus libri quatuor*. Lyon, 1561; Leiden, 1661.

—Modern English translation of his work in *Pierre Gilles Constantinople*. ed. and trans. Kimberly Byrd. New York: Italica Press, 2009.

Ginzburg, Carlo. *The Enigma of Piero*, with an Introduction by Peter Burke, trans. Martin Ryle and Kate Soper. London: Verso, 1985.

Graziano, Vittorio. *Ambasciate d'Italia in Turchia*. Catania: Mediterraneum, 1994.

Heyne, Gottfried. 'Priscae artis opera quae Constantinopoli extitisse memorantur'. *Commentationes Societatis Regiae Scientiarum Gottingensis,* 1790–1791.

—'Christian Got. Heynii pars commentationum de antiquitatibus byzantinis quae ad Hesychium illustrandum pertinent'. Imprint Lipsia: In libraria Weidmannia, 1820.

Homer, *Iliad*. ed. Monro, 3rd edn. Oxford: Oxford University Press, 1902.

Kieckhefer, Richard. 'Papacy'. In *Dictionary of the Middle Ages*. New York: Charles Scribner's, 1989.

Korolija Fontana-Giusti, Gordana. 'The Urban Strolling as a Measure of Quality'. In *Architecture Research Quarterly*. Cambridge: Cambridge University Press, No. 11, 2007, pp. 255–64.

Krautheimer, Richard and Ćurčić, Slobodan. *Early Christian and Byzantine Architecture*. London, and New Haven, CT: Yale University Press Pelican History of Art, 1986.

Jaynes, Julian. *The Origin of Consciousness in the Breakdown of the Bicameral Mind*. London: Allen Lane, 1976.

Lactantius. 'De Mort. Pers'. In O. F. Fritzsche ed., *Opera* (Bibl Patr. Ecc. Lat. XI), Vol. 4, translated in the University of Pennsylvania. Department of History, *Translations and Reprints from the Original Sources of European History*. Philadelphia, PA: University of Pennsylvania Press, 1897–1907.

Le Goff, J. 'Head or Heart? The Political Use of Body Metaphors in the Middle Ages', trans. Patricia Ranum. In *Fragments for a History of the Human Body*, Part Three. New York: Zone Books, 1989, pp. 12–27.

L'Orange, Hans Peter. *Art Forms and Civic Life in the Late Roman Empire*. Princeton, NJ: Princeton University Press, 1971, 1985.

McGilchrist, Iain. *The Master and Emissary – The Dividing Brain and the Making of the Western World*. New Haven, CT, and London: Yale University Press, 2009.

McManus, Stuart M. 'Byzantines in the Florentine Polis: Ideology, Statecraft and Ritual During the Council of Florence'. *The Journal of the Oxford University History Society* 6 (2008)/Hilary (2009): 1–22.

Mango, Cyril. *Byzantium: The Empire of New Rome*. New York: Charles Scribner's, 1980.

—*The Art of Byzantine Empire 312–1453 Sources and Documents*. Toronto: University of Toronto Press and Medieval Academy of America, 1986.

—*Le développement urbain de Constantinople (IV*–VII* siècles)*, 2nd edn. Études de topographie Byzantine, I–II, Paris, 1990.

—*Studies on Constantinople*. Aldershot: Ashgate Publishing, 1993.

—'The Triumphal Way of Constantinople and the Golden Gate'. *Dumbarton Oaks Papers* 54 (2000): 173–88.

Mango, Cyril and Dagron, Gilbert (eds). *Constantinople and its Hinterland*. Aldershot, 1995.

Morey, William C. *Outlines of Roman History*. New York, Cincinnati, OH, and Chicago, IL: American Book Company, 1901.

Müller-Wiener, Wolfgang. *Bildlexikon zur Topographie Istanbuls: Byzantion, Konstantinopolis, Istanbul bis zum Beginn d. 17 Jh*. Tübingen: Wasmuth, 1977.

Ostrogorski, Georgije. *History of the Byzantine State*. New Brunswick, NJ: Rutger University Press, 1986.

O'Sullivan, Timothy. 'The Mind in Motion: Walking and Metaphorical Travel in the Roman Villa'. In *Classical Philology*, Vol. 101. Chicago, IL: University of Chicago Press, 2006, pp. 133–52.

Pausanias. *Description of Greece*. English Translation by W. H. S. Jones and H. A.

Ormerod, 4 Vols. Cambridge, MA: Harvard University Press, and London: William Heinemann, 1918.

Perniola, Mario. 'Between Clothing and Nudity'. In *Fragments for the History of Human Body,* Vol. 2. New York: Zone Books, 1989, pp. 237–65.

Plato, *Timaeus. The Collected Dialogues*, ed. E. Hamilton and Huntington Cairns, Bollingen Series. Princeton, NJ: Princeton University Press, 1989.

Pollitt, J. J. *The Art of Rome (c. 753 BC–AD 337) Sources and Documents.* Cambridge: Cambridge University Press, 1983.

Quintillian, Marcus Fabius. *Institutio Oratoria,* trans. H. E. Butler. Loeb Classical Library. Cambridge, MA: Harvard University Press, 1920.

Riegl, Alois. *Late Roman Art Industry*, trans. Rolf Winkes. Archaeologica 36. Rome: Giorgio Bretschneider Editore, 1985.

—*Historical Grammar of the Visual Arts*, trans. Jacqueline Jung. New York: Zone Books, 2004.

Seneca, Lucius Annaeus. *Epistle 88*. Loeb Classics. Translation from Latin by Richard M. Gummere, 1917.

Stupperich, R. 'Das Statuenprogramm in den Zeuxippos-Thermen'. *Istambuler Mitteilungen* 32 (1982): 210–235.

Tafuri, Manfredo. *The Sphere and the Labyrinth. Avant-Gardes and Architecture from Piranesi to the 1970s*, trans. Pellegrino d'Acierno and Robert Connolly. Cambridge, MA, and London: MIT Press, 1987.

Vasari, Giorgio. *Vitae*, translated as *The Lives of the Artists*. Oxford World's Classics. Oxford: Oxford University Press, 1998.

Virgil. *Aeneid*, trans. John Dryden with Introduction and Notes. New York: P.F. Collier and Son, 1909.

Vitruvius, Marcus Pollio. *The Ten Books On Architecture*, trans. Morris Hicky Morgan. London: Dover Publications, 1960.

Westfall, Carroll William. *In This Most Perfect Paradise*. Philadelphia: Pennsylvania State University Press, 1974.

Yates, Frances. *The Art of Memory*. Chicago, IL: Chicago University Press, 1966.

Online resources

Encyclopaedia Britannica. 1911 edition. http://www.1911encyclopedia.org (accessed November 2010)

Encyclopaedia Coptica. http://www.coptic.net/EncyclopediaCoptica/ (accessed November 2010).

Eusebius.

The Life of the Blessed Emperor Constantine, trans. and revised by Ernest Cushing Richardson. http://www.fordham.edu/halsall/basis/vita-constantine.asp (accessed November 2010).

9

There and Back Again:

Cross-cultural Transmission of Clothing and Clothing Terminology

Timothy Dawson

The extravagantly misnamed 'Fall of the Roman Empire' greatly weakened, but by no means ended, the epic tale of the œcumenical empire. After a hiatus of a few centuries, contact between Western states and the enduring Roman Empire in the East resumed and became an increasing feature of the political, religious and cultural parameters of an expanding European worldview. In Rômania (as the residents of the Roman Empire had called it since at least the first century AD) the history and links with the West had never been forgotten, and various attempts had been made to reincorporate some Western provinces into the Empire, attempts which continued as late as the twelfth century. Over the centuries of Europe's Middle Ages the nature of the relationship between Constantinople and the West fluctuated and evolved. The political and religious aspects of this process are well known: the intrusion of the Normans into Italy and the Greek peninsula; the schism of the Churches; the Seljuk assault on Anatolia; the initiation of the Crusades and the creation of the Crusader states; the great crime of the Fourth Crusade and the collapse of Crusading. The economic factors are equally clear: principally the steady loss of Constantinople's trading wealth to the Italian city-states. Much less appreciated, but in many ways more pervasive and influential in the long term are the influences in material culture and language. The association of terminology with definable objects sheds a fascinating light upon how different linguistic groups hear and adapt words. An important cusp in the process of assimilation is the point at which either the foreign language term for an object is dropped in favour of a native term, or at which the foreign name may be seen to have come to be regarded as sufficiently indigenous. Another facet that makes material culture influences particularly interesting is the way it can be seen that they could be transmitted by more than one channel at any given time, and that the predominant direction of flow could also fluctuate.

Clothing is one area of material culture in which these processes can be traced with some facility. The most radical and enduring transformation of Western dress resulting from contact with the East was caused by the introduction of divided garments and the button fastening. The former carried a terminology with them, although more recent linguistic usage has confused that somewhat. Divided garments began with the Persians.[1] The Fahsi past participle meaning 'divided',[2] *kaftun* used for a long garment opening down the front ('coat' in modern English) gave Western languages, of course, *caftan*, either directly or via the Greek derivative *kavadion* (καβάδιον),[3] and became *qabâ* in Arabic. The ninth-century writer al-Aghani helpfully explained that 'when a man tears his tunic (*qamis*) from the opening below the neck to the foot it becomes a *qabâ*', thus making the nature of the garment explicit.[4] It is interesting to note that in Vyzantion there was an elite custom for a while to use a direct translation of the Persian, the nominalized past participle *diakoptês* (διακόπτης) for a coat in parallel to the vernacular use of the imported *kavadion*, but that practice seems not to to have survived the tenth century.[5] Less clear is the origin of the name of the shorter divided garment ('jacket') called *zoupa* (ζούπα) in Greek[6] and *djubba* in Arabic,[7] which migrated into French as *jupe* and *jupon*.[8] This garment offers a caution, in that one should not necessarily think that there need only be a single conduit of transmission. At the same time, the southern French were probably primarily influenced by contact with the Arabic-speaking Moors in al-Andalus, while others venturing further afield would have encountered both Greek and Arabic in the Levant, perhaps simultaneously, the two channels of influence converging to establish both the garment and the term in France before the end of the twelfth century.[9] One passage of poetry of that century reproduced by Goddard is specific that the *jupe* being described is 'made in the Saracen manner', suggesting the possibility that the author and audience may have been aware of *jupes* made in some other manner, such as Byzantine, or 'Greek', as they would most likely have thought of it.

Another novelty for Westerners was the padding of garments. In this case the area was military. The jacket just discussed, *zoupa/djubba*, could itself be padded, and it is apparent that in the thirteenth and fourteenth centuries there were both civilian and military *jupes*, perhaps distinguished by whether they were padded or not, or the degree to which they were padded. More distinctly, the Greek and Arabic terms for cotton fibre, *vamvakion* (βαμβάκιον)[10] and *al-qutun* respectively, gave medieval Latin, French and English specific terms for padded military garments, *wambasia*[11] and *gambais/gamboison*[12] from the Greek, and *auqueton/haqueton/aketon*[13] from the Arabic. The phonic divergences of the Latin and French terms from their Greek antecedent are very striking in this case.

These examples are all influences dating from the period when the West was coming into increasing contact with more sophisticated Levantine societies. From the thirteenth century we see the somewhat paradoxical trend of the collapse of the crusading movement and the loss of all the western colonized states on the Levantine mainland coinciding with an enormous and indeed imperialistic upsurge in European mercantile activity. Evidently, this was more culturally influential in the East than the military ventures had been, for through the next two centuries Eastern clothing and clothing terminology shows quite dramatic changes attributable to Western influence. Sometimes the changes are distinctly adverse. For example, in the earlier period in Rômania, the *esôforion* (ἐσωφόριον), that is, shirt or chemise, had had a sophisticated construction with a full closure at the neck and low-standing collar.[14] This arrangement is a great enhancement to the wearer's comfort, both keeping the neck warmer than it would otherwise have been and protecting it from irritation from heavy, often woollen, over-garments. Yet by the middle of the fourteenth century this feature had disappeared from Byzantine clothing, apparently in imitation of European custom.[15] On the terminological side, there is the case of the pre-eminent male cloak, a ubiquitous feature of court regalia in the tenth century, but confined to a few of the highest ranks at the end of the empire. Called *khlamus* (χλάμυς) from Antiquity through the middle Byzantine period (late ninth century to 1204), by the fourteenth century it had been renamed *tabarion* (ταμπάριον), a word derived from the Italian *tabarro* (also source of the French *tabart* and English tabard) without any indication of a change in nature, appearance or use.[16] *Tabarion* is also evidence for the evolution of medieval into modern Greek, being an early instance of the use of the combination *mu-pi* to represent the phoneme B, as has continued to the present.

These are all examples of unidirectional influence. In contrast there is one term which traced a remarkable journey over the course of thousands of years from Mesopotamia through Greek to diverse European languages and back again. It originates as a term for a now unknown item of clothing in the Akkadian language, between the mid-third millennium BCE and the early first century AD in the form *gônnaka* (γώννακα).[17] Late Akkadian begins to appear transliterated into Greek in the first century BCE and by that means the term enters common use in the Hellenistic world as *gaunakê* (γαυνάκη). The loose orthography of *koinê* and medieval Greek generated the alternate forms *kaunakês* and *kaunauges* (καυνάκης. καυναύγες), and the truncated forms *gauna, gouna* and *gounion* (γαύνα, γούνα, γούνιον).[18] The alternate forms are, in fact, much more commonly found in literature, yet we must infer that the expression was in much more common oral use simply from the way it migrated into European languages so widely. The garment *gaunakê* was applied to in Late Antiquity and the middle Byzantine era is somewhat clearer than in Akkadian. The tenth-century lexicon known as the *Suda*, admittedly not noteworthy for the technical precision of its definitions, merely says 'garment' using a term (*ampekhomenon*) which commonly indicates some sort of heavy outer garment.[19] The literary uses of the derivative terms support this. In numerous military sources from the *Stratêgikon* of *c.* 602 to the *Book of Ceremonies* in the mid-tenth century *gounion* and variants are heavy coats which are either worn over armour or in place of it.[20] The description in the *Stratêgikon* of a large garment with wide sleeves which covers all of a horseman's panoply protecting it from moisture yet allowing access to it and freedom of use indicates that it must be a coat rather than a cloak or a pull-over garment. It is also a distinct likelihood that these garments were sometimes hooded as hooded garments in civilian use are well attested.[21] In the prosaic terminology of later military manuals, protective garments go by updated technical names rather than by the older forms *epanoklivanon* and *epilôrikion* (ἐπανοκλίβανον, ἐπιλωρίκιον), literally 'upon the armour' (even though the latter could be used for an armour substitute), and a familiar term, *kavadion*, for those serving in lieu of armour. Their descriptions have slightly different details which can be seen to be relevant to Western and later evidence. In the tenth-century *Syllogê Taktikôn* freedom of movement in the *epilôrikion* was facilitated by passing the arms through slits at the elbows of the sleeves, while both the *kavadion* and *epilôrikion* (used in its proper sense as a surcoat) of the *Composition on Warfare* of Emperor Nikêforos Fôkas employ slits at the armpit for this purpose, a feature visible in illustrations of pull-over garments and surviving coats from Late Antiquity.[22] The Late Antique coats exhibit another feature shared with later coats – sleeves longer than the wearer's arms.[23]

Instances of *gaunakê* and derivatives as a civilian garment are rare in middle Byzantine literature. In the early twelfth century Kinnamos recounts a incident in which a dark linen *kuanauges* was mistaken for monastic robes.[24] Yet, as was noted above, we must infer that *gaunakê* was in more common spoken use at this time, since from the beginning of the thirteenth century it appears quite extensively in Latin as *garnachia/garnacia/guarnachia*,[25] in Italian as *guarnaccia*[26] and in French as *garnache*.[27] According to the early modern lexicographer Du Cange, all these refer to the sleeveless surcoat that had become a feature of European dress, both civil and military, from the late twelfth century, but pictorial sources suggest that the situation was no more simple in the West than it had been in Vyzantion. In the *Liber ad Honorem Augusti* of Peter of Eboli written no later than 1225 Richard the Lion Hearted is depicted twice in distinctive travelling garb.[28]

Figure 1 Richard I of England returning home from crusade
After the Liber ad Honorem Augusti de Pietro di Eboli.

Both pictures show a knee-length hooded tunic, but in one the king's arms emerge through slits in the elbows while in the other the slits are in the armpits. In these pictures we can surely see early examples of the *garnache* in forms still quite true to their Eastern precursors. It is significant that Richard is the only character in the *Liber* who wears such a garment. Various pieces of evidence suggest that there was a more ready conduit at the crucial juncture for the transmission of such material culture influences between Constantinople and Britain than to other parts of Europe. Anna Komnênê's remarks about the centrality of the English to the Varangian unit at the end of the eleventh century are well known. Less familiar is the fact that considerable numbers of Saxon refugees, including agricultural families, were settled in northern Anatolia after the Norman Conquest.[29] In 1176, Emperor Manuel wrote to King Henry II of England regretting the losses among Englishmen serving in the Roman Army at the Battle of Myriokefalon. These illustrate intensive contacts between Britain and Vyzantion over the course of more than a century, and while all refer to the English going East, those voyagers would not all have 'burned their boats' and never returned. It is to be expected that in doing so some carried Levantine custom back with them. Some 50 years after *Liber ad Honorem Augusti* in a manuscript illuminated in England, the *Gulbenkian Apocalypse*, we are presented with a great array of voluminous overgarments, most showing the characteristic of openings in the armpits, many sporting especially long sleeves, and some having other particularly Eastern characteristics.[30] There is ample evidence that through the thirteenth century such garments became increasingly popular across Europe, but the diversity of them shown in the *Gulbenkian Apocalypse* follows on from the *Liber's* depiction of King Richard in suggesting that clothing of this type had taken off more rapidly in England than on the Continent.

Thus we have seen a process whereby ample sleeved over-garments made their way to the West bearing with them some version of their Greek vernacular name. Yet such raiment had, of course, not vanished in the Levant, nor had the evolution or diversification in their styles ceased. We are, however, initially confronted with a near total hiatus in source material. In 1204 the Fourth Crusade was compelled by Venetian machinations to capture Constantinople. That would have been the end of many a political and cultural entity, but not the Roman Empire. With astonishing resilience scattered enclaves fought back, and after 57 years regained control of the city. Even after that it was a continuing struggle to restore the strength of the Empire, which left little surplus labour and wealth to sponsor artistic and literary output. Vast cultural heritage had been lost in the sack and a campaign of resurgence lasting more than an average lifetime of the period, and even materials from the earlier time which had been preserved were evidently no longer understood the way they had once been. Perhaps it was this that allowed familiar items to be rebranded with imported terms.

Between 1347 and 1368 the results of the reconstitution of Constantinopolitan court culture were encapsulated in the *Treatise on the Offices*. Besides the regalia, the most prominent informal male garments are *granatza* and *lapatza* (γράνατζα, λάπατζα).[31] These are described in some detail. They are almost identical, falling to the floor and with sleeves of the same length. There are traces of a coat showing this characteristic in a damaged fourteenth-century fresco in the crypt of the Church of the Holy Saviour in Khora.[32] We are told that the *granatza* was worn loose while the *lapatza* was encircled by a belt which also secured its sleeves. This information tells us much about what distinguished the two items. First, the wearer's arms in both cases must be freed in some way, since as for them to be fully enclosed in floor-length sleeves would be impossibly encumbering, and we have previously discussed means for achieving that – openings at the armpit or elbow. The *lapatza* must have the openings at the armpits, since otherwise having its sleeves constrained by the belt would make it something close to a strait-jacket. Hence the *granatza* would have its sleeve opening at the elbow. Happily, we find a pictorial source which confirms the use of just such a coat in a senior court context in the fourteenth century, the illuminated *Alexander Romance* manuscript.[33] The phonology of *granatza* as given in the *Treatise on the Offices*, that is, the interpolated or transposed 'r' and the equivalence of 'ch' to 'tz', is commonly observed in foreign terms imported into medieval Greek, and shows that this term had re-entered Byzantine usage from the West, evidently derived from the late Latin, and Italian vernacular forms *garnachia* and *guarnachia*. Thus the circle becomes complete.

Clothing is a profound marker of identity, both for the wearer and for observers. The initial motivation for Westerners adopting Levantine fashions was a mixture of indulgence of the exotic and appreciation of practical benefits. A *garnache* is a much more practical riding garment than a cloak, for example; yet for Peter of Eboli it became a marker of Englishness. Why the Rômiosi chose time and again to bestow foreign names on familiar garments and accessories is less clear. Exoticism making the mundane more interesting, perhaps? Sheer linguistic boredom? Whatever the reason, it is a phenomenon visible in many cultures. These examples illustrate that intercultural influences in material culture can be an intricate web, a multi-stranded and sometimes circular complex of processes, yet all the more fascinating for that.

Notes

1 Gervers-Molnár, Veronika. *The Hungarian Szur: An Archaic Mantle of Eurasian Origin*. Toronto: Royal Ontario Museum, 1973.

2 Steingass, Francis Joseph. *Persian–English Dictionary*. London: Routledge, 1977 (1892), p. 1037.

3   I employ a system of transliteration which in part reflects how the Greek sounded
    at the time, rather than how it was written. Hence, beta = v, eta = ê (but sounds
    i), omega = ô (but is indistinguishable from o), kh rather than ch for khi (chi),
    diphthongs were contracted and I have abandoned the traditional 'ph' in favour
    of 'f'. Thus, *kavadion* will be found as *kabadion* in other publications, and the
    Latinized Byzantium is Vyzantion.

4   Levy, Reuben. 'Notes on Costume from Arabic Sources'. *Journal of the Royal
    Asiatic Society* 1935, p. 324 n2. For numerous examples of *qabâ* in Arabic texts of
    this era see Serjeant, Robert Bertram. *Islamic Textiles: Material for a History up to
    the Mongol Conquest.* Beirut: Librairie du Liban, 1972.

5   *The Book of Ceremonies*, a manual of conduct and regalia for the court of
    Constantinople composed in various parts between 899 and 963, uses *diakoptês*
    (διακόπτης) for coats belonging to the Empress, and *kavadion* (καβάδιον)
    for coats worn by barbarians (Reiske, Johannes Jacob ed. *Constantine
    Porphyrogennêtus, De Cerimoniis Aulae Byzantinae.* Bonn: E. Weber, 1839,
    pp. 582 and 749 respectively) while the dream interpreter Achmet uses *kavadion*
    throughout (Drexl, Francis ed. *Achmetis Oneirocriticon.* Leipzig: B. G. Teubner,
    1925, pp. 88, 114, 218) and the term is common in tenth-century military manuals
    (for example, Nikêforos Fôkas' *Compostion on Warfare*, (a.k.a. *Praecepta Militaria*)
    I.3; McGeer, Eric (ed. and trans.). *Sowing the Dragon's Teeth.* Washington, DC:
    Dumbarton Oaks, 1995, p. 12). *Diakoptês*, in contrast, does not appear elsewhere
    in surviving literature of the period.

6   Achmet gives a highly informative commentary on the *zoupa* (ζούπα) in civilian
    use, including the various fibres with which it might be padded: op. cit., p. 117.

7   Again, Serjeant, op. cit., provides diverse references to *djubba*.

8   Robert, Paul. *Dictionnaire alphbetique et analogique de la Langue Francaise.* Paris:
    Société du Nouveau Littre, 1972, p. 956 cites *djubba* as the source for *jupe* in the
    twelfth century, with *jupon* emerging in the fourteenth century. Since then, *jupe*
    has been reallocated from an upper torso garment to one extending from the
    waist downwards.

9   Goddard, Eunice Rathbone. *Women's Costume in French Texts of the Eleventh and
    Twelfth Centuries.* New York: Johnson Reprint Corporation, 1973 (1927), p. 145.

10 βαμβάκιον (see note 3 on transliteration). The *Composition on Warfare* (note
    5) mentions *vamvakion* as the padding for military coats in several places, and a
    tenth-century treatise on siege defence lists it as an essential raw material (Van
    Den Berg, Hilda ed. *Anonymus De Obsidione Toleranda*, Leiden: E. J. Brill, 1947,
    p. 49). The adjectival form *vamvakêros* (βαμβάκηρος), denoting 'made of cotton
    cloth', is much rarer, and was not conspicuous until very late in the eleventh
    century: headscarves listed in the Will of Kalê Pakouriani, in Lefort, Jacques,
    Oikonomides, Nicholas and Papachryssanthou, Denise (eds) *Actes d'Iviron II.*
    Paris: P. Lethielleux, 1990.

11 Baxter, J. G. and Johnson, Charles. *Medieval Latin Word-list from British and Irish Sources*. Oxford: Oxford University Press, 1934, p. 187 finds *gambizonium, gambiso, wambasia, wambiso* and *wanbasia* in medieval sources from *c.* 1166 onward. Niermeyer, J. D. *Mediae Latinitatis Lexicon Minus*. Leiden: E. J. Brill, 1976, p. 1126 gives *wambesio* citing the Greek antecedent.

12 Greimas, H. J. *Dictionnaire de l'ancien Francais jusqu'au milieu de XIVe siecles*. Paris: Librairie Larousse, 1969, p. 307.

13 Stone, George Cameron. *A Glossary of the Construction, Decoration and Use of Arms and Armour in all Countries and in all Times*. New York: Jack Russell, 1934, p. 6.

14 ἐσωφόριον, found in *De Cerimoniis*, 576, 635, 661, 677. Dawson, Timothy. 'Concerning an Unrecognised Tunic from Eastern Anatolia'. *Byzantion* 73, 1 (2003): 201–10.

15 See, for example, the magnificently detailed donor portraits in the *Lincoln Typikon* of the Bodleian Library, Oxford.

16 χλάμυς, ταμπάριον. Verpeaux, Jean (ed. and trans.) *Traité des Offices de Pseudo-Codinos*. Paris: Centre National de la Recherche Scientifique, 1966, *passim*.

17 γώννακα. Du Cange, Charles du Fresne. *Glossarium ad Scriptores Mediae et Infimiae Gaecitatis*. Graz: Akademische Druck-U. Verlagsanstalt, 1958, col. 200; Liddell, Henry George, Scott, Robert and Jones, Henry Stuart. *A Greek–English Lexicon* (ninth edition). Oxford: Clarendon Press, 1963 (1843), p. 339; Hemmerdinger, Bertrand. '158 noms communs Grecs d'origine Iranienne'. *Byzantinoslavica* 30 (1969): 19.

18 καυνάκης, καυναύγες, γαύνα, γούνα, γούνιον.

19 γαυνάκη: ἀμπεχόμενον. Adler, Ada ed. *Suidae Lexicon*, 5 vols. Stuttgart: B.G. Teubner, 1971, Vol. I, p. 509; Liddel, Scott and Jones, op. cit., p. 86.

20 Dennis, George T. ed. and Gamillscheg, Erst (trans.) *Das Strategikon des Maurikios*. Vienna: Verlag der Österreichischen Akademie der Wissenschaften, 1981, p. 80; Alder, *De Obsidione*, p. 48; Reiske, *De Cerimoniis*, p. 381.

21 Various collections around the work hold surviving hooded tunics from Egypt, and hooded, loose-sleeved over-tunics (μαφορτοδελματίκιον, *mafertodelmatikion*) are listed in Diocletians *Edict on Prices*: Frank, Tenney. *An Economic Survey of Ancient Rome*. Princeton, NJ: Pageant Books, 1959, p. 371. In the middle Byzantine era there are sporadic illustrations of hooded garments, for example, Dionysiou Monastery codex 587m f. 13v.

22 Fluck, Cäcilia and Vogelsang-Eastwood, Gillian (eds). *Riding Costume in Egypt: Origin and Appearance*. Leiden: E. J. Brill, 2004.

23 A later long-sleeved garment was the *skaramangion* (σκαραμάγγιον) which could be a coat or a tunic. Dawson, Timothy. 'Oriental Costumes in the Byzantine Court Reconsidered'. *Byzantion* 75 (2006): 97–114.

24   Meinke, Augustus ed. *Iôannês Kinnamos, Epitome Rerum ab Ioanne et Alexio [=Manuel] Comnenis Gestarum*. Bonn: Edward Weber, 1836, bk. II, ch. 4.

25   Du Cange, Charles du Fresne. *Glossarium Mediae et Infimiae Latinitatis*. Graz: Akademische Druck-U. Verlagsanstalt, 1954, Vol. IV, pp. 34–5.

26   Macchi, Vladimiro ed. *Standard Italian and English Dictionary*. London: George Harrap & Co, 1970, p. 608.

27   Greimas, *Dictionnaire*, p. 309. A notable occurrence in French is in the *Rule* of the Order of the Temple of Solomon, paras 132, 142, 314, 425 and 558: Upton-Ward, J. M. (trans.) *The Rule of the Templars: The French Text of the Rule of the Order of the Knights Templar*. Woodbridge: Boydell and Brewer, 1992.

28   Siragusa, G. B. ed. *Liber ad Honorem Augusti de Pietro di Eboli*. Rome: Instituto Storico Italiano, 1905, p. 129.

29   Sheppard, Jonathon. 'The English in Vyzantion'. *Traditio* 29 (1974): 53–93.

30   On folio 43v a garment is shown closed with a slit running down from the left side of the neck fastened at the top with a single button, an adaptation of the most common neck opening employed on pull-over garments in the Eastern Roman Empire. See Dawson, 'tunic', note 14.

31   γράνατζα, λάπατζα, Verpeaux, *Traité*, 219.

32   Back wall of tomb F: Underwood, Paul Atkins. *The Kariye Djami*. New York: Bollingen Foundation, 1966, Vol. 3, p. 547.

33   Trahoulias, Nicolette S. *The Greek Alexander Romance: Venice Hellenic Institute Cod. Gr. 5*. Athens: Exandas, 1997, *passim*, for example, f. 160v.

References

Adler, Ada ed. *Suidae Lexicon*, 5 vols. Stuttgart: B. G. Teubner, 1971.

Baxter, J. G. and Johnson, Charles. *Medieval Latin Word-list from British and Irish Sources*. Oxford: Oxford University Press, 1934.

Dawson, Timothy. 'Concerning an Unrecognised Tunic from Eastern Anatolia'. *Byzantion* 73, 1 (2003): 201–10.

—'Oriental Costumes in the Byzantine Court Reconsidered'. *Byzantion* 75 (2006): 97–114.

Dennis, George T. ed. and Gamillscheg, Erst (trans.) *Das Strategikon des Maurikios*. Vienna: Verlag der Österreichischen Akademie der Wissenschaften, 1981.

Drexl, Francis ed. *Achmetis Oneirocriticon*. Leipzig: B. G. Teubner, 1925.

Du Cange, Charles du Fresne. *Glossarium Mediae et Infimiae Latinitatis*. Graz: Akademische Druck-U. Verlagsanstalt, 1954.

—*Glossarium ad Scriptores Mediae et Infimiae Gaecitatis*. Graz: Akademische Druck-U. Verlagsanstalt, 1958.

Fluck, Cäcilia and Vogelsang-Eastwood, Gillian (eds). *Riding Costume in Egypt: Origin and Appearance*. Leiden: E. J. Brill, 2004.

Frank, Tenney. *An Economic Survey of Ancient Rome*. Princeton, NJ: Pageant Books, 1959.

Gervers-Molnár, Veronika. *The Hungarian Szur: An Archaic Mantle of Eurasian Origin*. Toronto: Royal Ontario Museum, 1973.

Goddard, Eunice Rathbone. *Women's Costume in French Texts of the Eleventh and Twelfth Centuries*. New York: Johnson Reprint Corporation, 1973 (1927).

Greimas, H. J. *Dictionnaire de l'ancien Francais jusqu'au milieu de XIVe siecles*. Paris: Librairie Larousse, 1969.

Hemmerdinger, Bertrand. '158 noms communs Grecs d'origine Iranienne'. *Byzantinoslavica* 30 (1969).

Lefort, Jacques, Oikonomides, Nicholas and Papachryssanthou, Denise (eds). *Actes d'Iviron II*. Paris: P. Lethielleux, 1990.

Levy, Reuben. 'Notes on Costume from Arabic Sources'. *Journal of the Royal Asiatic Society* (1935).

Liddell, Henry George, Scott, Robert and Jones, Henry Stuart. *A Greek–English Lexicon* (ninth edition). Oxford: Clarendon Press, 1963 (1843).

McGeer, Eric (ed. and tr.). *Sowing the Dragon's Teeth*. Washington, DC: Dumbarton Oaks, 1995.

Meinke, Augustus ed. *Iôannês Kinnamos, Epitome Rerum ab Ioanne et Alexio [=Manuel] Comnenis Gestarum*. Bonn: Edward Weber, 1836.

Niermeyer, J. D. *Mediae Latinitatis Lexicon Minus*. Leiden: E. J. Brill, 1976.

Reiske, Johannes Jacob ed. *Constantine Porphyrogennêtus, De Cerimoniis Aulae Byzantinae*. Bonn: E. Weber, 1839.

Robert, Paul. *Dictionnaire alphabetique et analogique de la Langue Francaise*. Paris: Société du Nouveau Littre, 1972.

Serjeant, Robert Bertram. *Islamic Textiles: Material for a History up to the Mongol Conquest*. Beirut: Librairie du Liban, 1972.

Sheppard, Jonathon. 'The English in Byzantium'. *Traditio* 29 (1974).

Siragusa, G. B. ed. *Liber ad Honorem Augusti de Pietro di Eboli*. Rome: Instituto Storico Italiano, 1905.

Steingass, Francis Joseph. *Persian–English Dictionary*. London: Routledge, 1977 (1892), p. 1037.

Stone, George Cameron. *A Glossary of the Construction, Decoration and Use of Arms and Armour in all Countries and in all Times*. New York: Jack Russell, 1934.

Trahoulias, Nicolette S. *The Greek Alexander Romance: Venice Hellenic Institute Cod. Gr. 5*. Athens: Exandas, 1997.

Underwood, Paul Atkins. *The Kariye Djami*. New York: Bollingen Foundation, 1966.

Upton-Ward J. M. (trans.) *The Rule of the Templars: The French Text of the Rule of the Order of the Knights Templar*. Woodbridge: Boydell and Brewer, 1992.

Van Den Berg, Hilda ed. *Anonymus De Obsidione Toleranda*. Leiden: E. J. Brill, 1947.

Verpeaux, Jean (ed. and trans.). *Traité des Offices de Pseudo-Codinos*. Paris: Centre National de la Recherche Scientifique, 1966.

Index

Page numbers in italic indicate a figure.